NORTH CAROLINA
STATE BOARD OF COMMUNITY COLLEGES
LIBRARIES
ASHEVILLE-BUNCOMBE TECHNICAL COLLEGE

DISCARDED

JUN 2 2025

LIBRARY AUTOMATION SYSTEMS

BOOKS IN
LIBRARY AND INFORMATION SCIENCE

A Series of Monographs and Textbooks

EDITOR
ALLEN KENT

Director, Office of Communications Programs
University of Pittsburgh
Pittsburgh, Pennsylvania

Volume 1. CLASSIFIED LIBRARY OF CONGRESS SUBJECT HEADINGS, Volume 1—CLASSIFIED LIST, edited by James G. Williams, Martha L. Manheimer, and Jay E. Daily.
Volume 2. CLASSIFIED LIBRARY OF CONGRESS SUBJECT HEADINGS, Volume 2—ALPHABETIC LIST, edited by James G. Williams, Martha L. Manheimer, and Jay E. Daily.
Volume 3. ORGANIZING NONPRINT MATERIALS, by Jay E. Daily.
Volume 4. COMPUTER-BASED CHEMICAL INFORMATION, edited by Edward McC. Arnett and Allen Kent.
Volume 5. STYLE MANUAL: A GUIDE FOR THE PREPARATION OF REPORTS AND DISSERTATIONS, by Martha L. Manheimer.
Volume 6. THE ANATOMY OF CENSORSHIP, by Jay E. Daily.
Volume 7. INFORMATION SCIENCE: SEARCH FOR IDENTITY, edited by Anthony Debons.
Volume 8. RESOURCE SHARING IN LIBRARIES: WHY • HOW • WHEN • NEXT ACTION STEPS, edited by Allen Kent.
Volume 9. READING THE RUSSIAN LANGUAGE: A GUIDE FOR LIBRARIANS AND OTHER PROFESSIONALS, by Rosalind Kent.
Volume 10. STATEWIDE COMPUTING SYSTEMS: COORDINATING ACADEMIC COMPUTER PLANNING, edited by Charles Mosmann.
Volume 11. USING THE CHEMICAL LITERATURE: A PRACTICAL GUIDE, edited by Henry M. Woodburn.
Volume 12. CATALOGING AND CLASSIFICATION: A WORKBOOK, by Martha L. Manheimer.
Volume 13. MULTI-MEDIA INDEXES, LISTS, AND REVIEW SOURCES: A BIBLIOGRAPHIC GUIDE, by Thomas L. Hart, Mary Alice Hunt, and Blanche Woolls.
Volume 14. DOCUMENT RETRIEVAL SYSTEMS: FACTORS AFFECTING SEARCH TIME, by K. Leon Montgomery.
Volume 15. LIBRARY AUTOMATION SYSTEMS, by Stephen R. Salmon.

Additional volumes in preparation

LIBRARY AUTOMATION SYSTEMS

Stephen R. Salmon

University of Houston
Houston, Texas

MARCEL DEKKER, INC. *New York*

COPYRIGHT © 1975 by MARCEL DEKKER, INC. ALL RIGHTS RESERVED.

Neither this book nor any part may be reproduced or transmitted in any form or by any means, electronic or mechanical, including photocopying, microfilming, and recording, or by any information storage and retrieval system, without permission in writing from the publisher.

MARCEL DEKKER, INC.

270 Madison Avenue, New York, New York 10016

LIBRARY OF CONGRESS CATALOG CARD NUMBER: 75-25168

ISBN: 0-8247-6358-0

Current printing (last digit):
10 9 8 7 6 5 4 3 2

PRINTED IN THE UNITED STATES OF AMERICA

TO MY WIFE CHRISTINA

expert editor,
staunch supporter,
apt critic,
and fellow sufferer through it all

INTRODUCTION

There are few librarians today who are not wondering how computers and networks will affect the operation of their libraries tomorrow. Questions are raised regarding automation--what to automate; when to automate; how to automate. Should work on automation proceed individually or in consortia; should services be purchased from others; or should automation not be considered at all, and why?

In a sense, these questions cannot be answered unless and until a library establishes evaluation criteria. But before criteria can be developed rationally, there must be a foundation of understanding as to how the field developed, where it is today, and where it might be going tomorrow.

This book provides such a foundation. It will be useful not only to practitioners, but also to their administrators, who must judge proposals that would change the world of libraries, and would frequently require risk capital to be expended.

Finally, this book will be useful to professors in library schools who are obliged to teach their students how to cope in a brave new world.

Allen Kent

PREFACE

This book is intended as a reasonably comprehensive discussion of library automation systems for the librarian without previous knowledge or experience in the field, and for the intelligent layman. Library automation systems, in the context of this work, are combinations of electronic data processing machines and appropriate programs and operating procedures, organized to work together in carrying out, with a minimum of human intervention, some well-defined library process. It is a field that many thoughtful observers feel has reached a certain maturity, and so deserves to have its portrait made.

The approach throughout most of the book is historical, or to be more precise, developmental. There are three reasons for this. In the first place, it is convenient, not only for the author but hopefully for the reader as well; unless one is to pick up and examine systems at random, some rational order is necessary (even if arbitrary), and the historical serves as well as any. Second, library automation systems are seldom independent achievements; those who work in the field stand on the shoulders of those who went before. The work of Fasana and others in automatically generated codes for controlling card production, which led to the MARC format recognition technique, and the use of "traveling cards" in special library serials systems, which led to Voigt's pioneering "arrival card" serials system in San Diego, are only two examples. Finally and more generally, it seems to the author that we must understand the way in which the field of library automation has developed if we are to understand fully where we are today, and why. Library automation systems do not exist in a vacuum, and what we do today is partly determined by what was done yesterday, as well as by the mechanical and social circumstances in which we find ourselves. Library automation, that is to say, like any other development, is inextricably tied to its history.

I have avoided the "cookbook" approach, with instructions on how to automate a library, not only because such works already exist, but also because such an approach inevitably runs the risk of being narrow and restrictive, of describing only one technique for mechanizing particular areas of library automation when in fact several methods are available and appropriate. With few exceptions, I have also omitted descriptions of data processing equipment and the way in which such equipment operates, since this information is readily available in a number of standard works.

The principal argument of the book is stated in the first chapter: that the story of library automation is best told through a description of actual operating systems. As even the casual reader must be aware, the literature is replete with descriptions of proposed systems, plans, and projects under way. Many of these projects were never implemented, and those that were implemented underwent substantial changes before actually doing the jobs for which they were designed. In order to avoid misleading the reader with seemingly logical schemes which in practice may be flawed, therefore, I have with few exceptions omitted discussion of any system that is not yet operational. The obvious exception is Chapter 9, which discusses only those projects and practices that failed to withstand the test of practicality.

A secondary thesis which I have attempted to demonstrate throughout the work is that there is a central key to understanding the development of library automation systems to date, and this is the gradual yet dramatic improvement in communications between man and machine. A review of the reports, documentation, and actual operations of the hundreds of library automation systems now installed leaves this impression most strongly: that the improvement

Preface

in communications is perhaps the most significant trend discernible, and certainly the most encouraging.

One obvious difficulty with a book that attempts to cover this large and still-changing field is that portions of it will be out of date as soon as it is written. I have tried to include as much material as possible without delaying completion of the manuscript unduly, and the method of page composition and printing has been chosen deliberately to enable publication of the information in as timely a fashion as possible. Nevertheless there will be omissions as well as other errors, and I can only hope that my readers will point them out so that they can be rectified in any subsequent edition.

A second limitation arises from the fact that any book must draw a line at some arbitrary point not only in time but also in subject matter. For example, this discussion of library automation is limited to activities customarily performed within the library, and hence excludes such important functions as computer searching of the machine-readable data bases constructed by various indexing and abstracting services, even though few librarians would question the fact that the rapid growth of commercially-available data base services has major implications for reference and information services in libraries of all sizes and types. Readers who explore the literature further will find many such related matters of interest.

For practical reasons, it has not been possible to visit each project personally, and the information given on many systems is thus based solely on the published literature. Some of this may be considerably out of date, and I will greatly appreciate receiving more current information.

My debts are many. Michael Bruer, Ronald Naylor, Karen Latimer, Marvine Brand, Joe Rosenthal, Paul Fasana, William Cole and Wesley Simonton read the manuscript and offered valuable suggestions and comments. Allen Kent prodded me, as a good editor should, to write an earlier version of some of the material that appeared in the *Encyclopedia of Library and Information Science*. Allen Veaner and

Frederick Kilgour corrected errors in the text dealing with the BALLOTS Project and OCLC. And Bobbie Anderson and Jane Hays struggled mightily through the world's worst handwriting and often-scrambled notes to produce not only the manuscript but the final composition. To all, my heartfelt thanks.

Stephen R. Salmon

CONTENTS

Introduction   v
Preface   vii

Chapter 1

BACKGROUND AND BEGINNINGS   1

   In the beginning was Billings
   Punched-card library systems
   Computerized library systems
   The context of development
   Intrex and MARC
   On-line systems
   Total and integrated systems

Chapter 2

ACQUISITION SYSTEMS   13

   Acquisition systems based on unit record equipment
   Off-line computerized acquisition systems
   On-line interactive systems

Chapter 3

CATALOGING SYSTEMS BEFORE MARC   39

   Cataloging systems based on unit record equipment
   Automatic typewriter systems
   Sequential card camera systems
   Off-line computer systems
   Off-line catalog card systems
   Off-line book catalog systems
   Photocomposed book catalogs

Chapter 4

MARC AND OFF-LINE SYSTEMS AFTER MARC   73

    The MARC Pilot Project
    MARC II
    Format recognition
    Expansion of MARC
    Post-MARC cataloging systems
    Off-line catalog card systems
    Off-line book catalog systems
    Combined book catalog and catalog card systems

Chapter 5

ON-LINE CATALOGING SYSTEMS   103

    On-line input, off-line catalog cards
    OCLC
    Chicago and Stanford
    Commercial cataloging systems
    The New York Public Library book catalog system
    On-line input, off-line catalog cards and book catalogs
    On-line catalog reference, without cards or book catalogs

Chapter 6

THE EFFECT OF AUTOMATION ON CATALOGING PRACTICE   127

    Typographical presentation of cataloging information
    Extent of information given
    Choice of information given
    Arrangement of catalog information
    On-line techniques

Chapter 7

SERIALS SYSTEMS   147

    Types of serials systems
    Other functions
    Unit record systems
    Off-line computer listings
    Off-line computerized accessioning systems
    Other off-line computerized serials systems
    On-line computerized serials systems
    MEDLARS
    National Serials Data Program and CONSER

Contents   xiii

Chapter 8

CIRCULATION SYSTEMS   181

   Unit record systems
   The Montclair system
   Computerized 357-type systems
   On-line circulation systems
   On-line circulation systems with full inquiry capabilities
   Light-pen systems
   On-line light-pen systems with full inquiry capabilities

Chapter 9

THE PROBLEMS OF LIBRARY AUTOMATION SYSTEMS   219

   The computer center and systems personnel
   Suppliers
   Library staff
   Poor planning
   Poor design
   Poor implementation
   A final word

Chapter 10

THE PROSPECTS OF LIBRARY AUTOMATION SYSTEMS   235

   Networks
   Standards
   Mini-computers
   Commercial systems
   Future developments

Bibliography   245
Index   281

LIBRARY AUTOMATION SYSTEMS

Chapter 1

BACKGROUND AND BEGINNINGS

Library automation is the use of automatic and semiautomatic data processing machines to perform such traditional library activities as acquisitions, cataloging, and circulation. Although these activities are not necessarily performed in traditional ways, the activities themselves are those traditionally associated with libraries; library automation may thus be distinguished from related fields such as information retrieval, automatic indexing and abstracting, and automatic textual analysis.

Linguistic purists have argued rightly that the term "automation" applies more correctly and narrowly to automatic process control, and indeed this was historically the first use of the term. The broader meaning, however, has had the sanction of widespread usage for a number of years, and "library automation" is now by far the most commonly used term for mechanization of library activities using data processing equipment.

In the beginning was Billings

The whole automation phenomenon in our society began with a librarian, in a way. Herman Hollerith, the Census Bureau employee who invented punched-card machinery, attributes the idea to a suggestion by Dr. John Shaw Billings, director of the Surgeon-General's Library (now the National Library of Medicine). According to the *Dictionary of American Biography*, Hollerith's "work on the census brought him into contact with Dr. John Shaw Billings, from whom came the suggestion of Hollerith's main invention. In a letter to a friend written nearly forty years later he described the origin of the idea: 'One evening at Dr. B's tea table he said to me, "There ought to be a machine for doing the purely mechanical work of tabulation and similar statistics."'"[1] Hollerith agreed, and by 1890 had invented equipment using the now-familiar punched cards for tabulating the census figures of that year. In 1896, he formed the Tabulating Machine Company, which later became the International Business Machines Corporation, or as we know it, IBM. Hollerith offered Billings a share in the venture, but apparently Billings declined.

Punched-card library systems

Librarians continued to be mildly interested in such machinery for most of the first half of the next century. Ralph Parker installed a Hollerith punched-card system for circulation control at the University of Texas in 1936[2] and by the middle 1940s had also experimented with its use in serial record control. In 1942, the Montclair Public Library of Montclair, New Jersey, installed "two specially designed book charging machines," which recorded individual transactions automatically in punched cards.[3] The Library of Congress produced a book catalog using punched cards in 1950, and the King County (Washington) Public Library produced another one in 1951.

These were scattered instances of mechanized systems, however. More were installed in the late 1950s, but most of these were in small, specialized libraries. Typically, such systems used standard punched-card equipment, sometimes called "unit record" equipment because the punched card as a unit record was central to its operation. A common assortment was a card punch, a sorter, a collator, and a tabulator such as the IBM 403.

Except experimentally, computers were not used before about 1961, and in this respect, library automation lagged behind business, industry, and science. The lag was not because of lack of interest and

1. Background and Beginnings

enthusiasm on the part of librarians, however; computers were still assumed by most people to be satisfactory only for numerical work, and computer programs were still oriented toward business and scientific applications. Even unit record equipment was difficult for most libraries to obtain until their parent institutions--universities, local governments, and businesses--had obtained computers. And unit record equipment, by its nature, was limited in the amount of processing that could be done: only fairly simple tasks could be performed, one at a time, under the control of a wired control panel in the tabulator. The only means of "communication" with the machines was by punching holes in cards (or in paper tapes), and communication back to the users of the system was limited to printed reports or to more punched cards. The capacity for manipulation and analysis of data was small, and of course there was no provision for storing data for later retrieval--except, again, on punched cards.

Computerized library systems

The general-purpose computers that became widely available in the 1960s changed all that, and made possible a second era of library automation systems. Punched-card equipment remained, but played only a secondary and gradually diminishing role. Most of the systems common in the 1960s used punched cards for input, so information was fed into the system in a way not very different from unit record systems, but once the data were entered many more operations could be performed during a single processing, or "run." More importantly, the system could now "remember," storing information regarding book orders in progress, books held or on loan, periodicals received, and so forth, all on magnetic tape. Further, the information could be transferred automatically in and out of the computer's "core" storage as needed for complete operations. The speed of operations and the capacity for manipulation and analysis of data were greatly increased, often by several orders of magnitude.

The context of development

The increased availability of computers and the improvements in data processing they made possible were only two of the reasons for the rapid development of library automation systems in the 1960s. Another was the growing realization in many quarters that the computer could be used effectively for non-numerical work. To some, in fact, the marriage of the computer and the library seemed a natural alliance; as one writer phrased it, "A library is a place for storing knowledge under a system that facilitates identification and retrieval as needed, which is also a definition of a computer."[4] The growth in the sheer mass of published information to be handled has also been offered as an explanation for the increased activity in library automation. Undoubtedly all these were factors, but it also seems likely that the increasingly felt urgency of the need for answers--answers for many things, but particularly answers to medical, military, and social problems--contributed strongly to the impetus. Jesse Shera's quotation from a doctor friend sums up what many seem to have felt: sooner or later, "we all die of a lack of information."[5]

Whatever the reasons were, library automation projects burgeoned in the early 1960s. The National Library of Medicine began a project to mechanize its handling of medical literature (the MEDLARS project); the University of California at San Diego began its pioneering work in serials control; and Southern Illinois University in Carbondale began studies on its landmark circulation system, all in 1961. The Ontario New Universities Library Project was established at the University of Toronto in 1963 to produce computerized book catalogs for five new university libraries, and the same year saw the publication of "the King report," *Automation and the Library of Congress*,[6] which established the feasibility of automating many of the activities of that largest and most prestigious of libraries.

Intrex and MARC

Many who heard a siren song in the King report undoubtedly heard it again in the *Report of a Planning Conference on Information Transfer Experiment, September 3, 1965*,[7] a conference that brought together librarians, engineers, industrialists, publishers, government officials, and information scientists to formulate a program of

1. Background and Beginnings

experiments called "Intrex," which, it was hoped, would "provide a design for evolution of a large university library into a new information transfer system that could become operational in the decade beginning in 1970."[8] One of those present at the conference was Vannevar Bush, who in 1945 had foreseen a "memex," "a device in which an individual stores his books, records, and communications, and mechanized so that it may be consulted with exceeding speed and flexibility ... an enlarged intimate supplement to his memory," consisting of "a desk ... translucent screens ... a keyboard, and sets of buttons" with "provisions for consultation of the record by the usual scheme of indexing."[9] Now, twenty years later, when his colleagues at M.I.T. had accomplished much--but by no means all--of what he foresaw, he challenged them again:

> The benefits of the great advance in analytical machinery thus far have flowed largely, but not quite completely, to men of business, science and engineering. The program in the minds of you gentlemen reaches far beyond this. It will influence, perhaps revolutionize, the methods of every professional group--in law, medicine, the humanities. It will support every phase of our general culture.[10]

Intrex was to last for eight years, and although it failed to accomplish what Bush envisaged its influence as the first large-scale experiment in library automation was immediate, and seems likely to grow as the results of the project are assessed.[11]

The enormous influence of another project that began in 1965 is already clear. Project MARC (for Machine-Readable Cataloging) was initiated at the Library of Congress to provide a format for cataloging data that would be machine-readable, acceptable as a national standard, and usable interchangeably on all of the different computers likely to be used in library automation. Its success laid the foundation for advances in the field that would otherwise have been impossible, and as an international, ever-expanding standard and service its contribution is only beginning to be exploited.

On-line systems

MARC and Intrex laid the groundwork for the next era of library automation, but it could not begin until another important technical step had been taken: the introduction of on-line, interactive computer systems. Most of the computerized library automation projects of the mid-1960s, including those based on MARC, were off-line, batch-processing systems. In such systems, the data and the programs are delivered to the computer in machine-readable form (whether punched cards, punched tape, or magnetic tape), the computer processes the job, and the desired output (whether printed lists, printed catalog cards, reports, punched cards for circulation, or what have you) is then produced. During the processing, the entire computer or some defined portion of it is dedicated to the job.

In an on-line system, the computer has one or more terminal devices connected permanently to it (by cables or telephone wires) for the performance of particular jobs; the library user is "connected" to the computer and is capable of communicating with it at all times. The computer will ordinarily be doing other jobs as well, but the system and the hardware allow virtually simultaneous processing by allocating each user and each job a small fraction of a second at a time, going on to the next and the next, and returning finally to the first without its attentions to other matters being evident to the user.

The terminals connected to the computer may have keyboards like a typewriter, or cathode-ray tube (CRT) screens like a television set, or slots that accept and read book cards or borrower's cards, or printing devices, or a combination of these. They may also have considerable circuitry or even a small computer built into them to provide some editing or other processing capabilities without accessing the computer, or to "buffer" (i.e., store temporarily) the information to be conveyed until the computer is ready to accept it. The key fact is that the information stored by the computer (usually on magnetic disks) is available at all times, usually within a few seconds at most, and without having to punch cards in order to communicate with the machine. Most such systems provide for "interaction" or even "conversation" with the computer: in response to a keyboard inquiry, the computer program asks for further information, the user supplies

1. Background and Beginnings

it, and the computer proceeds with the conversation depending on the answers to its questions. Communication between man and the machine is thus considerably improved over off-line batch-processing systems. The necessity for producing numerous large reports is eliminated, as is the necessity for manually searching through such print-outs. The desired information can be called up on the screen or the typewriter, the appropriate action taken, and the results of the action seen immediately for visual verification. Considering the complexities of bibliographic information and the editorial operations that libraries perform, these are enormous advantages. In fact, from simple unit record systems to off-line computer systems and then to on-line systems, it is the dramatic improvement in communication between the user and the system, between man and machine, that is the most distinctive and decisive element in the development of library automation.

At least one experiment in the use of on-line systems for library-related purposes had already begun by the time of the Intrex conference. At the same institution that hosted the conference (M.I.T.), the Technical Information Project had indexed several dozen physics journals and was using one of the first experimental on-line time-sharing systems to search this body of citations using typewriter terminals. In 1967 two large-scale projects began that would culminate several years later in on-line systems providing access in seconds to a much larger body of bibliographic data. The Ohio College Library Center (OCLC) and Stanford University's BALLOTS (Bibliographic Automation of Large Library Operations using a Time Sharing System) were both designed to access most of the hundreds of thousands of cataloging records made available by Project MARC, plus additional records created by each system. By the next year, landmark on-line systems were in regular operation in a handful of libraries. Bell Telephone Laboratories and Eastern Illinois University had on-line circulation systems, Université Laval in Quebec was using an on-line serials control system, and Washington State University had implemented one for acquisitions.

"Total" and "integrated" systems

One controversy regarding system design should be mentioned before actual systems are discussed. Much of the early literature of library automation speaks of "total systems" or the "total systems approach." The philosophy behind this terminology varied with the user. In some cases, it implied that libraries should be automated completely or perhaps not at all; proponents of this theory argued that to automate only one portion of a library's activities was to invite incompatibility with systems that might later be developed for other activities. Others, less radical in approach, used such terms to apply only to design, not to implementation. They argued that the library should be studied as an integrated whole, its entire operations thoroughly understood and flow-charted if possible, and a complete system designed to automate the whole. The parts of the system could then be implemented one at a time, as funds permitted.

For several reasons, these theories have never been tested. For one thing, it has never been completely clear what all the activities that might be automated are, and as the field of library automation developed, new potentials were revealed, old assumptions abandoned. Approaches thought to be advantageous in some areas--such as the commonest designs for serials control--were found to be impractical, and discarded. In any case, no library ever had the money to be "totally automated" even if it had known how, and the one library that proclaimed its intention to do so failed completely.[12]

In later years, a variation of the philosophy has appeared in the idea of "integrated technical processing" systems. Its proponents argue that good design demands the elimination of redundant keyboarding operations as much as possible, and that in library systems, therefore, bibliographic data entered into the system at the time an item is ordered should be reused if possible, or modified as necessary, to produce various cataloging products, such as catalog cards or book catalogs; even, perhaps, to provide reference to the cataloging data through on-line terminals.

1. Background and Beginnings 9

Some of the largest and most sophisticated systems are based on this philosophy. In one, for example, the design concept is specifically "to be able to create a record and to update it at any point in the technical processing operations; to enter data, partial or complete, at any time and subsequently be able to use, amend, or correct these data; to signal desired output at any time and get it at the desired time in the proper format, and positioned in an array designed for easiest use."[13]

Despite widespread practice, however, the technique remains controversial. An opposing point of view holds that the application of present cataloging rules results in a degree of change in data elements sufficiently high in many instances to warrant re-keyboarding of the data.[14] Lorenz, for example, in describing the Library of Congress Order Division system, notes that "the question of whether acquisitions records produced by this system may be useful for later cataloging operations ... will be explored, but the disparity between acquisitions data and cataloging data may be too great to make this use practical in the Library of Congress."[15]

This book makes no attempt to decide the issue. The story of library automation is the story of actual, working automated library systems, and these are described, insofar as possible, as they exist. A few integrated technical processing systems do exist, and are discussed under headings that seem most appropriate. The vast majority of existing systems, however, fall readily into four major categories:

1. Acquisition systems
2. Cataloging systems
3. Serials systems
4. Circulation systems

Each type is discussed from a general historical viewpoint, in an attempt to make clear the implications of various developments in each category. With that as a basis, a look at general problems and prospects for the future can then be essayed.

NOTES

1. *Dictionary of American Biography, Supplement One*, Charles Scribner's Sons, New York, 1944, p. 415.

2. Ralph H. Parker, "The Punched Card Method in Circulation Work," *Library Journal*, 61, 903-905 (December 1, 1936).

3. Margery Quigley, "Ten Years of IBM," *Library Journal*, 77, 1152-1157 (July 1952).

4. Lowell A. Martin, "The Changes Ahead," *Library Journal*, 93, 711 (February 15, 1968).

5. Jesse H. Shera, "Librarians against Machines," *Science*, 156, 748 (May 12, 1967).

6. Gilbert W. King et al., *Automation and the Library of Congress*, Library of Congress, Washington, D.C., 1963.

7. *Intrex; Report of a Planning Conference on Information Transfer Experiments, September 3, 1965*, Carl F. J. Overhage and R. Joyce Harman, eds., M.I.T. Press, Cambridge, Mass., 1965.

8. *Ibid.*, p. xv.

9. Vannevar Bush, "As We May Think," *Atlantic Monthly*, 176, 106-107 (July 1945).

10. *Intrex; Report...*, pp. 144-145.

11. M. M. Kessler et al., "The M.I.T. Technical Information Project-- a Prototype System," *Proceedings of the American Documentation Institute, 1964, v.1: Parameters of Information Science*, the Institute, n.p., 1964, pp. 263-268; M. M. Kessler, "The M.I.T. Technical Information Project," *Physics Today*, 18, 28-36 (March 1965); Sanborn C. Brown, "A Bibliographic Search by Computer," *Physics Today*, 19, 59-64 (May 1966); M. M. Kessler, "The Technical Information Project of the Massachusetts Institute of Technology," in *Proceedings of the 1966 Clinic on Library Applications of Data Processing*, University of Illinois Graduate School of Library Science, Urbana, 1966, pp. 7-17.

12. Florida Atlantic University: see Chapters 3 and 9.

13. Charles Payne, "The University of Chicago's Book Processing System," in *Stanford Conference on Collaborative Library Systems Development; Proceedings*, Stanford University Libraries, Stanford, California, 1969, p. 120.

14. Of interest on this point is an analysis at Columbia University, which indicated that many of the data elements submitted at order time are later determined to be unacceptable in the final catalog record, particularly such data items as pagination, series title, and publication date. [Nathalie C. Bates, "Data Analysis of Science Monograph Order/Cataloging Forms," *Special Libraries*, 57, 583-586 (October 1966)]. Markuson notes that "of most importance is the fact that only about 25% of the author names submitted at

1. Background and Beginnings   11

>   order time were used in the same form in the final catalog entry
>   --a fact that should give systems designers some concern."
>   (Barbara Evans Markuson, "Automation in Libraries and Informa-
>   tion Centers," in *Annual Review of Information Science and Tech-
>   nology*, v. 2, John Wiley & Sons, New York, 1967, p. 267).

15. John Lorenz, "The Library of Congress and Library Automation,"
    in *Collaborative Library Systems Development*, M.I.T. Press, Cam-
    bridge, Mass., 1971, p. 131.

Chapter 2

ACQUISITION SYSTEMS

Most automated library acquisition systems are designed to handle the considerable amount of paperwork involved in buying books. Typically they

1. Print purchase orders
2. Maintain book fund accounts and print book fund reports of various types
3. Provide information on orders outstanding, and sometimes on works in process--that is, books received but not yet cataloged
4. Prepare vouchers or checks to pay for the books

Many also print other reports derived from the order information; one system described below, for example, produces 32 separate products. These may include lists of orders by order number, by author, by country, by language, or by any other element of data that has previously been coded and entered into the system; claims or cancellation notices to be sent to a dealer when the book has not been received within a predetermined period of time; and notices to the original requester of a book that it has been ordered or received. Some of the more elaborate systems also provide for such functions as conversion of foreign currencies to dollars; automatic checking for possible duplicate orders; "holding" orders until funds become available; reordering from a second vendor if the first cannot fill the order; computation of such dealer performance measures as average length of time to fill an order, or average discount; and provision of information for cataloging or circulation functions.

Acquisition systems also vary in other respects:

1. By type of material handled (most handle monographs, but many do not handle serials)
2. By type of orders handled (many do not handle standing, blanket or approval orders, or gifts and exchanges)
3. By type of payment possible (some cannot accommodate payments in advance, deposit accounts, or memberships)
4. By type of language representable (most cannot deal with nonalphabetic languages such as Chinese, and many do not provide for diacritics)

Despite these differences, most acquisition systems fall readily into one of three broad categories representing the major technical developments discussed earlier:

1. Those based exclusively or primarily on unit record equipment
2. Off-line, batch-processing systems using computers
3. On-line systems using various types of remote terminals for communication with a computer

Acquisition systems based on unit record equipment

The typical punched-card or unit record acquisition system uses a keypunch, a sorter, a collator, and a tabulating machine such as the IBM 402, 403, or 407. Cards are punched with order information, and are then sorted and passed through the tabulator to print orders. The punched cards are then placed, with the help of the collator, in the file of cards used for previous orders, to create an orders outstanding file; this file may also be printed out in list form on the tabulator. When the books are received, the price paid for each item

2. Acquisition Systems

is punched into one of the cards, which then serves to update financial records, and in some cases to write vouchers or checks.

The public libraries of Decatur, Illinois and Lake County, Indiana provide early examples of such systems. Decatur began late in 1959 with an inexpensive set of equipment (the IBM Series 50) costing $375 per month, and used it to produce not only purchase orders but 14 other products as well, including accounting records, statistics, shelflist cards, and book cards. By 1963/1964, the cost for machine rental, material, and equipment had risen to $798 per month, but payroll, budgeting, and circulation functions had been added, the total staff of the library had been reduced, and the library was operating on less money than it had five years previously.[1]

Lake County began in 1962 with a similar system, using a 403 rather than a 402, and including book plates and book catalogs among its products. The library claimed a processing cost of only 24 cents per volume in 1964, handling approximately 2,000 volumes per month.[2]

Among university libraries, the University of Missouri, St. Louis University, and the Joint University Libraries of Vanderbilt, Peabody, and Scarritt were early pioneers with punched-card systems. The Missouri system was unique in its use of an IBM machine no longer being manufactured, the "Cardatype," rather than the customary accounting machine. The Cardatype combined a typewriter-like keyboard and printing platen with the ability to read unit record cards, punch them, and perform modest computational chores. Data entered through the keyboard, read from punched cards, or computed in the arithmetic unit could be utilized in the production of printed orders and other records, and as many as four additional typewriter units could be attached to the central unit, each preparing distinctive documents.

The application at Missouri is an excellent example of a unit record system in which the same punched cards are used repeatedly to produce various products. The Cardatype, used at the beginning of the process to prepare purchase orders, also produced temporary cards for the public catalog, Library of Congress card orders, order records, and report slips (see Fig. 2-1). A collator was used periodically to

Library Automation Systems

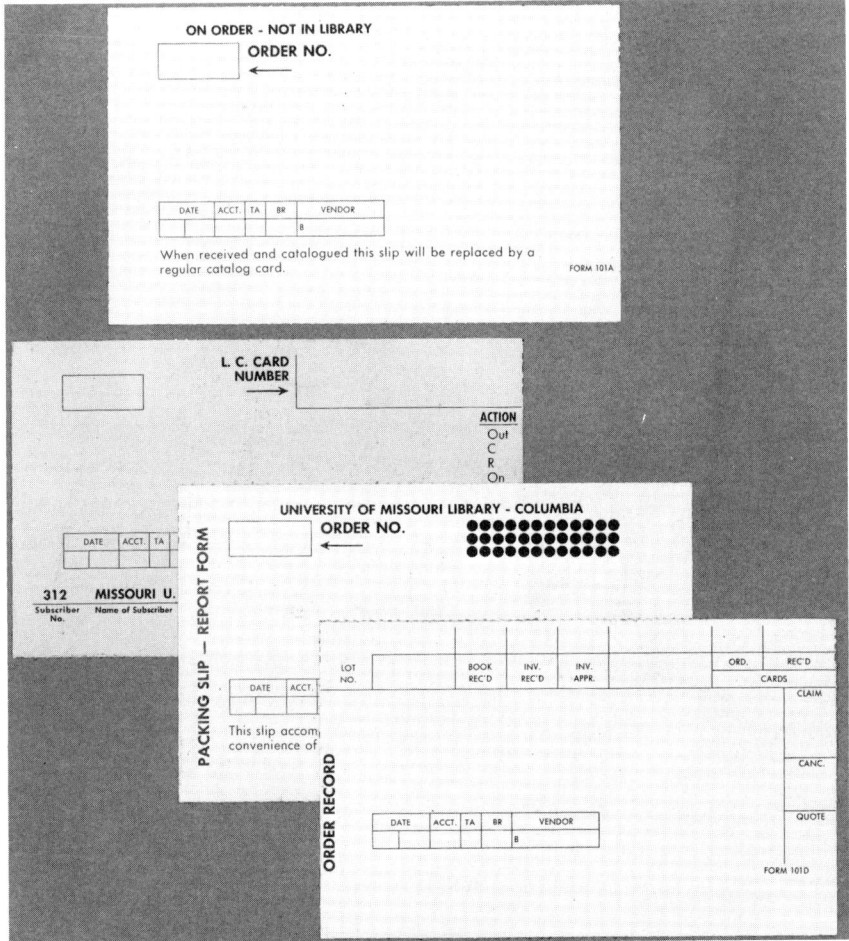

FIG. 2-1. By-products of the University of Missouri acquisition system.

search the file of cards for the books on order, and if items were not received within a specified period of time the same cards were used to produce cancellation notices or claim notices (see Fig. 2-2). If the items were reported out of print, the cards could also be used to request quotations from out-of-print book dealers, in which case a copy of the request form was again placed in the public catalog as well as in a desiderata file (see Fig. 2-3).[3]

2. Acquisition Systems

FIG. 2-2. Claim notice, University of Missouri acquisition system.

In the St. Louis University application, the order date was recorded in so-called "Julian" or "shop" date form--that is, the number of the day of the year--and this was used to trigger claim notices. The files were so arranged that if the items ordered were not received within ninety days of the time ordered, a claim notice was automatically produced. After operating for several years, the system was abandoned for lack of sufficient volume to justify its cost.

The Joint University Libraries system handled fund accounting, produced orders for Library of Congress catalog cards as well as for books, printed lists of books on order and in process, and produced temporary cards to be filed in the public catalog. A special card punch, the IBM 526 summary punch, was connected to the 402 tabulator so that when purchase orders were printed, cards could be punched with the total amounts of each order for use in encumbering funds.[4] The system was converted to a computer operation in 1966 using IBM 1401 and 7072 computers, and is still in operation at this writing.

Numerous special libraries had also begun such systems by the mid-1960s, typically using company equipment for a few hours per week. The one at IBM's Watson Research Laboratory is of particular interest. Punched cards produced at the time the items were ordered were manually arranged in a "processing information file" subdivided into the following categories:

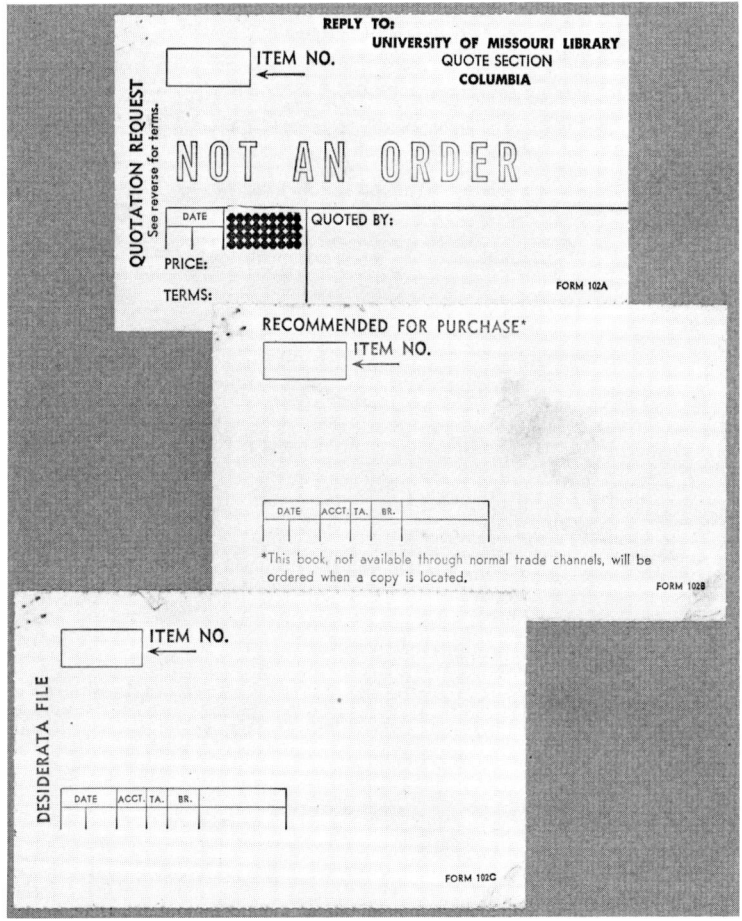

FIG. 2-3. Quotation request, University of Missouri acquisition system.

    Ordered but not yet published
    Ordered but not yet received
    Overdue and claimed
    Received but not yet cataloged
    Cataloged but catalog cards not yet reproduced and filed
    Recent additions to the collections

As books moved from one step to another, the appropriate cards were manually shifted. Three times a week, an IBM 407 tabulator was used

2. Acquisition Systems

```
                        AUGUST 23, 1963

                    PIL (PROCESSING INFORMATION LIST)

           NOT YET PUBLISHED

                1963  COP. 1AIZERMAN    THEORY-AUTOM CCN              P1228 317 C
         VOL.1        COP. 1BEREZIN     COMPUTING METH                TC765     C
         VOL.2        COP. 1BEREZIN     COMPUTING METH                TC765     C
                1961  COP. 1COTTRELL    MOLECULAR ENER TRANSF C1711             C
                      COP. 1CRYOGENIC TECH                            P162      C
                      COP. 1DANTZIG                                   P170  303 E
  QD411.D72 VOL.1 1961 COP. 1DUB        ORGANOMETALLIC COMPOU SH111 320 R
  QD411.D72 VOL.2 1961 COP. 1DUB        ORGANOMETALLIC COMPOU SH111 320 R
  QA251.D8 PT.2 1963   COP. 1DUNFORD    LINEAR OPERATORS      C1098 301 S
  QA251.D8 PT.2 1963   COP  ??????      ?????  ?????????              301 C

           ORDERED NOT RECEIVED

                1963  COP. 1ABRAGAM     LEFFET MOSSBAUER              P1231 317 C
                1960  COP. 1ABSTRACTS-THESIS ACCEPTED-PARTIAL FULF GIFT  334 E
                1961  COP. 1ABSTRACTS-THESIS ACCEPTED-PARTIAL FULF GIFT  334 E
                1961  COP. 1ACHERKAN    ANGLO-RUSSKII SLOVAR                333 E
        B             ADVANCEMENT-SCI VOL.18 NUM.76 MARCH 1962  39889 320
  QD251.A36 VOL.4 1963 COP. 1ADV-ORG CHEM METH + RESULTS       P1254 319 C
         VOL.3  1963  COP. 1ADV-POLYMER SCI                    SH121 329 C
                1961  COP. 1ACAD NAUK SSSR  BIBL PO AVTOMATICHLSK  39654 319 C

           OVERDUE AND CLAIMED

                1961  COP. 1KELLOGG     ATMOSPHERES-MARS + VE 37418 310 F
                1961  COP. 2KELLOGG     ATMOSPHERES-MARS + VE 37418 310 S
         VOL.2  1962  COP. 1KATZ        VACUUM MICROBALANCE T SH38        C
                1961  COP. 1KEYES       INTERNAT HANDBOOK-UNI 36670 30, C
   P ZEISS-NACHRICHTEN      MESSNER     BEDEUTUNG-INTERFERENZ 38402 312 C
                1960  COP. 1MOSKOVSKII UNIV  TRUDY UCHENYKH FILOLO 37190 307 C
                      COP. 1NIDDITCH    PROPOSITIONAL CALCULU P1188

           RECEIVED NOT YET CATALOGED

   LB1777.A52 1962       COP. 1AMER ASSOC-ADV-SCSECONDARY SCHOOL SCI  GP172 325 R
   LB1777.A52 1962       COP. 2AMER ASSOC-ADV-SCSECONDARY SCHOOL SCI  GP172 325 C
   QD1.A513 NO.143 1963  COP. 1AMER CHEM SOC   ABSTRACTS-PAPERS       GIFT  333 C
   QD1.A513 NO.144 1963  COP. 1AMER CHEM SOC   ABSTRACTS-PAPERS       GIFT  333 C
   ZZ.PAM.A33 1961/62    COP. 1AMER INST-ELEC ENDEVELOPMENTS + TRENDS GIFT  333 C
   QA76.A66 VOL.3 1963   COP. 1ANNUAL REV-AUTOM PROGR                 C1346 327 C
   Q129.A57 1961         COP. 1ANTHONY       SCIENCE + ITS BACKGRO P1379 330 C
         VOL.5  1963  COP. 1ARMOUR RES FOUND HANDBOOK-THERMOPHYSIC 16638 333 C
         VOL.1  1963  COP. 1AUTOMATIC DICT-STENOTYPE-ENG TRANSCRIPT GIFT       R
```

FIG. 2-4. Processing Information List, IBM Watson Research Library.

to print the file, creating a "Processing Information List," or "PIL," which made information on the processing status of any item readily available (see Fig. 2-4). The system was later transferred to an IBM 1401 computer, with "recent additions" in one list and the other five categories combined in a second list, still called "PIL." The status of each item was noted in columns corresponding to the five categories, with the "Julian" or "shop" date shown for the day each item moved into each category (see Fig. 2-5). By observing which column had the most recent date, one could see at a glance the status of each item. The computer was programmed to identify items which stayed too long in one category, and produced notices of items that required claiming or expediting.[5] "PIL" lists, increasing in sophistication of typography and production, were to become a common feature of later systems until superseded in the 1970s by terminal displays of the same information.

Off-line computerized acquisition systems

As general-purpose computers became widely available in the 1960s, off-line, batch-processing computerized systems became (and

Library Automation Systems

IBM RESEARCH
RECENT ADDITIONS
293 10 09 64

LINE #	CALL NUMBER		AUTHOR	TITLE	PO.#	DES	ORDER	NOTPUB	CLAIM	RECD	CNC	RCADD
1355	T 55.A1B4	964	BESTS SAFETY MAINTENANCE DIRECT		P1983	E	118	135				272
1356	QA 263.B42	964	BICKLEY	MATRICES	P1201	R	210				226	237
1357	QA 263.B42	964	BICKLEY	MATRICES	P1201	C	210				226	237
1358	LB 17.B55	956	BLOOM	TAXONOMY-EDUC OBJECTI	51662	R	232			234	238	244
1359	LB 17.B55	956	BLOOM	TAXONOMY-EDUC OBJECTI	51662	E	232			234	238	244
1360	QA 331.B645	964	BOAS	POLYNOMIAL EXPANSIONS	SH148	C	078			244	262	274
1361	QD 281.P6B67	955	BOVEY	EMULSION POLYMERIZATI	P1280	C	233			245	266	274
1362	QD 606.B58	963	BOWEN	RADIOACTIVITATION ANA	HEI75	E	216			253	258	268
1363	QD 606.B58	963	BOWEN	RADIOACTIVITATION ANA	HEI75	C	216			253	258	268
1364	QA 191.B6	962	BOWMAN	INTRO-DETERMINANTS &	P1216	C	212				226	237
1365	HM 251.B62	964	BRADFORD	T-GROUP THEORY & LAB	P1235	C	219			230	237	244
1366	QC 753.B71	960	BRAILSFORD	MAGNETIC MAT	P1247	S	225			232	237	244
1367	QC 753.B71	960	BRAILSFORD	MAGNETIC MAT	P1247	S	225			232	237	244
1368	QA 433.B62	964	BRILLOUIN	TENSORS-MECH & ELASTI	TC549	C	233			241	266	274
1369	QC 661.B73	953	BRILLOUIN	WAVE PROPAGATION IN P		C						232
1370	Q 149.U6B76	964	BUREAU-LABOR STATSCIENTISTS, ENGS, & T			C				230	231	234
1371	HT 108.B8		BURGESS	CONTRIBUTIONS-URBAN S	TC517	C	216			241	260	268
1372	QA 76.5B69	964	BURNETT-HALL	COMPUTER PROGR & AUTO	P1248	R	225			238	244	254
1373	HB3730.B77		BUSINESS & DEF SEUNITED STATES INDUST		GP305	R	219			237	260	268
1374	QA 241.C25	900	CAHEN	ELEMENTS-THEORIE-NOMB	47578	C	076			226	233	244
1375	TK7872-L3C14	962	CALIF UNIF	LASERS-BIBLI	RECAT	R				225		237
1376	QD 5.C33	947	CALLAHAM	RUSSIAN-ENG TECH & CH	RECAT	C				230		232
1377	TK7872-L3C26	964	CARROLL	STORY-LASER	P1249	C			195	231		244
1378	Z 55.5C3	958	CARTER	BRIEFHAND DICT	RECAT	C				227		232
1379	Z 56.C33	957	CARTER	CARTER BRIEFHAND	RECAT	C	225			227		232
1380	B 3216.C3	955	CASSIRER	PHILOSOPHY-SYMBOLIC F	P1202	C	210			238		237
1381	QC 303.C31	964	CHALMERS	PRINCIPLES-SOLIDIFICA	TC536	S	231			231	247	254
1382	QH 221.C52	940	CHAMOT	HANDBOOK-CHEM MICROSC	RECAT	C				231	233	244
1383	QH 221.C52	940	CHAMOT	HANDBOOK-CHEM MICROSC	RECAT	C				232	244	254
1384	ZZ.PAM.C325	964	CHEM & ENGG NEWS	REVOLUTION-OFF COPYIN	51403	C	211			232	244	254
1385	ZZ.PAM.C325	964	CHEM & ENGG NEWS	REVOLUTION-OFF COPYIN	51403	C	211			253	258	268
1386	TK7872-V3C48	964	CHODOROW	FUNDAMENTALS-MICROWAV	P1301	S	238			253	258	268
1387	TK7872-V3C48	964	CHODOROW	FUNDAMENTALS-MICROWAV	P1301	C	238			240	266	274
1388	Z T164.C81C75	964	CODMAN	SOURCES-BUS INF	P1124	R		213		209		238
1389	T 50.C65	962	CONF-ACCURACY-INDUST MEASUREMENT-LENGT		HE172	C	176			247	220	255
1390	TK7815.C5	959	CONF-PHYS ELECTRONICS		51650	C	225			247		255
1391	TK7815.C5	960	CONF-PHYS ELECTRONICS		51650	C	225			247		255
1392	TK7815.C5	961	CONF-PHYS ELECTRONICS		51650	C	225			247		255
1393	TK7815.C5	962	CONF-PHYS ELECTRONICS		51650	C	225			247		255
1394	TK7815.C5	963	CONF-PHYS ELECTRONICS		51650	C	225			247		252

FIG. 2-5. Later version of Processing Information List, IBM Watson Research Library.

2. Acquisition Systems

as of this writing, remain) the most common and popular form of acquisition system. Most such systems still use punched-card input, feeding order information into the system in a way not greatly different from unit record systems, but once data input has taken place, information is normally transferred back and forth between magnetic tapes or magnetic disk files without the necessity of repeated manual handling of cards. The typical acquisition system of this type, in addition to printing orders, automatically updates the file of information on orders outstanding, encumbers the necessary funds and updates the appropriate financial records, stores the bibliographic information for later use, and gathers statistics. As noted earlier, computer systems make possible better communication from the machine back to the user, but in the case of acquisition systems this has been a dubious blessing; most such systems are characterized by the production of numerous and massive reports which seldom get consulted or read.

Two public library systems are of interest as examples of the transition from unit record systems to computers. Both used a Univac machine, the 1004 Card Processing System, which had capabilities about halfway between the unit record systems and a small computer such as the IBM 1401. The Suffolk County (New York) Cooperative System began with an IBM 403 tabulating system in 1963, and switched to the Univac 1004 a year later, adding tape drives for storage. A unique feature was the use of mark-sensing pencils to record and input some elements of data, such as the list price and discount in lieu of keypunching the information. The magnetic tape drives allowed the system to store fiscal data and bibliographic information for production of catalog cards. The Nassau County (New York) Library System began with a similar system in 1964; the system was transferred to a Univac 1005 with magnetic tape drives in 1968 so that orders and other reports could be printed faster and the information for them stored more conveniently.[6-8]

By far the most popular computers for acquisition systems in the mid-1960s, however, were those in IBM's 1400 series, particularly the 1401. The University of Illinois at Chicago Circle began using a 1401 for an off-line acquisition system in 1964, incorporating the "Processing Information List" feature pioneered at the IBM Watson Research Library. The UICC list was arranged not strictly alphabetically, but according to a computer-generated code word composed of the first four letters of the author's last name, the author's initials, and the initials of the first two words of the title (see Fig. 2-6).

```
          PROCESSING INFORMATION LIST 24MAY63    19

     WHEEBJBL1443    01     000420 140300 8300 1      ORD#
WHEELER-BENNETT, JOHN WHEELER, 1902-
    BREST-LITOVSK, THE FORGOTTEN PEACE, MARCH 1918.
    LONDON, MACMILLAN, 1938.


     WINGSEKC1443    01     000175 753725 8300 1      ORD#
                    CATALOG 117, NUMBER 87. #
WINGFIELD-STRATFORD, ESME CECIL, 1882-
    KING CHARLES AND KING PYM, 1637-1643. LONDON,
    HOLLIS AND CARTER, 1949.
    942.06 C474YW


     WINSF  SC1443   01     000350 105075 8400 1      ORD#
WINSOR, FREDERICK.
    SPACE CHILDS MOTHER GOOSE. NEW YORK, SIMON AND
    SCHUSTER, 1958.


     WRIGF VS1443    01     000750 105075 8300 1      ORD#
WRIGHT, FRANCES.
    VIEWS OF SOCIETY AND MANNERS IN AMERICA.
    CAMBRIDGE, MASSACHUSETTS, BELKNAP PRESS,
    6/14/1963.
    %JOHN HARVARD LIBRARY¤


     WYTRJAAP1403    01     000650 105075 3930 1      ORD#
WYTRWAL, JOSEPH ANTHONY, 1924-
    AMERICAS POLISH HERITAGE, A SOCIAL HISTORY OF THE
    POLES IN AMERICA. DETROIT, MICHIGAN, ENDURANCE
    PRESS, 1961.


     ZARIO  CA1443   01     001690 105075 3500 1      ORD#
                    001-002 #
ZARISKI, OSCAR.
    COMMUTATIVE ALGEBRA. BY OSCAR ZARISKI AND PIERRE
    SAMUEL. PRINCETON, NEW JERSEY, VAN NOSTRAND, 1958,
    1960.
```

FIG. 2-6. Processing Information List, University of Illinois at Chicago Circle Library.

2. Acquisition Systems

Orders were printed on three-by-five-inch slips, which were manually sorted by vendor and attached to cover letters for mailing.[9] Pennsylvania State University implemented a similar system the same year, using a 407 tabulator as well as a 1401 and a 7074 computer. A unique feature was the use of "change cards," five cards punched with the order number each time an order was prepared, and later used to report changes in the status of a book on order or in process. These cards were placed in cardboard packets and kept in a manually arranged file; if the status of an order changed, one of the cards was withdrawn, a code for the change was written on the card, the card was sent to a keypunching section where the code was punched in the card, and the card was then used by the computer to update the master magnetic tape record of orders outstanding. Codes were established for some twenty-five different changes, including "not yet published," "out of print," "claim sent," "defective copy received," "invoice approved," "book in cataloging," and "processing completed." In addition to a listing of orders in process, with the status of each order shown, the system produced daily lists of books requested by faculty but not yet ordered for each university department or separate fund, about 250 lists in all; when the system was later redesigned, however, this feature was dropped.[10-12]

Perhaps the best example of an off-line batch-processing system of the mid-1960s is the one at the University of Michigan, implemented in 1965 on an IBM 1401, converted a year later to a 1460 and soon after to an IBM 360, and still running strong at this writing. A ten-part order form is generated, which includes slips for the official and public catalogs. The orders outstanding file is automatically updated, but instead of printing it out the university now produces it on a computer-output microfiche (COM) for both economy and ease of handling. Entries for Slavic language works have "Slavic" punched at the beginning of each entry, and orders for music recordings similarly begin with the word "Recording" in order to create separate sections in the list for such works; other entires are alphabetized through the first 83 characters. A list of items on order arranged by fund is also produced and distributed to academic departments and division librarians. Bibliographic information on outstanding orders is stored on tape, but the fund files, statistical data, and vendor files are all stored on disks for easier access.

The Michigan system is one of the few projects for which good cost figures are available. About a year after the initial implementation, an analyst from outside the library evaluated the system in terms of both overall efficiency and costs. The results indicated that the system did indeed perform efficiently and economically; almost fifty percent more orders were handled by the automated system than by the previous manual system, and the cost per order, when like activities were compared, dropped by seven cents (from $1.59 to $1.52) over a two-year span. The librarian principally involved with development of the system has cautioned, however, that "while the information gathered was informative, it can, at best, only be considered as a guide since it is impossible to compare accurately an existing system with something that might have been."[13-16]

In the same year that Michigan's system was first implemented (1965), Washington University in St. Louis designed a system to control technical processing routines after books left the Acquisitions Department and until they had been fully cataloged and processed. Building on Penn State's "change card" idea, the system was designed to generate "process control cards" that could be inserted in IBM 357 terminals along with a plastic prepunched "badge" indicating the particular change in status to be recorded: for example, that the book had been received, or reported not yet published, or cancelled, or forwarded to a particular cataloging station, or to the card preparation unit, or (finally) that the book was under control of the public catalog and could be removed from the system. The information would be automatically recorded by a high-speed card-punch (an IBM 1034) in a remote location, and then be transmitted to the computer.[17] The system was not fully implemented until 1968, using a 1401 for production of the orders and an IBM 360 Model 50 computer for processing.

Two years earlier, in 1966, Yale University picked up the idea of "process control" and used it in the design of an acquisition system that later served as a model for the automated acquisition

2. Acquisition Systems 25

system at the Library of Congress.[18,19] As implemented at Yale, the technical processing "monitor" checks the status of each order during each day's run, and notifies the library of orders delayed past a predetermined length of time, and of other actions that need to be taken as a result of changes in status. The system represents an improvement in communications for off-line systems, presaging the later development of on-line systems; the insertion of prepunched cards in remote terminals eliminates the necessity of manually punching the information in a data processing department and carrying the cards to the computer, and the computer "talks back" by automatically printing action reports regarding particular items when needed.

A remarkable thirty-two different outputs were originally produced by the Yale system, including notices to requesters of the status of their orders (now discontinued because of lack of interest) and large in-process and order number listings, both of which were changed to microfilm form in 1971 because of their size and cost. First implemented on an IBM 7094-7040 "direct-coupled system," the system was converted in 1972 to run on an IBM 360 Model 67 and a short time later to an IBM 370 Model 155. IBM 357 data collection devices are still used for recording the status and location of items, and IBM 826s (typewriters coupled with keypunches) are used to prepare order forms while simultaneously punching the same information into cards.[20,21]

Other examples of batch-processing off-line systems in university libraries are legion. By 1966, the Joint University Libraries system had converted to a 1401 and the University of Missouri had converted its unit record system to a 1440 computer, in this case not a university computer but one used solely by the library.[22] In California, the Honnold Library, which serves the six Claremont Colleges, implemented a computerized acquisition system using an IBM Model 40. The fullest bibliographic information available was entered as early in processing as possible, and a book catalog was produced as the final step in the system.[23] The University of Maryland, which had a unit record system modeled after Missouri's, converted to an off-line system using several computers in succession, most recently a Univac 9300.[24,25]

Other Ivy League universities were not to be outdone by Yale. Harvard implemented a successful system in 1967, Cornell in 1968, and Columbia between 1968 and 1971. The Harvard system automatically edits order information for obvious mistakes such as lack of vendor, unusually high price, and invalid fund coding before producing orders. Prices need not be in United States dollars, since the computer has been programmed to convert all foreign currencies into dollars at the current rate of exchange, which can be altered daily if needed. The system checks the outstanding order file periodically, and claims are automatically produced if orders have not been received in the time specified by the selecting librarians; if an item has still not been received after two claims have been produced and a third survey of the files made, the order is automatically cancelled. Data for almost 600 separate library accounts are maintained. The system

> has speeded up the ordering process to a point where what used to take weeks now requires only a day or so. Indeed, large quantities of 'Rush' orders have been completely processed and mailed in less than a day without seriously inconveniencing the system. Furthermore, book selectors can now know the up-to-the-minute status of their book fund rather than be forced to guess from quarterly reports.[26,27]

The Columbia system is remarkable particularly for the size and power of the equipment used: two IBM 360s, a Model 91 coupled with a Model 75, one of the most powerful complexes in the world at the time it was installed. Input is prepared on IBM magnetic tape Selectric typewriters (MTSTs) and converted to machine-readable form on a Digidata System 30 converter. Records for materials in all Roman alphabet languages and in transliterated Cyrillic languages are handled by the system, as are microforms, maps, and speech records, but not serials; and material received through purchase, blanket order, standing order, gift, exchange, deposit, and cooperative acquisition programs are all included. As in the Yale system, the flow of materials is monitored through acquisitions and cataloging departments and until catalog cards are filed in the public catalog. About 65,000 orders are processed annually for an impressively low 93 cents per order.[28]

2. Acquisition Systems

An acquisition system differing from others in its extensive use of paper tape was implemented in 1968 at the University of British Columbia. Friden Flexowriters were used to punch the paper tapes as a by-product of such activities as typing orders, processing invoices, and receiving books. The paper tape then served as input to a PDP-11 computer which, in conjunction with a Honeywell 200, did the processing. The usual orders outstanding lists, claims, cancellation notices, and fund reports were produced, as was a list of current accessions, later discontinued for lack of user interest.[29]

A system originally developed in 1968 at Florida Atlantic University for use on an IBM 360 was transferred to Arizona State University and implemented there, on a Honeywell 200, in 1971. "Introduction of the system," claims one study, "resulted in a substantial transfer of personnel from technical processing to public services ... Costs on a per volume circulated basis for 1971/1972 were $3.79 as opposed to $4.03 for 1969/1970 ... There was also a substantial reduction of backlog in the technical processing operation."[30]

Of later off-line, batch-processing systems, one in particular may be noted because of the unusually small size of both the system and the institution involved. This is the acquisition system implemented in 1971 on an IBM 360 Model 30 at Parkland College, a two-year community college in Champaign, Illinois. The system has required the addition of an extra staff member for keypunching, plus $170 per month for a model 129 keypunch, $400 per year for punch cards and magnetic tape, and several hundred dollars more per year for specially printed forms, but the library staff apparently believes these costs are offset to some extent by the fact that it no longer orders items preprocessed at a cost of $2.05 per item.[31]

Among special libraries, perhaps the best-known batch-processing system is at the Washington University School of Medicine Library in St. Louis. The system was begun in 1965 in conjunction with a book catalog project. Cards punched with the order information were used to produce orders on an IBM 870 Document Writer (a machine similar to the Cardatype described earlier, which it made obsolescent). The cards were then used to update the magnetic tape record of orders outstanding and orders received, using the university's 1401 computer. Later changes in the status of particular orders were indicated on copies of the order form, then punched into cards, which again were used to update the magnetic tape file. Some seventeen different lists were printed out from the file at periodic intervals.[32]

After living with the system for several years, the library decided to redesign the system during 1969.

> The old system had been predicated on the belief that the data collected at the time of the book order need only be slightly amended for catalog purposes. This attractive idea, unfortunately, was found wanting in practice. Thus, the first step was the separation of the acquisitions from the cataloging system. This was accomplished in December 1968. All incomplete acquisition transactions (i.e., all 'on order, not received' items) were taken from the master tape and put on a smaller tape. This became the acquisition tape; what remained was cataloging data. The acquisition system is now running as a separate system independent of the catalog function but still using the original program.[33]

Very few computerized acquisition systems of this type have been reported in public libraries. Several that developed from unit record systems have already been noted, but only one that was initiated as a computerized system has received wide attention. This is the batch-processing system of the Orange County (California) Public Library. It began as a straightforward book purchasing system in 1966, using an IBM 1460 computer. After converting the system to run on a 360 Model 30 and then on an RCA Spectra 70 Model 45 computer, the library decided to redesign the system entirely in order to incorporate additional features, including a book catalog. Both library staff and a commercial software firm were used to accomplish the design and programming tasks. The new system, termed BIBLIOS (for Book Inventory Building Library Information Oriented System) was implemented in 1969, also on the RCA Spectra 70 computer owned by the county. Development costs were just over $100,000 for the acquisitions portion of the system, and the cost of ordering and receiving a title under the system has been calculated at approximately $2.23.[34-36]

2. Acquisition Systems

On-line interactive systems

In 1967, Connie Dunlap, developer of the University of Michigan system and at that time head of their acquisitions department, spoke to an ALA Preconference on Library Automation regarding the status of acquisition systems. No on-line systems were then in use, she pointed out, and although several were planned, it appeared likely that most institutions would find such systems too expensive.[37] By 1975, however, the costs of on-line storage and the necessary terminal equipment had declined dramatically, and over a dozen such systems were in operation.

Perhaps the earliest to be implemented was at Washington State University in 1968, using three IBM 1050s (terminals with typewriter-like keyboards) on-line to an IBM Model 67. Paper-tape readers and punches are attached to the 1050s to provide an alternative means of entry, and as backup to the on-line system. As purchase order information is entered, each field of information is "tagged" (assigned a unique code) by the terminal operator, and the computer edits each field for valid order number, correct budget information, and so forth. When the information has been entered, the operator visually edits the resulting typed version and makes any necessary corrections on the spot. A code indicating that the record has been edited is then entered on the record, without which the record cannot be processed. The entry and editing process requires an average of about three minutes per title.

The 1050 terminals are also used to input receiving and invoice information, to enter accession numbers, and to indicate that orders can be cleared from the in-process file. Washington State has adopted the Washington University-Yale University process control technique, and as a by-product of the order entry procedure a book card is created for insertion in IBM 357 card readers to indicate when a book is received and moves through various stages in processing.

Because both on-line and off-line input (through the paper-tape devices) are possible, the library has made comparative studies of the two methods. The results indicate that operators prefer to work on-line, and make fewer errors as a result. Most errors are identified immediately by the computer, or are recognized by the operator, so they can be corrected at once and the amount of erroneous information flowing through the system is drastically reduced. The increased efficiency made possible by improved communication between man and machine is thus concretely demonstrated.[38]

By 1969, M.I.T. was using another keyboard terminal, the IBM 2741, to enter corrections to orders previously input on paper tape. The use of the terminal was limited to a seven-day period beginning on the 17th of the month, however, and appears to have been merely a means of avoiding the necessity for correcting the paper tapes and re-inputting them. No searching was done via the terminal, and although the device could print out information from the computer no real interaction appears to have taken place or been intended. The project was funded through the Computer Center, not the library, and when the funds were cut off in September of 1972 the system was discontinued.[39]

Meanwhile, also in 1969 and also in Massachusetts, terminals with visual display screens were being used for the first time in an acquisition system. The "Book Order and Selection System" (BOSS) of the University of Massachusetts in Amherst uses four such devices (in this case, IBM 2260s--see Fig. 2-7) on-line to an IBM 370/145 computer. Design of the system began in 1968, and less than twelve months elapsed before the system was operational. Currently BOSS processes about 90,000 orders per year, maintains the on-order file, provides both receiving and invoicing information, and produces claims for items not received. The original order information as well as changes are entered via the terminal; since the visual display shows an outline or "mask" of the information to be entered, no special coding forms are required. If a keying error is caught by the computer, the visual display screen immediately indicates it. After the error is corrected and the computer determines that all required information has been entered, a mask for the next order is displayed. The orders outstanding file can be searched on the 2260 by order number, author, title, or Library of Congress card number. The unit

2. Acquisition Systems

FIG. 2-7. IBM 2260 visual display terminal.

cost for acquisition of an item has been calculated at $2.55, which includes the cost of searching (not normally a function handled by a batch-processing system) and some costs properly assignable to cataloging. Manual file maintenance has been substantially reduced, and the backlog of processing eliminated.[40-42]

A smaller system was implemented at Oregon State University in 1970 using a CDC 3300 computer and a CDC 210 (later 211) terminal with a visual display screen as well as a 35 KSR teletype (keyboard) terminal. Dubbed LOLITA (for Library On-Line Information and Text Access), the system was developed over a three-year period for around $90,000, a modest figure compared to most other early on-line systems. In part this low cost was possible because an existing time-sharing system at the university's computer center was used, and "programming efforts could be concentrated exclusively on the design of LOLITA and an earlier pilot project ... No time was needed to design, debug or redesign the operating system software, as was necessary at Washington State University and the University of Chicago."[43]

One report indicates that "acquisitions personnel have been transferred to other duties, bookkeeping loads on the college bookkeeping operation have been reduced, lists of new books are more complete and are produced with less labor, and the system provides input to the cataloging operation which has resulted in some further saving there. The fund accounting system is sound and is now accepted by the state for legal accounting purposes."[44] An interesting feature is a provision for entering orders into the system and "holding" them until funds become available. In a recent fiscal year, the library received enough funds in the last ten days to double monographic purchases for the year, and despite the shortness of time the library was able to encumber the funds using this capability.[45]

Syracuse and Northwestern Universities both implemented on-line acquisition systems during 1971 using keyboard terminals in the IBM 2740 series, and both connected to IBM 370 computers. Despite some similarity in equipment, however, the systems have marked differences. Northwestern's provides input from MARC tapes, converts foreign currency, and writes checks, whereas Syracuse's does not; on the other hand, Syracuse's system automatically issues cancellation notices, checks for duplicate billing and duplicate orders, assigns funds based on the subject matter of the item being ordered, offers access by vendor, fund, series, and date ordered, produces accession lists and delinquent order lists, and provides a wide variety of other management information, none of which is provided at Northwestern. Unfortunately, no costs for either system have been published.[46]

Perhaps the most sophisticated system presently in operation is Stanford University's BALLOTS (for Bibliographic Automation of Large Library Operations using a Time-Sharing System). BALLOTS is a combined or "integrated" technical processing system, and includes both acquisition and cataloging functions. By 1975, over $2.5 million in grants from the Office of Education, the Council on Library Resources, and the National Endowment for the Humanities had been spent on its

2. Acquisition Systems

development. Design began in 1967, but the first production operations did not occur until 1972, when the first part of the acquisition system (the "MARC module") was implemented. The first segment provided the capability of searching machine-readable cataloging data supplied by the Library of Congress, and using it to order and catalog books. During the first year only MARC titles could be handled, but by late 1973 other parts of the system had been implemented, and non-MARC titles could also be acquired and cataloged. Serials, standing orders, and approval orders are also now handled by the system, although in contrast to most other acquisition systems fund accounting is not.

The equipment used is a large IBM 360 Model 67 computer, a small PDP 11 computer as an intermediary, and a number of Sanders 804 programmable display terminals; cataloging and acquisition departments share 11 terminals, and others are located at the reference desks in the main and undergraduate libraries, where library staff assist the public in searching the files.

The searching capabilities of the system are in fact its most elegant feature, with many indexes on-line and numerous automatic hints and instructions from the computer as a search progresses. There is also a program for training new users of the system via the terminal itself.[47-52]

A similarly sophisticated system implemented the same year (1972) at Dartmouth College is also of interest. This one handles acquisitions but not cataloging, since Dartmouth uses the Ohio College Library Center (OCLC) program described in Chapter 5. Two cathode-ray tube terminals and two Model 33 teletype machines are used for communication with the computer (a Honeywell GE-635). Searching is performed primarily on two files, an in-process file and a vendor file, the latter providing such vendor performance statistics as the average time to fill an order, average number of claims, and average discount. Perhaps because the number of orders in process at any one time is relatively low (compared to the large university and public libraries in which such on-line systems are more commonly found) an in-process list is still printed out weekly, even though the same information is available through terminal inquiry. The relatively low volume may also account in part for the fact that the costs of the automated system appear substantially higher than for the previous manual system: about $8.75 per item processed, versus $6.21 before. One observer has commented that "a tauter, less complex system could provide adequate speed and control at a substantially lower cost," and it is possible that the library is paying a significant premium for the sophistication or the system.[53]

A useful contrast, to cite one final example, is the on-line system in operation since 1972 at the Cleveland Public Library. Cleveland had previously used batch-processing systems: an IBM 1401 system from 1965 to 1968, and an IBM 360 Model 20 system from 1968 to 1972. In 1972 it purchased not one, but two LIBS 100 minicomputer systems from Computer Library Services Inc. (CLSI), complete with all programs necessary to run the systems, for a total price of $57,000 per system. Cleveland's objectives in switching to on-line minicomputers were "to escape from a batch processing system" with separate data processing and acquisitions departments and the many problems arising from split responsibilities, "to get away from the massive generation of reports and listings that were of little value for management purposes," and "to keep track of the flow of materials and dollars at a reasonable price."[54]

The heart of each of the new systems is a Digital Equipment Corporation PDP-11 with specially designed terminals. Input, receiving, searching, and updating may all be performed on-line. In-process control and a variety of management information are also provided. During the first two years of operation, each system had been out of operation less than 5 percent of the time, and never had both been out of operation at the same time. Published cost figures reflect an annual cost of $55,668 per year versus $123,360 per year for the former IBM system; the cost per item processed was an impressive forty-six cents.[55]

2. Acquisition Systems 35

NOTES

1. Mary T. Howe, "Mechanization in the Decatur Public Library," in *IBM Library Mechanization Symposium, Endicott, New York, May 25, 1964*, International Business Machines, White Plains, N.Y. [1965], pp. 1-13.
2. Lorin R. Burns, "The Use of IBM Unit Record Equipment in the Lake County Public Library," in *IBM Library Mechanization Symposium, Endicott, New York, May 25, 1964*, International Business Machines [1965], pp. 15-35.
3. Ralph H. Parker, "Development of Automatic Systems at the University of Missouri Library," in *Proceedings of the 1963 Clinic on Library Applications of Data Processing*, University of Illinois Graduate School of Library Science, Urbana, 1964, pp. 46-48.
4. Eleanor F. Morrissey, "A Mechanized Book Order and Accounting Routine," *Southeastern Librarian*, 15, 143-148 (Fall 1965).
5. G. E. Randall and Roger P. Bristol, "PIL (Processing Information List) of a Computer-Controlled Processing Record," *Special Libraries*, 55, 82-86 (February 1964).
6. Guenter A. Jansen, *Univac Electronic Data Processing in the Public Library Systems of Long Island*, Univac Division, Sperry Rand Corporation, Washington, D.C. [1968?]
7. *Univac Data Processing Procedures for Library Systems*, Univac Division, Sperry Rand Corporation, Washington, D.C. [1968?]
8. *The Year We Pushed the Button*, Nassau Library System, Hempstead, New York [1965?]
9. Louis A. Schultheiss, "Data Processing Aids in Acquisition Work," *Library Resources & Technical Services*, 9, 66-72 (Winter 1965).
10. Thomas L. Minder, "Automation--the Acquisitions Program at the Pennsylvania State University Library," in *IBM Library Mechanization Symposium, Endicott, New York, May 25, 1964*, International Business Machines, White Plains, N.Y. [1965], pp. 145-156.
11. Thomas Minder and Gerald Lazorick, "Automation of the Penn State University Acquisitions Department," in *IBM Library Mechanization Symposium, Endicott, New York, May 25, 1964*, International Business Machines, White Plains, N.Y. [1965], pp. 157-163.
12. Joseph Becker, "System Analysis--Prelude to Library Data Processing," *ALA Bulletin*, 59, 293-297 (April 1965).
13. Connie Dunlap, "Automated Acquisitions Procedures at the University of Michigan Library," *Library Resources & Technical Services*, 11, 192-202 (Spring 1967).

14. James W. Thomson and Robert H. Muller, "The Computer-Based Book Order System at the University of Michigan Library: a Review and Evaluation," in *Proceedings of the 1968 Clinic on Library Applications of Data Processing*, University of Illinois Graduate School of Library Science, Urbana, 1969, pp. 54-78.
15. Connie Dunlap, "The Automation of Acquisitions Systems," in *Library Automation, a State of the Art Review*, American Library Association, Chicago, 1969, p. 41.
16. Connie Dunlap, "Mechanization of Acquisitions Processes," in *Advances in Librarianship*, Melvin J. Voigt, ed., Academic Press, New York, 1970, vol. 1, pp. 44-48.
17. Stephen R. Salmon, "Automation of Library Procedures at Washington University," *Missouri Library Association Quarterly*, 27, 13-14 (March 1966).
18. Sally Alanen, David E. Sparks and Frederick G. Kilgour, "A Computer-Monitored Library Technical Processing System," in *Progress in Information Science and Technology; Proceedings of the American Documentation Institute 1966 Annual Meeting, October 3-7, 1966, Santa Monica, California*, Adrianne Press, Woodland Hills, California, 1966, pp. 419-426.
19. Sandra E. Stone, *History of Automation at Yale University Library*, Yale University Library, New Haven, Connecticut, 1973, pp. 6, 10.
20. *Ibid.*, pp. 5-6.
21. Lawrence R. Buckland, James Dolby and Mary Madden, *Final Report, Phase I: Survey of Automated Library Systems*, Inforonics, Inc., Maynard, Mass., 1973, pp. F 1-4.
22. Ralph H. Parker, "Not a Shared System," *Library Journal*, 92, 2967-2970 (November 1, 1967).
23. Robert F. Teare, "Experience to Date in Automated Acquisitions at Honnold Library," in *Proceedings of the American Society for Information Science*, v. 6, *Cooperating Information Societies*, Greenwood, Westport, Conn., 1969, pp. 29-37.
24. Carl R. Cox, "Mechanized Acquisitions Procedures at the University of Maryland," *College & Research Libraries*, 26, 233-236 (May 1965).
25. Carl R. Cox, "The Mechanization of Acquisition and Circulation Procedures at the University of Maryland Library," in *IBM Library Mechanization Symposium, Endicott, New York, May 25, 1964*, International Business Machines, White Plains, New York [1965], pp. 206-225.
26. Richard De Gennaro, "Automation in the Harvard College Library," *Harvard Library Bulletin*, 16, 231 (July 1968).
27. *Widener Library Acquisitions System*, Harvard University Library, Cambridge, Mass., [1969?] pp. 1-2.

2. Acquisition Systems

28. Richard Phillips Palmer, *Case Studies in Library Computer Systems*, R. R. Bowker, New York, 1973, pp. 149-160.
29. Buckland, *op. cit.*, table following p. 38 and pp. P 2-3.
30. *Ibid.*, p. W 1.
31. Ruth C. Carter, "Automation of Acquisitions at Parkland College," *Journal of Library Automation*, 5, 118-136 (June 1972).
32. Evelyn A. Moore, Estelle Brodman, and Geraldine S. Cohen, "Mechanization of Library Procedures in the Medium-Sized Medical Library: III. Acquisitions and Catalog," *Bulletin of the Medical Library Association*, 53, 305-328 (July 1965).
33. Glyn Evans and Estelle Brodman, *The Redesign of the Automated Acquisitions-Catalog System at Washington University School of Medicine Library*, the Library, St. Louis, 1969, p. 1.
34. John C. Kountz and Robert Norton, "BIBLIOS--A Modular Approach to Total Library ADP," in *American Society for Information Science: Proceedings*, v. 6, *Cooperating Information Societies*, Greenwood, Westport, Conn., 1969, pp. 39-50.
35. John C. Kountz, "BIBLIOS Revisited," *Journal of Library Automation*, 5, 63-86 (June 1972).
36. Buckland, *op. cit.*, table following p. 38 and pp. 1-2.
37. Connie Dunlap, "The Automation of Acquisitions Systems," in *Library Automation, a State of the Art Review*, American Library Association, Chicago, 1969, p. 39.
38. Dunlap, "Mechanization of Acquisitions Processes," pp. 50-52. See also Thomas K. Burgess, "Criteria for Design of an On-line Acquisitions System at Washington State University Library," in *Proceedings of the 1969 Clinic on Library Applications of Data Processing*, University of Illinois Graduate School of Library Science, Urbana, 1970, pp. 50-66.
39. Palmer, *op. cit.*, pp. 161-176.
40. *Ibid.*, pp. 140-148.
41. James H. Kennedy and James S. Sokoloski, "Man-Machine Considerations of an Operational On-line University Library Acquisitions System," in *Proceedings of the American Society for Information Science*, 7, 65-67 (1970).
42. Buckland, *op. cit.*, pp. D 1-5.
43. Frances G. Spigai and Thomas Mahan, "On-line Acquisitions by LOLITA," *Journal of Library Automation*, 3, 277 (December 1970); see also Larry Auld and Robert Baker, "LOLITA: An On-Line Book Order and Fund Accounting System," *Proceedings of the 1972 Clinic on Library Applications of Data Processing*, University of Illinois Graduate School of Library Science, Urbana, 1973, pp. 29-53.

44. Buckland, *op. cit.*, pp. R 1-2.
45. *Ibid.*, p. R 2.
46. Buckland, *op. cit.*, table following p. 38 and pp. A 1-2.
47. "BALLOTS-MARC Operations at Stanford University," *Library of Congress Information Bulletin*, 32, 130-131 (April 13, 1973).
48. Glee Cady et al., *System Scope for Library Automation and Generalized Information Storage and Retrieval at Stanford University*, Stanford University, Stanford, California, 1970.
49. Allen Veaner, Hank Epstein, and John Schroeder, "The Stanford Experience," in *Collaborative Library Systems Development*, M.I.T. Press, Cambridge, Mass., 1971, pp. 42-68.
50. Buckland, *op. cit.*, table following p. 38 and pp. Q 1-2.
51. Project BALLOTS and the Stanford University Libraries, "Stanford University's BALLOTS System," *Journal of Library Automation*, 8, 31-50 (March 1975).
52. Wayne Davison, "Minicomputers and Library Automation: The Stanford Experience," in *Proceedings of the 1974 Clinic on Library Applications of Data Processing: Applications of Minicomputers to Library and Related Problems*, University of Illinois Graduate School of Library Science, Urbana, 1975, pp. 55-79.
53. Palmer, *op. cit.*, pp. 188-204.
54. *Ibid.*, p. 186.
55. *Ibid.*, pp. 177-187, and Buckland, *op. cit.*, pp. G 1-3 and table following p. 38.

Chapter 3

CATALOGING SYSTEMS
BEFORE MARC

In no other area of library automation has activity been so intense as in the manipulation of cataloging data. A survey conducted by the LARC Association in 1970 revealed a total of 158 cataloging systems and 112 systems involved in the production of special catalogs and bibliographies;[1] there are undoubtedly more, since many libraries did not respond to the questionnaire, including some with cataloging systems reported in the literature. The intellectual work of describing the physical book or item and analyzing its subject content has been largely untouched, but machines have been used to produce a wide variety of products derived from such description and analysis, to control the clerical and technical processes involved, and to promote the exchange and use of cataloging data regionally and nationally.

The principal activity of cataloging systems remains the production of catalog cards, but the availability of high-speed printers driven by computers has sparked a remarkable revival of interest in an older way of presenting cataloging information, the book catalog. Other printed products, created usually as by-products rather than as a primary goal, include spine labels, book plates, book pockets (or labels for placement on book pockets), and book cards for use in either manual or automated circulation systems. In recent years, there has also been a growing recognition that substantial economic benefits would result if cataloging data could be provided to individual libraries in a timely fashion from a centralized source, thus lowering the cost of the intellectual effort of cataloging in the individual libraries; this in turn has resulted in an increased emphasis on the ability to search centralized cataloging "data bases," usually via terminals linked to computers.

Other functions performed by cataloging systems include

1. Creation of worksheets for cataloging, or for input of cataloging data
2. Prompting of system operators, typists or catalogers by displaying possible input "tags," noting misspellings and illogical combinations of data, and leading operators from one step to the next
3. Maintenance of name and subject authority files, i.e., lists of terms used in the system, the sources of the terms, and the cross-references made to and from the terms
4. Production of catalog cross-reference cards
5. Provision for editing of data for corrections and revisions
6. Arrangement of entries in filing sequence, both for catalog cards and book catalogs
7. Controlling the movement or location of material, during cataloging or physical preparation, or while in a cataloging arrearage
8. Ordering of catalog cards from a central source
9. Selective listing of catalog records by specified criteria, such as subject, geographical area covered, date of publication, or combinations of such criteria

The mechanical means used to perform these functions have generally followed the technological developments described in the previous chapter, but with some important differences and additions. The following types are identifiable:

3. Cataloging Systems Before MARC   41

    1. Systems based on unit record equipment
    2. Systems based on automatic typewriters and associated equipment driven by punched tape, magnetic tape, or punched cards
    3. Systems using card-actuated sequential cameras
    4. Off-line batch-processing systems using computers
    5. On-line systems using various types of terminals for searching for initiating catalog card or book catalog production (with the production itself usually done off-line); and sometimes for reference by users to the catalog data

This chapter discusses the first three categories, as well as off-line systems implemented before the development of the MARC (Machine-Readable Cataloging) Project at the Library of Congress. Chapter 4 discusses MARC and off-line systems based on MARC, and Chapter 5 completes the discussion of cataloging systems with coverage of the Ohio College Library Center (OCLC) and other on-line cataloging systems.

Cataloging systems based on
unit record equipment

The earliest cataloging applications used unit record equipment to produce catalogs in book form. Typically, the cataloging information was keypunched, and the resulting punched cards were then sorted into filing sequence (either manually or with the assistance of mechanical sorters) and passed through a tabulator to produce printed pages. In many cases, these printed pages were photographed and then reproduced by offset printing to provide a large number of copies of the catalog. The method is simple, and once created the machine record can be reused many times. There are marked disadvantages to this method, however:

    1. Large files of punched cards must be kept in sequence and handled manually every time a catalog is produced, or when additional records are sorted into the file;
    2. The typography available is primitive, without lowercase letters, diacritics, or special characters;

3. Only a limited amount of data can be placed on each card, so either extremely brief entries must be used, or multiple cards must be used for each entry, with the cards tied together by a special number created for each entry and punched in each card;

4. Only the simplest filing arrangements can be handled mechanically; the rest must either be done by hand, or simplified filing rules must be adopted.

Despite these limitations, a large number of book catalogs have been produced in this manner. The Library of Congress began experimenting with the process in 1946, and the catalog of *Serial Titles Newly Received* (now called *New Serial Titles*), which the Library began publishing in 1950, was probably the first successful, nonexperimental punched-card catalog.[2] Only a year later, in 1951, the King County (Washington) Public Library system began a book catalog system with separate catalogs for each individual library, supplemented by weekly lists. The punched cards were reproduced on an IBM 513 Reproducer for as many added entries as needed, arranged in the desired sequence, then run through an IBM 402 tabulator to produce the pages.[3] Only one punched card was used for each book producing what later came to be called a "short-title" catalog or "book list."

Similar catalogs were produced by the University of Rochester,[4] the New York State Library, and a number of special libraries. In most cases, the book form was not intended as a replacement for the library's traditional card catalog, but was issued in order to make bibliographic information more available to widely scattered patrons. At Rochester, for example, the "primary purpose" was "to put an accurate list of all books and journals in the science libraries on the desk of each member of the faculty and research staff in the departments served by each library."[5] Not every library keeps its card catalog, however; since the 1960s, the Lake County (Indiana) Public Library has relied entirely on a brief-entry book catalog produced on an IBM 403 with 15-part paper. The catalog is in three sections--author, title, and subject--which simplifies sorting and consultation

3. Cataloging Systems Before MARC 43

(see Fig. 3-1). A closed-circuit teletype system connecting the 14 branches and their Technical Processing Center is used to provide additional information, as well as for other purposes.[6]

Perhaps the earliest example of a machine-produced book catalog with reasonably full entries was the Los Angeles County Public Library catalog produced in 1955. At that time, there were 114 branches and

Author & First Initial		Title		Classification	Copies Available
BECHDOLT	J	ON THE AIR	J		10
BECK	H	GOING TO CAMP	J	796.54	1
BECK	L	ANNE BOLEYN			1
BECK	L	DIVINE LADY			2
BECK	L	HUMAN GROWTH		611013	8
BECK	S	SIMPLICITY OF SCIENC		500	2
BECK	V	LOVE ON THE RUN	Y		1
BECK	H	HOW TO BECOME AMERIC		32361	2

Author Catalog

Title	Author & First Initial		Classification	Copies Available
E M FORSTER	TRILLING	L	829.91	1
EACH BRIGHT RIVER	MCNEILLY	M		1
EACH IN HIS WAY	GALL	A J		2
EACH MANS SON	MCCLENNAN	H		1
EACH TO THE OTHER	LAFARGE	C	811.5	1
EAGLE OF NIAGARA	BRICK	J		2

Title Catalog

Subject Class	Author & First Initial		Title	Year
AIR CONDITIONING				
62156	ANDERSON	E	AUDELS REFRIGERATIO	59
69793	DERMAN	J	HOME AIR CONDITIONI	58
697	GRAHAM	F	AUDELS HOUSE HEATIN	48
69790	SEVERNS	W	AIR CONDITIONING AN	58

Subject Catalog

FIG. 3-1. Book catalog, Lake County (Indiana) Public Library.

service outlets, only 25 of which had card catalogs, and even these were incomplete and costly to maintain. Meetings with the branch librarians resulted in decisions to include the full author, full title, edition (other than the first), date of publication, volumes if more than one, and a short annotation where appropriate for the subject catalog. Most conventional notes and the collation were omitted. The catalogs were issued in eight parts: for adults, there were separate author, title, subject, fiction, and foreign language catalogs; and for children there were separate author, title, and subject catalogs. The subject catalogs were the most complete, as they included annotations as well as "see" and "see also" references, and analytics for anthologies. The author catalogs contained most of the bibliographic data except for annotations, and the title catalogs were even briefer--a straight alphabetic listing, with only the authors and class numbers given in addition to the titles.[7]

A number of other public libraries adopted the Los Angeles County system or one similar to it in the early 1960s, including the Montgomery County (Maryland) Public Library, which (in a noteworthy example of library cooperation) was able to obtain from Los Angeles County a full set of the latter's book catalogs, the subject heading code book, a detailed description of keypunching procedures, 220,000 subject heading cards, and even the wired control panels for the IBM 407 tabulator to be used! Studies indicated that the cost of the Montgomery County catalog was about the same as its card catalogs, with the added advantages of multiple copies for the branches (and incidentally for the county's secondary and elementary schools) and centralized control of error correction and filing.[8,9]

A few unit record cataloging systems produced catalog cards instead of book catalogs. One example is the library processing center for the Albuquerque Public School system, which in 1964 began producing catalog cards, book cards, and labels on a 407 (see Fig. 3-2). Most unit record systems, however, concentrated on book catalogs.

Automatic typewriter systems

In contrast, automatic typewriter systems were used almost exclusively for production of catalog cards. In such systems, keying

3. Cataloging Systems Before MARC   45

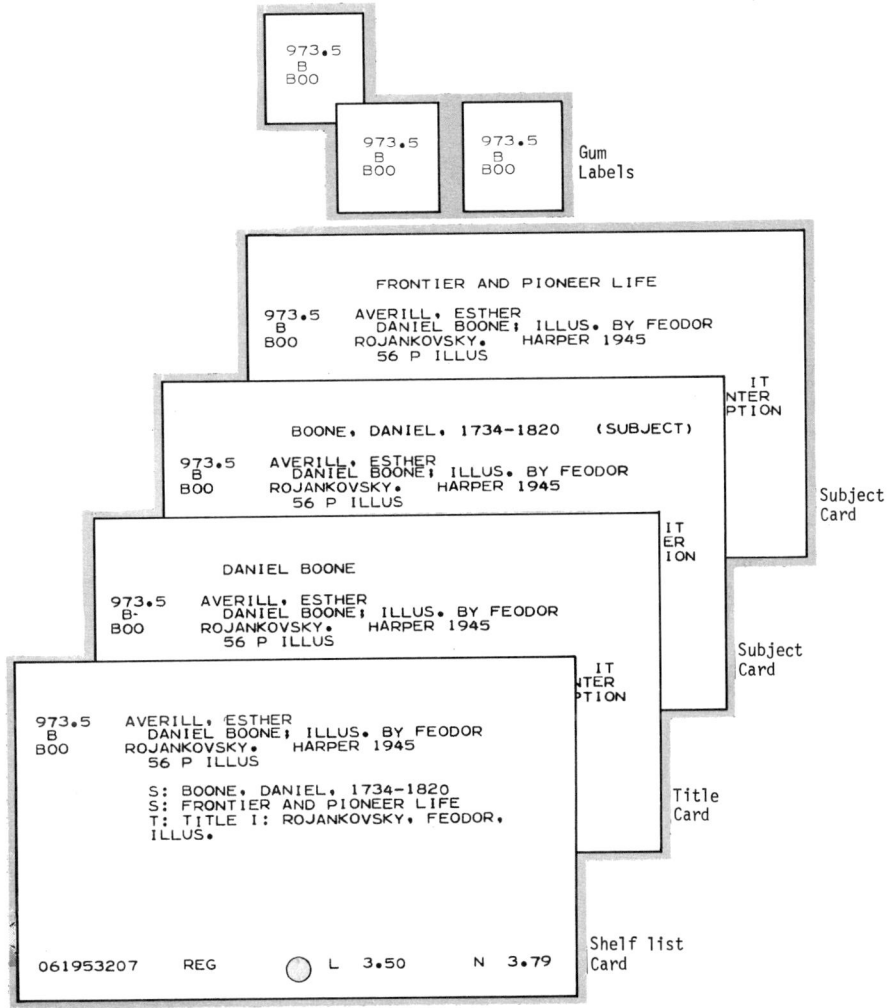

FIG. 3-2. Catalog cards and labels, Albuquerque Public School system.

the data does not produce punched cards; instead, a spool of either punched paper tape or magnetic tape is produced, and printing is done not on a separate machine like the tabulator, but on the same machine that does the input--that is, on an automatic typewriter. The primary advantage of such systems is the improved typography: lower case as well as upper case is normally available, diacritical marks can be used, and some such systems even provide subject headings in red, mimicking manually typed cards to such an extent that they are indistinguishable. Other advantages are the elimination of the need for great care in keeping sets of punched cards together, and the ability of most libraries to justify having the equipment housed in the library for its exclusive use, rather than having to depend on a centralized data processing facility for machine time and assistance.

Most of these early systems used Flexowriters (paper tape machines) and auxiliary devices that made it possible to program most of the operations involved in producing sets of catalog cards. The U.S. Naval Postgraduate School in Monterey, California began using such a system in the mid-1950s[10] and the California State Library in 1958. In the latter system, the cataloging data were typed on the Flexowriter, which simultaneously prepared two tapes, one for the unit card data and a second one containing the added entry headings. The unit card tape was spliced into a loop and placed on an auxiliary paper tape reader, and the heading tape was placed on a second reader. The unit card tape had switch codes which, when the typewriter was operating automatically, caused the machine to switch from reading the unit card tape to reading the heading tape at the proper points in the operation. The heading tape contained similar codes for carriage returns and indentations, so that the headings as well as the rest of the data were located properly on continuous catalog card stock. Later, the continuous stock was separated into individual cards.[11]

The University of Missouri began a more extensive Flexowriter system in 1963, and developed a special cutter to separate individual cards from the continuous stock, thereby eliminating the objectionable serrated edges associated with pre-perforated stock. At one time as many as 250,000 cards per year were being produced with the system at an average cost of six cents per card. A similar system, based on Missouri's, was developed at Washington University and began operation in 1964. All operation codes were inserted automatically

3. Cataloging Systems Before MARC

by the machine itself from special "program" tapes, so that the operators were relieved of the need to memorize codes and detailed procedures. Programs were also developed which automatically adjusted the spacing of the data for exceptional circumstances; if an added entry heading required three or more lines, for example, the rest of the catalog card information was automatically lowered the required number of spaces. As the Flexowriters typed the main entry cards during the automatic production phase, they also produced yet another tape, which was used to create several by-products of the system. The tape was accumulated on a self-winding reel until cards had been produced for all books on a book truck, and was then passed through an IBM 047 tape-to-card converter to produce book cards, in punched-card format, for use in an automated circulation system. Next, the tape accompanied the book truck to the processing room, where it was placed on a specially built Flexowriter, equipped with a Se-Lin labeling device, which automatically produced the labels for the books. The by-product tape could also be passed through the 047 to produce decks of punched cards for processing by computer to produce accession lists and specialized bibliographies, although in actual practice this capacity was never used except for demonstration purposes.[12]

Other Flexowriter systems were installed at the University of Colorado,[13] the University of British Columbia,[14] Cleveland State University,[15] and Georgia Institute of Technology,[16] the latter two based on the Washington University and Missouri systems. Another brand of automatic typewriters--the Dura Mach 10--formed the basis for similar systems at Boston University[17] and UCLA.[18] Virtually all of the automatic typewriter systems were later abandoned, however, because of constant difficulties in keeping the machines running properly and because of their relatively slow speeds compared to computer-driven printers.

A closely related group of machines called the IBM 870 Document Writing System was also used by a number of libraries in the early 1960s to produce catalog cards. The machinery was operated by punched

cards instead of paper tape, but in other respects was similar to
Flexowriter systems. The Los Angeles City Schools began using the
870 system in 1962, with the initial goal of reducing serious backlogs in catalog card production. The backlogs were indeed eliminated,
but for this type of application the machines had many of the same
drawbacks as tabulating equipment. Keeping sets of punched cards
together for each catalog record was cumbersome, and the number of
characters available, although greater than with tabulating equipment,
was still less than adequate. The librarian in charge saw this not
only as an operational difficulty, but also as an educational problem:
"Since the cards are produced for teaching-learning situations as
well as for finding purposes," she pointed out, "this is a serious
drawback, especially since there is an increase in the study of foreign languages in the schools."[19] The cost per set of catalog cards
for the new system was about the same as for the previous manual
system.

Other 870 systems were implemented the following year (1963) at
the Anaheim (California) Public Library and Yale University's Medical
School, but by the mid-1960s the 870 was largely superseded by IBM's
new 1050 system, a similar set of equipment that could use either
punched cards or paper tape (or both), and could be operated independently or connected to a computer. It also used a ball-shaped
printing mechanism like that of the IBM Selectric typewriters, which
permitted the substitution of interchangeable printing elements,
and thus different type fonts; a special typing element and keyboard
were even designed for library use. Early library users of the 1050
equipment were the Washington University School of Medicine and the
University of Chicago; both of these later abandoned the equipment,
however, because of frequent mechanical difficulties.

By the late 1960s, the 1050 system was itself superseded by
another new IBM system, the MTST (for Magnetic Tape Selectric Typewriter). As the name implies, it is also based on IBM's Selectric
typewriters, and operates by means of magnetic tape rather than
either punched cards or paper tape. The equipment has been widely

3. Cataloging Systems Before MARC   49

used for the production of catalog cards, using procedures similar to the earlier Flexowriter systems described above.[20] The University of California at Irvine installed such a system in 1968, Cornell University in 1969, and the University of Houston in 1970.[21] At Cornell and Houston, however, the MTSTs have since been replaced because of their cost, and Houston has installed a set of similar automatic typewriters called CPTs at about two-thirds the cost of the MTSTs. Tape-oriented automatic typewriters are becoming increasingly popular for business office use, and several models competitive with the MTSTs have recently become available.

One unique system of historical interest should also be mentioned here. In 1961 the Itek Corporation developed a system for the Air Force Cambridge Research Library in Bedford, Massachusetts, which used Flexowriters for input of the cataloging data and for printing of the catalog cards, but not for programming or arrangement of the cataloging information. Instead, a special prototype machine called the "crossfiler" was used to expand and arrange the data after input and before printing it out on the Flexowriters. Input techniques were based on what its developers called a "machine-interpretable natural format;" that is, the natural typing operations (carriage returns, tabulating shifts, and spaces) were used in a fixed sequence to format the data during the input phase and to identify and control data elements during processing as well. The technique was simple and effective, reducing greatly the amount of coding that had to be added to the record and in this respect presaging the development of "format recognition" by the MARC project at the Library of Congress some years later (see Chapter 4).[22,23]

Sequential card camera systems

While the development of catalog card systems was in a phase dominated by automatic typewriters, book catalog systems passed from the unit record era to the use of another type of specialized equipment, the card-actuated sequential camera, some examples of which are still in use at this writing. There are several varieties, but in all such systems, the cataloging data is typed directly onto cards.

VariTyper Corporation's Foto-List camera and Kodak's List-O-Matic camera use standard-size punched cards, with the information typed in the center, usually by a VariTyper (a typewriter which permits use of various type faces and sizes) or a standard typewriter. The Foto-List photographs only one line at a time, whereas the List-O-Matic camera takes one, two, or three lines at a time. Normally numbers are also punched into these cards to provide the capability for sorting them into the desired sequence mechanically on standard punched-card sorters and collators, although in most applications some hand-sorting is also required. A third type, Lithoid's Compos-O-Line camera, accepts standard three-by-five-inch catalog cards, instead of punched cards, which has the disadvantage that no mechanical sorting is possible.

Regardless of how the cards are arranged, all such cameras then photograph the typed portions of the cards, in sequence, and produce photographic negatives which are cut and formatted into pages for printing by photolithography.

The principal advantage of the sequential card camera technique for producing book catalogs is the appearance of the final product, which is much more attractive and readable than the product of a punched-card system or computer print-out. A second advantage is that the photographing of cards takes place at a much faster rate (between 7,000 and 14,000 cards per hour) than the process of printing on a tabulator such as the 403 or 407. In the 1960s the cost of getting started was also less than with computer-produced systems.

The disadvantages of the sequential camera approach, on the other hand, are also substantial. Each separate entry must be typed--added entries cannot be generated automatically from a single typing of the main entry. The catalog information itself is not in machine-readable form, so that there is no possibility of manipulating it by machine, or using the data for other products. The method also shares with punched-card tabulating systems the disadvantage that large and increasing quantities of cards must be manually handled to produce each catalog; as Cartwright has noted, this becomes more and more cumbersome, expensive, and prone to error as the size of the file increases.[24]

3. Cataloging Systems Before MARC   51

The Los Angeles County Public Library, which as noted earlier began its book catalog with punched-card equipment, switched to the sequential card method in 1962, using a Foto-List system provided by a company called Econolist. The Free Library of Philadelphia began a book catalog program in 1963 using the Compos-O-Line camera in order to use the three-by-five-inch catalog cards already in its catalog and to avoid disruption of existing cataloging routines.[25] Many others--primarily public libraries--followed suit.

Off-line computer systems

As with acquisition systems, the increased availability of computers for library applications ushered in a new era for both card production and book catalog systems. Typically in such systems, the catalog data elements are punched into cards in much the same way as in unit record systems, although in some cases the data are punched into paper tape or recorded directly on magnetic tape. From this point on, however, the operations are performed differently. The information is fed into a computer, which normally checks for obvious errors in format and logic, and then stores the data on magnetic tape, magnetic disks, or occasionally on a variety of other storage devices. Since the information is stored in machine-readable form on machine-manipulable devices, there is no further necessity for physical handling of the data to produce cataloging products, apart from the computer operator's routine handling of magnetic tapes, disks, etc. In early systems, the computer programs for manipulating the data and producing output were normally punched in cards, which did require repetitive handling, but in later systems the programs are also on tapes or disks, and often are called up automatically as needed. All formatting is done by machine, and normally in book catalog systems the filing arrangement is also done automatically. In many catalog card systems, the entries are arranged in rough filing sequence by the computer before the cards are printed, thus speeding the manual filing process. The primary advantage of such systems is the freeing of library personnel from clerical routines; the primary disadvantage is the limited typography available, as with unit record systems, although computer printers with upper and lower-case chains and computer-driven photocomposition devices have lessened this problem.

Off-line catalog card systems

One of the earliest computerized catalog card systems was developed in the early 1960s as a by-product of an information retrieval system called SHARP (Ships Analysis and Retrieval Project), a joint venture of the Navy's Bureau of Ships Technical Library and the David Taylor Model Basin Applied Mathematics Laboratory. In addition to subject searches and information retrieval, various printed products were generated, among them catalog cards for all documents entered in the system (see Fig. 3-3).[26] By 1963, IBM had also begun to produce catalog cards using computers.[27]

From the standpoint of its influence on later developments, however, the most influential of the early systems was without doubt the one developed at Yale University. As noted earlier, the Yale Medical Library had begun producing cards on an IBM 870 system as early as 1963. By 1964, the library was using an IBM 1401 computer to "expand" the catalog data and create a full set of punched cards, with a "decklet" of cards representing all the information on each catalog card in the set. These punched cards were then used to drive the 870 system described earlier. Later the same year, an IBM 709 computer was also incorporated into the system to sort the data into filing order before the cards were punched.[28] By 1965, the library had abandoned the 870, and was using the computer printer with a special chain containing an expanded character set to print the cards (see Fig. 3-4).[29] This system was used until 1971, when it was finally discontinued, for two reasons: maintaining the growing data base on magnetic tapes (as opposed to disks) had become increasingly cumbersome, and the computer center had brought in an IBM 360 computer to replace the 7094 for which the system was designed. By this time, personnel at Yale had come to feel that systems designed for one library alone were rapidly becoming obsolete, and that the expense of reprogramming the system for the 360 could not therefore be justified.[30] The influence of the Yale system, however, was to be felt long after its discontinuance, as we shall see.

3. Cataloging Systems Before MARC

```
HYDROFOIL BOATS
GRUMMAN AIRCRAFT ENGINEERING CORPORATION. U104210
REPORT XAR-A-45.
EXPERIMENTAL STUDY OF HIGH SPEED
HYDROFOILS. VOLUME I.
PARTS I-III. WITH APPENDICES.
WRIGHT, H.A.
NOBS 84454                    8.26.63
                                      001V
     HYDROFOIL BOATS         HYDRODYNAMICS
     HYDROFOIL BOATS-DESIGN  HYDROFOILS
     MATHEMATICAL ANALYSIS   CONTRACT NOBS 84454


HYDROFOIL BOATS-DESIGN
GRUMMAN AIRCRAFT ENGINEERING CORPORATION. U104210
REPORT XAR-A-45.
EXPERIMENTAL STUDY OF HIGH SPEED
HYDROFOILS. VOLUME I.
PARTS I-III. WITH APPENDICES.
WRIGHT, H.A.
NOBS 84454                    8.26.63
                                      001V
     HYDROFOIL BOATS         HYDRODYNAMICS
     HYDROFOIL BOATS-DESIGN  HYDROFOILS
     MATHEMATICAL ANALYSIS   CONTRACT NOBS 84454


HYDRODYNAMICS
GRUMMAN AIRCRAFT ENGINEERING CORPORATION. U104210
REPORT XAR-A-45.
EXPERIMENTAL STUDY OF HIGH SPEED
HYDROFOILS. VOLUME I.
PARTS I-III. WITH APPENDICES.
WRIGHT, H.A.
NOBS 84454                    8.26.63
                                      001V
     HYDROFOIL BOATS         HYDRODYNAMICS
     HYDROFOIL BOATS-DESIGN  HYDROFOILS
     MATHEMATICAL ANALYSIS   CONTRACT NOBS 84454


HYDROFOILS
GRUMMAN AIRCRAFT ENGINEERING CORPORATION. U104210
REPORT XAR-A-45.
EXPERIMENTAL STUDY OF HIGH SPEED
HYDROFOILS. VOLUME I.
PARTS I-III. WITH APPENDICES.
WRIGHT, H.A.
NOBS 84454                    8.26.63
                                      001V
     HYDROFOIL BOATS         HYDRODYNAMICS
     HYDROFOIL BOATS-DESIGN  HYDROFOILS
     MATHEMATICAL ANALYSIS   CONTRACT NOBS 84454
```

FIG. 3-3. Catalog cards, Bureau of Ships Technical Library.

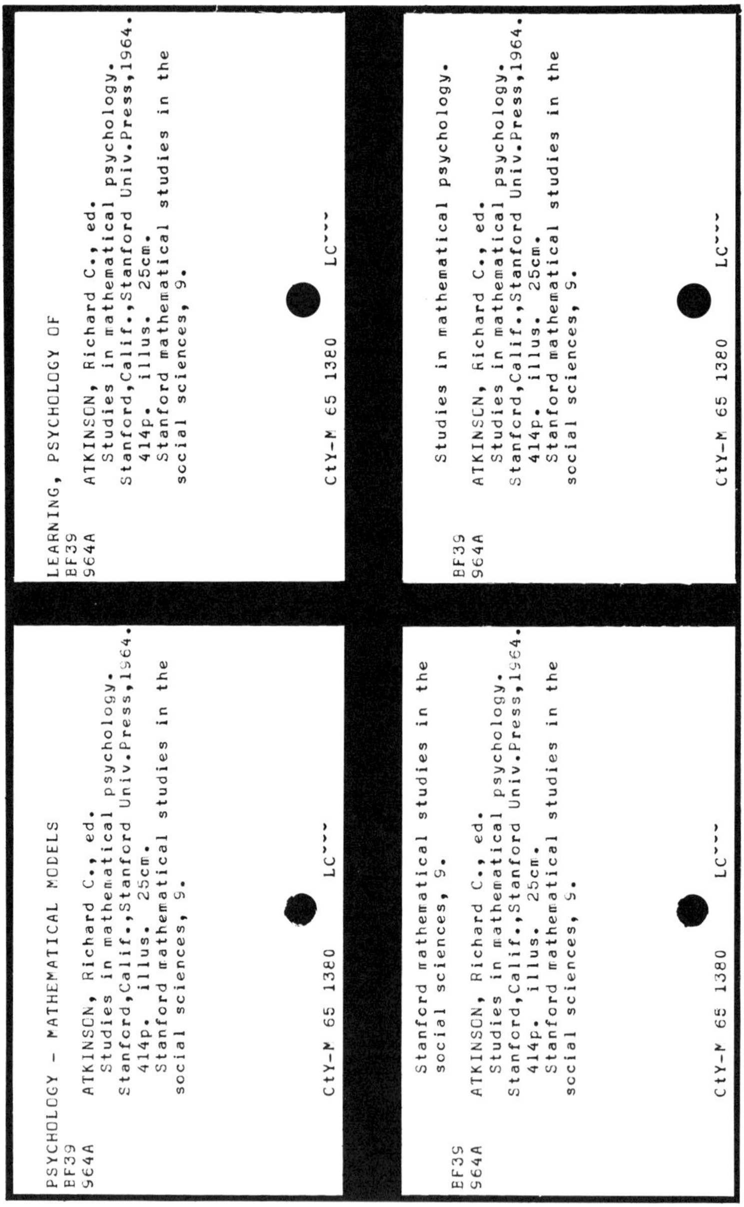

PSYCHOLOGY - MATHEMATICAL MODELS
BF39
964A ATKINSON, Richard C., ed.
Studies in mathematical psychology.
Stanford,Calif.,Stanford Univ.Press,1964.
414p. illus. 25cm.
Stanford mathematical studies in the
social sciences, 9.

CtY-M 65 1380 LC***

LEARNING, PSYCHOLOGY OF
BF39
964A ATKINSON, Richard C., ed.
Studies in mathematical psychology.
Stanford,Calif.,Stanford Univ.Press,1964.
414p. illus. 25cm.
Stanford mathematical studies in the
social sciences, 9.

CtY-M 65 1380 LC***

Stanford mathematical studies in the
social sciences, 9.
BF39
964A ATKINSON, Richard C., ed.
Studies in mathematical psychology.
Stanford,Calif.,Stanford Univ.Press,1964.
414p. illus. 25cm.
Stanford mathematical studies in the
social sciences, 9.

CtY-M 65 1380 LC***

Studies in mathematical psychology.
BF39
964A ATKINSON, Richard C., ed.
Studies in mathematical psychology.
Stanford,Calif.,Stanford Univ.Press,1964.
414p. illus. 25cm.
Stanford mathematical studies in the
social sciences, 9.

CtY-M 65 1380 LC***

FIG. 3-4. Catalog cards, Yale University Medical Library.

3. Cataloging Systems Before MARC   55

Other pre-MARC computerized catalog card systems include those of the Indiana University Regional Campus Libraries,[31] the Phillip Morris Research Library in Richmond, Virginia,[32] the Albuquerque, New Mexico public school libraries,[33] and the public library systems of Suffolk and Nassau Counties in New York.[34]

Off-line book catalog systems

Although the general procedures are the same, computerized book catalog systems differ from card production systems in several important ways: storage of the bibliographic data between issues of the book catalog is normally required; entries input between editions must be interfiled; and arrangement of individual entries in the desired filing sequence for book catalogs is complex, whereas most card systems arrange, if at all, only a relatively small number of cards in rough filing sequence before printing them out.

Early book catalog systems were characterized by the use of elaborate input coding forms, ruled into 80 columns like an IBM card. Catalogers or their assistants were required to print each letter carefully in a box, and to learn and assign a large number of codes identifying particular data elements. Later systems used worksheets with the codes (or "tags" as they came to be called) already pre-printed on the forms, and still later systems employed techniques which allowed conventional catalog cards to be "edited," that is, to have the tags merely added to data already printed on catalog cards or slips.

Processing of the catalog entries after input normally involves not only duplication of the entries under each heading, but also a significant amount of computer editing (noting missing data or illogical coding, for example) and several proofreading and error correction cycles. The computer must also sort entries into multiple sequences, since most book catalogs are divided catalogs--that is, instead of being arranged with all entries in a single filing sequence, the entries are divided into an author catalog, a title catalog, and a subject catalog, or some similar combination.

When all of the data have been edited, proofread, corrected, "expanded," sorted, and arranged in the proper sequence, the final step--production--can begin. This may be done on a conventional computer line printer (sometimes with a special uppercase and lowercase chain); with a computer-driven photocomposition device; or on a computer-output microfilm (COM) device.

The earliest project to use computer line printers to produce full-scale book catalogs was also one of the most successful. In 1963, the University of Toronto was asked by the Ontario government to develop basic collections of approximately 35,000 volumes each, complete with the necessary catalogs, for five new Ontario universities. In the ONULP (Ontario New Universities Library Project) that resulted, complete bibliographic information for the volumes purchased (including even the thickness of each volume) was keypunched; stored on magnetic tape by an IBM 1401 computer; edited, sorted and arranged on an IBM 7094 computer; and printed out in book catalog form on the 1401. The computer printer was equipped with a specially designed chain which contained uppercase and lowercase letters and a large number of diacritical marks (100 characters in all). The computer print-out was reduced to 60 percent of the original before printing plates were produced so that more information would be contained on each page (see Fig. 3-5).[35] Programs were written in COBOL (Common Business Oriented Language), so that the five new institutions could modify them more easily at a later date if they wished, and to make the initial programming task easier and more convenient, but the resulting programs were unusually lengthy in terms of processing time, a common problem with COBOL programs.[36] The first catalogs were produced in 1964, in 150 copies, and were followed by monthly supplements with quarterly, semiannual and annual cumulations until the project ended, in 1967, as planned. By that time, the university estimated that the book catalogs had cost a million dollars less than would have been required to create five new card catalogs.

3. Cataloging Systems Before MARC

FIG. 3-5. Book catalog, Ontario New Universities Library Project.

Another early computerized book catalog project was especially significant in terms of the formatting and programming techniques employed. The Boeing "SLIP" system was one of the first to provide a generalized set of programs which could produce a variety of printed products with only minor changes in the specifications incorporated in the input to the system, and it was also one of the earliest to use so-called "table-driven" programs for library automation purposes. A total of twelve different tables were constructed by the system's programs in the computer memory, and used to sort input data into various categories, depending both on the nature of the data (whether it was author, title, subject or imprint data, for example) and the eventual use to be made of it. At the production stage, the programs then used the tables to rearrange the data by the broad groups specified for the final product, and to arrange data within these groupings by filing sequence.

The book catalog produced by the system was divided into an author catalog and a title-subject catalog, the latter containing both conventional subject headings and "alternate title entries ... generated by rotation of the complete titles about the normal indexing locus, the left margin" (see Fig. 3-6).[37] These so-called "permuted" titles, which placed various significant words in the titles at the filing position and thus used the titles themselves to construct a different sort of subject approach, were to become common features of later systems. A modified form of the Library of Congress filing rules was used for the book catalog. Titles and permuted titles were sorted full length, continuing on to the first six characters of the author's name if necessary; similarly, authors were sorted on their full length, continuing into the first six characters of the title if necessary.

Friden Flexowriters were used for input, because the typewritten copy created at the same time made proofreading and correction easier, but the system was also designed to accept punched-card input. The paper tape from the Flexowriters was converted to magnetic tape using an IBM 1401 computer, the subsequent processing being done on an IBM 7094 computer as in the Toronto system.

3. Cataloging Systems Before MARC 59

STATISTICS ... GUIDE TO UNITED STATES GOVERNMENT
  ANDRIOT, JOHN L.. ARLINGTON, VA.. DOCUMENTS INDEX, 1961.. Z7554.U5G8
STATISTICS MANUAL, WITH EXAMPLES TAKEN FROM ORDNANCE DEVELOPMENT ...
  CROW, EDWIN L.. DAVIS, FRANCES A.. N.Y.. DOVER, 1960.. QA276.C885
STATISTICS OF EXTREMES ...
  GUMBEL, EMIL J.. N.Y.. COLUMBIA UNIV. PRESS, 1958.. QA276.G82
STEEL
  AMERICAN SOCIETY FOR METALS.. METALS HANDBOOK, 1948-DATE .... 4 V.. CLEVELAND, OHIO. PRO ALSO.. TA459.A5.R
STEEL- HEAT TREATMENT
  GROSSMANN, MARCUS A.. AMERICAN SOCIETY FOR METALS.. PRINCIPLES OF HEAT TREATMENT .... 4TH ED. CLEVELAND,
  A.M.S.. 1953.. TN672-G91.53
STEEL- SPECIFICATIONS
  AMERICAN INSTITUTE OF STEEL CONSTRUCTION.. STEEL CONSTRUCTION MANUAL .... 5TH ED., N.Y., 1946.. TA684.A47.46
STEEL- TESTING
  FREEMAN, JAMES W.. VOORHEES, HOWARD R.. RELAXATION PROPERTIES OF STEELS AND SUPERSTRENGTH ALLOYS AT ELEVATED
  TEMPERATURES .... PHILA., AMER. SOC. TESTING MATERIALS, 1956. PRO.. TA473.F58
STEEL, STRUCTURAL- HANDBOOKS
  AMERICAN INSTITUTE OF STEEL CONSTRUCTION.. STEEL CONSTRUCTION MANUAL .... 5TH ED., N.Y., 1946.. TA684.A47.46
STEEL CONSTRUCTION MANUAL ...
  AMERICAN INSTITUTE OF STEEL CONSTRUCTION.. 5TH ED., N.Y., 1946.. TA684.A47.46
STEEL FRAMES ... PLASTIC DESIGN OF
  BEEDLE, LYNN S.. N.Y.. WILEY, 1958. PRO.. TA684.B36
STELLAR ATMOSPHERES ...
  GREENSTEIN, JESSE L.. UNIV. OF CHICAGO PRESS. 1960.. QB809.G7
STELLAR DYNAMICS ... PRINCIPLES OF
  CHANDRASEKHAR, SUBRAHMANYAN.. ENL. ED., N.Y., DOVER, 1960.. QB351.C48.60
STELLAR INTERIORS, AND NEBULAE ... ASTROPHYSICS - NUCLEAR TRANSFORMATIONS,
  ALLER, LAWRENCE H.. N.Y.. RONALD PRESS, 1954.. QB801.A5
STELLAR INTERIORS ... PHYSICAL PROCESSES IN
  FRANK KAMENETSKII, D A.. JERUSALEM, ISRAEL PROGRAM FOR SCIENTIFIC TRANSLATIONS, 1962.. QB895.F85
STELLAR STRUCTURE ... INTRODUCTION TO THE STUDY OF
  CHANDRASEKHAR, SUBRAHMANYAN.. N.Y., DOVER, 1957.. QB461.C45.57
STENOGRAFIIA ...
  GILDEBRAND, A G.. MOSKVA, UCHPEDGIZ, 1960.. Z90.G38.R

FIG. 3-6. Book catalog, Boeing SLIP project.

Two early book catalog projects at other institutions were failures, although the problems they encountered were instructive. The most publicized of the two was begun at Florida Atlantic University in the mid-1960s. Its design included the concept of variable-length records with field indicators much like those developed for the MARC program discussed in the next chapter, and the early issues were produced with the same special printing chain employed by the Toronto project. Use of this chain had to be abandoned by FAU, however, because of the high production costs associated with its use. The machine time required using the IBM 1460 computer then available at FAU was over three times the amount of time required using a conventional 48-character chain, and this extra increment of time had become difficult to schedule as well as expensive. Special, simplified filing rules were adopted as another means of cutting costs, but the library was still able to produce only irregular supplements on regular computer print-out paper. The catalog was finally abandoned entirely in 1967.[38]

In retrospect, one aspect of the Florida Atlantic system that seems especially curious is that despite its elaborate coding forms and input procedures, no proofing or editing procedures were established and no correction program was written. Not surprisingly, the first edition of the catalog contained a remarkable number of errors; blind cross-references abounded, and William Shakespeare "appeared in at least four different places in the subject catalog and at least four in the author catalog due to variant spellings."[39] More serious was the fact that although its automation efforts were well publicized before implementation (eleven articles on FAU appeared between April 1963 and July 1964), no attempt was made to inform the rest of the library community of its subsequent experiences.

By contrast, the difficulties encountered by the Washington University School of Medicine library in its book catalog project have been frankly and fully publicized. The first WUSM catalog was issued in 1965, and contained only entries cataloged between January and September of that year. The computer print-out used for production

3. Cataloging Systems Before MARC   61

of the pages was not photographically reduced in size before the printing masters were made, so even for the relatively small number of titles (1,050 items) there were 267 pages (see Fig. 3-7). This contributed to one of the problems mentioned in the preface of the catalog itself:

*S 16

BLOOD PRESSURE
    1964
MALMCRONA, RAOUL. HAEMODYNAMICS IN MYOCARDIAL INFARCTION. GOTEBORG, 1964. 54 P.   JNLS   ACTA MED SCAND 1964

BLOOD PROTEINS
    1964
LEEUWEN, A. M., VAN. NET CATION EQUIVALENCY (BASE BINDING POWER) OF THE PLASMA PROTEINS. A STUDY OF ION-PROTEIN INTERACTION IN HUMAN PLASMA BY MEANS OF IN VIVO ULTRAFILTRATION AND EQUILIBRIUM DIALYSIS. AMSTERDAM, 1964. 212 P.   JNLS   ACTA MED SCAND 1964

BLOOD PROTEINS - CONGRESSES
    1963
APPLIED SEMINAR ON THE SERUM PROTEINS AND THE DYSPROTEINEMIAS, WASHINGTON, D. C., 1963. SERUM PROTEINS AND THE DYSPROTEINEMIAS. PHILA., LIPPINCOTT, 1964. 461 P.   WH 400 A652S 1963

BLOOD SUBSTITUTES
    SEE PLASMA SUBSTITUTES.

BONE AND BONES
    1965
HALL, MICHAEL C. THE LOCOMOTOR SYSTEM FUNCTIONAL HISTOLOGY. SPRINGFIELD, THOMAS, 1965. 436 P.   WE 101 H178L 1965
SIMON, GEORGE. PRINCIPLES OF BONE X-RAY DIAGNOSIS. 2D ED. WASHINGTON, BUTTERWORTHS, 1965. 193 P.   WE 200 S594P 1965

BONE DISEASES - CONGRESSES
    1964
PEARSON, O. H. DYNAMIC STUDIES OF METABOLIC BONE DISEASE. PHILA., DAVIS, 1964. 229 P.   WE 200 P362D 1964

BONE NEOPLASMS - CONGRESSES
    1963
CLINICAL CONFERENCE ON CANCER, 8TH, ANDERSON HOSPITAL AND TUMOR INSTITUTE, HOUSTON, 1963. TUMORS OF BONE AND SOFT TISSUE. CHICAGO, YEAR BOOK, 1965. 448 P.   WE 258 C641T 1963

BOOK INDUSTRY
    1964
BARROW (W. J.) RESEARCH LABORATORY, RICHMOND. PERMANENCE/DURABILITY OF THE BOOK - III, SPRAY DEACIDIFICATION. RICHMOND, 1964. 62 P.   PAM   P 2476B 1964
BARROW (W. J.) RESEARCH LABORATORY, RICHMOND. PERMANENCE/DURABILITY OF THE BOOK - II, TEST DATA OF NATURALLY AGED PAPERS. RICHMOND, 1964. 79 P.   PAM   P 2476A 1964

FIG. 3-7. Book catalog, Washington University School of Medicine Library.

> The catalog printed here represents only 8 months of acquisitions and cataloging in a comparatively small specialized library. It runs close to 300 pages, or would be close to 250 pages had we photo-reduced it the usual 40%. Just printing and binding it, once we had the offset masters produced by the computer, cost about $600 for 200 copies. Were we to print such a catalog each year at our present rate of growth, we would need to budget $800 yearly. But it is unthinkable that we should not wish to cumulate the list. This means that the second year our printed catalog would cost about $1,600; the third year, $2,400; and so on in arithmetic progression for as long as we wish to cumulate.[40]

Another difficulty noted was the surprising lack of interest on the part of users:

> We would be willing to spend the large amounts of money noted above and to suffer the trauma of throwing away out-of-date, printed, bound volumes if we were convinced that scientist-users of our collections found such catalogs useful and desirable in their offices, laboratories, or homes [but] the scientists at this Medical Center have shown no desire to have a library catalog at their fingertips ... The Washington University School of Medicine Library has provided free copies of its semi-annual cumulated serial holdings list ... to all departments of the Medical Center for almost 3 years now, and has offered (by signs on bulletin boards) free copies of these lists to any registered reader who has need of them. The response has been deafening by its silence, and the number of copies of these records we produce has therefore steadily diminished. We do not believe a book catalog will be any more desired by our readers. ...
>
> But now we know we can produce this printed catalog, we are under no compulsion to continue to do so. "Good lord, keep us from doing efficiently what doesn't need to be done at all."[41]

Despite these reservations, another book catalog covering the years 1965 to 1967 was later produced, with annual supplements in 1967 and 1968. These were used merely as supplements to the traditional card catalog, not as replacements for it, but in 1968 it was decided to test the feasibility of the book catalog by relying on it alone. For the most part, users "accepted the new system with resignation, except for a few who objected to the necessity for searching multiple alphabets when the dates for an item were not known."[42]

3. Cataloging Systems Before MARC   63

The staff, on the other hand, found dealing with the new system a serious difficulty. Part of the problem apparently arose from the fact that the system had been designed with the assumption that bibliographic information generated at the acquisitions step could be used for the cataloging step without rekeyboarding, but in the experience of this library the idea did not work out. Series might be ordered under a series title, and cataloging personnel were then faced with the necessity of expanding the single record into the necessary number of individual ones; on the other hand, acquisitions personnel might create separate records for volumes ordered separately, but considered by cataloging as part of a set.[43]

Another problem noted was the difficulty of changing printed records; once the catalog had been produced, the records were there until the catalog had been reprinted or superseded. The Nursing School Library was disbanded, but the records for it in the catalog could not be readily deleted, so "it became necessary to paste a general statement on the cover of each copy in the Library. Copies already distributed could not even have that updating."[44] Problems also were attributed to the small size of the computer memory used (8,000 characters of storage, on an IBM 1401 computer); the Dental Library holdings were to be added, for example, but only by inputting them little by little could this be accomplished.

After four months of struggling, the library abandoned the book catalog system entirely. Fortunately (and wisely in this case), the production of catalog cards had been continued all along.

By the mid-1960s, computer-produced book catalogs also became available from commercial firms. One of the first libraries to obtain a book catalog in this way was the Baltimore County Public Library, which contracted with Documentation, Inc., of Bethesda, Maryland for one containing the 50,000 entries cataloged by the library since 1959. Input was done on Flexowriters, processing was done on the firm's IBM 1401 and 1410 computers, and the printing was done with the same "expanded character set" printing chain mentioned earlier. The first catalog indicated which works were held by which branches, but these location indicators were later eliminated.

The time consumed and the cost involved in updating them were out of all proportion to their use, [and] in addition they were never accurate. If a book is not in one agency it can be reserved through intra-library loan and, under ideal conditions, it can be in the hands of the borrower within two days. If a borrower has to have the book immediately he can call intra-library loan and get the names of the branches owning it. He can then call the branch and have it held for him to pick up.[45]

Some 250 copies of the catalog were produced, over half of them for the county's 125 public schools.[46] By 1971, at least two other public library systems in the area were using the BCPL data base for titles also in their libraries, thus avoiding the costs of converting these entries to machine-readable form.[47]

The St. Louis Junior College District reported in 1965 that it had contracted with the Alanar division of Bro-Dart Industries to produce a similar catalog with brief entries. A code number was added to each entry, referring the user to fuller information on the same titles in a photographic reproduction of Library of Congress cards.[48] And in New England, the New Bedford (Massachusetts) Public Library arranged with a local service bureau to produce a book catalog, again using very brief entries. The library estimated that approximately $9,000 per year was saved in salaries formerly required for clerical filing of cards, plus about $2,250 per year through the elimination of catalog card reproduction.[49]

Although book catalogs were (and have continued to be) of interest primarily to public libraries, Toronto and Florida Atlantic were not the only universities to initiate book catalog projects during this period. In 1964, Stanford University had commissioned one of the landmark studies in this field,[50] comparing the costs of various methods of book catalog production, followed by another study comparing the costs of a book catalog with the costs of a card catalog.[51] Based on these studies, a project was begun to produce a book catalog for the Meyer Memorial Undergraduate Library, which was scheduled to open in 1966. The first edition was produced in time for the opening, and subsequent editions have been produced annually, supplemented on a quarterly basis. The first edition contained entries for 25,000

3. Cataloging Systems Before MARC 65

titles, and by the fourth edition in 1969 the total had reached 60,000; a limit of 100,000 is planned. Each edition is divided into three parts: author-title, subject, and shelflist.

Input is by punched cards, with an IBM 7090 used for the sorting and a 1401 to print, again employing the special printing chain mentioned earlier. A cost analysis based on the 41,000-title second edition issued in 1967 indicated total costs of $38,670, some 50 percent more than original estimates but very close to the estimates made during the system design stage.[52]

Photocomposed book catalogs

As an alternative to printing the final page copy on a computer printer, a computer-driven photocomposition device may also be used. Photocomposers of this type read information from tape and by projecting an electron beam on the surface of a cathode ray tube produce pictures of each character in turn, much like the images on a television screen. These images are copied on photosensitive paper at a very high rate of speed (several thousand characters per second) and at a very high resolution (hundreds of lines per inch). The legibility of the characters, combined with the fact that many different type fonts are often available interchangeably, means that the resulting pages are much more attractive and readable than those produced by computer line-printers (see Fig. 3-8). The costs of this method prevented widespread use in the earlier days of book catalogs, but the cost per page has now been reduced to the point that the number of catalogs produced in this fashion is rapidly increasing.

A good example of the transition from computer print-out to photocomposition and an interesting use of the book catalog technique are represented by the Harvard University shelflist project. The Widener Library of Harvard College as late as 1964 still had its shelflist in the old sheaf form common in the nineteenth century--that is, handwritten in loose-leaf volumes rather than on cards. This form and its size (some 1.6 million entries in 200 main classes) made it difficult to maintain and almost impossible for scholars to consult. Realizing the potential value to libraries and scholars of a classified listing of Widener's holdings that

AUTHOR/TITLE CATALOG

AME, MAURICE U.
   Science for progress by Maurice U. Ames, Arthur O. Baker and Joseph F. Leahy. 2d ed. Prentice-Hall, c1961.   610 p. illus., maps. (Science for progress series)   Includes bibliographies. A textbook for junior high school courses in general science.
                              7-12   500   Ame

AMELIA EARHART: FIRST LADY OF THE AIR. Seibert, Jerry.
                                             921   Ear

AMERICA.   **SEE**
   Whitman, Walt. Walt Whitman's America.   811   Whi

AMERICA, AMERICA, AMERICA. Giniger, Kenneth Seeman,
                                             973   Gin

AMERICA BEGINS. Dalgliesh, Alice.   973.1   Dal

AMERICA GROWS UP. Johnson, Gerald W.   973   Joh

AMERICA IN THE MAKING.
   Reinfeld, Fred. Pony Express.   383   Rei

   Wade, William W. From barter to banking: the story of money.
                                         332.4   Wad

AMERICA IS BORN. Johnson, Gerald W.   973.2   Joh

AMERICA MOVES FORWARD. Johnson, Gerald W.   973   Joh

AMERICA, PORTRAIT OF FREEDOM. (FILMSTRIP - SOUND)
   Long Filmslide Service (1964)   90 fr. color. 35 mm. and phonodisc: 1 s. 12 in. 33 1/3 rpm. microgroove.   With teacher's guide. For 30/50 cycle automatic or manual advance projector. Summary: Survey of our nation as it is today, as well as some of our past heritage, with emphasis on the contribution freedom of choice has made to our strength and security.
                            3-8   FSS 973   Ame

AMERICA THE BEAUTIFUL. (STUDY PRINT)   U. S. Govt. Print. Off., 1965.   52 col. photos. 20 x 24 in. Each photograph portrays a scene from one of the United States, Puerto Rico, or the Virgin Islands.   k-1259-9053970   SP 917.3   Ame

AMERICA THE BEAUTIFUL. (KIT)   The heart of America in poetry. Brunswick Productions, c1964; Columbia ML 5668 (c1961)   60 fr. 35mm. and phonodisc: 2 s. 12 in. 33 1/3 rpm. microgroove.   Spoken by Vincent Price. Filmstrip for Paul Revere's ride, by H. W. Longfellow.   Contents. - side 1. The landing of the Pilgrim fathers, by F. D. Hemans. Thanksgiving day, by L. M. Child. Paul Revere's ride, by H. W. Longfellow. The village blacksmith, by H. W. Longfellow. The star-spangled banner, by F. S. Key. The house by the side of the road, by S. W. Foss. Tress, by J. Kilmer. The barefoot boy, by J. G. Whittier. - side 2. A visit from St. Nicholas, by C. C. Moore. O captain! My captain! By W. Whitman. Jesse James, by W. R. Benet. Casey at the bat, by E. L. Thayer. Casey Jones. The new colossus, by E. Lazarus. Chicago, by C. Sandburg. America for me, by H. van Dyke. In Flanders fields, by J. McCrae. America the beautiful, by K. L. Bates.   5-12   KT 811   Ame

AMERICA'S ABRAHAM LINCOLN. McNeer, May.   973.792   Mac

AMERICA'S CULTURAL REVOLUTION. (FILMSTRIP)   New York Times, Office of Educational Activities (c1966) 50 fr. b&w. 35 mm. (Filmstrip on current affairs)   Summary: Discusses the surge of cultural activities in the United States from the great complexes in the cities to the theatre groups and art shows of the small towns. Studies the development of jazz, folk music, museums, and new trends in reading, movies and television.
                        6-12   FS 301.2   Ame

AMERICA'S ETHAN ALLEN. Holbrook, Stewart.   973.392   Hol

AMERICA'S FIRST ARMY. Davis, Burke.   973.2   Dav

AMERICA'S FIRST SPACEMAN. Smaus, Jewel Spangler.
                                             629.4   Sma

AMERICA'S FIRST TRAINED NURSE. Baker, Rachel.   500.092   Bak

AMERICA'S OWN MARK TWAIN. Eaton, Jeanette.   921   Twain, M.

AMERICA'S PAUL REVERE. Forbes, Esther.   973.392   For

AMERICA'S ROBERT E. LEE. Commager, Henry Steele.
                                             973.792   Com

AMERICA'S STORY RETOLD. (PHONODISC) Ellis, Lois Prante.
                                           PD 973   Ell

AMERICA'S TRIAL AND AGONY.   IN
The Civil War. (FILMSTRIP - SOUND).   FSS 973.7   Civ

AMERICA'S WONDERLANDS. National Geographic Society, Washington, D. C.   333.7   Nat

AN AMERICAN ABC. Petersham, Maud.   973   Pet

AMERICAN AUTHORS. (FILMSTRIP)   Encyclopaedia Britannica Films (1958)   6 filmstrips (50 fr. ea.) color. 35 mm. Summary: Presents brief biographical sketches of early American literary persons with classroom discussion outlines included.
                        6-12   FS 810.9   Ame

AMERICAN BIRTHRIGHT BOOKS.
   Lewis, Anthony. The Supreme Court and how it works.
                                        323.42   Lew

THE AMERICAN BOOK OF DAYS. Douglas, George William.
                                          394.2   Dou

THE AMERICAN CITIZENS HANDBOOK. Morgan, Joy Elmer,
                                       342.73   Mor

AMERICAN COMPOSERS. Posell, Elsa Z.   780.920   Pos

AMERICAN CONQUEST OF CALIFORNIA.   IN
California history, set 2. (FILMSTRIP).   FS 979.4   Cal

AMERICAN FOLK SONGS FOR CHILDREN. (PHONODISC)
   Folkways Records FC 7001 (c1953)   2 s. 10 in. 33 1/3 rpm. microgroove.   With lyric sheet. Selections from American folk songs for children, by Ruth Crawford Seeger. Pete Seeger, vocalist.   Contents. - side 1. Jim along Josie. There was a man and he was mad. Clap your hands. She'll be coming 'round the mountain. All around the kitchen. Billy Barlow. - side 2. Bought me a cat. Jim crack corn. Train is a-coming. This old man. Frog went a-counting.   2-6   PD 784.4   Ame

AMERICAN FOLK SONGS FOR CHILDREN AT HOME SCHOOL AND NURSERY SCHOOL. Seeger, Ruth Crawford.   784.4   See

AMERICAN HERITAGE.
   Adventures in the wilderness, by the editors of American heritage. Author: Rutherford Platt; consultant: Horace M. Albright. American Heritage Pub. Co., c1963.   153 p. illus. (part col.) maps. (American heritage junior library)   Quarto volume. Bibliography: p. 149. An account of the exploration and exploitation of the North American wilderness from the time of European discovery until recent years, when the need for preservation of our great natural resources has become more apparent; illustrations are from early paintings and drawings.   6-8   500.9   Ame

   The American Indian. Adapted for young readers by Anne Terry White from the text by William Brandon for the American heritage book of Indians. Ed. by Alvin M. Josephy, Jr.; introd. by John F. Kennedy.Random House (c1963)   200 p. illus. (part col.), maps, ports. (Landmark giants) An historical survey of the Indians of the western hemisphere from ancient times to the present, with emphasis on the Indians north of the Rio Grande.
                        4-8   4-8   970.1   Ame

   Americans in space, by the editors of American heritage. Author: John Dille. Consultant: Philip S. Hopkins. American Heritage Pub. Co., c1965.   153 p. illus. (part col.) ports. (part col.) (American heritage junior library) Quarto volume. Bibliography: p. 149. An account of the space flight research and development program in America, including the pioneering work of Robert H. Goddard, some aspects of the race with Russia, the training of the original seven astronauts, and concluding with the flight of Gordon Cooper.   7-12   629.4   Ame

   The Battle of Gettysburg, by the editors of American heritage. Author, Bruce Catton. American Heritage Pub. Co., c1963.   153 p. illus. (part col.), maps, ports. (American heritage junior library)   Quarto volume. Bibliography: p. 149. Pictures and text combine to reveal the glory and horror of a battle which marked a turning point in the Civil War.   6-8   973.7   Ame

8

FIG. 3-8. Photocomposed book catalog.

3. Cataloging Systems Before MARC 67

13486.46 - .51	Individual authors, etc. - 1558-1660 - Shakespeare - Individual plays - Merry wives of Windsor - Editions	
	13486.46	Pamphlet box. Shakespeare, William. Merchant of Venice.
	13486.46.01	Pamphlet vol. Shakespeare, William. Merchant of Venice. 2 pam.
	13486.46.02	Pamphlet vol. Shakespeare, William. Merchant of Venice. 4 pam.
	13486.46.03	Lang, Andrew. The comedies of Shakespeare: The merchant of Venice. n.p., 1890.
Htn	13486.46.4*	Samuels, P.F. Comedy of Shylock v. Merchant of Venice. Vatican, n.d.
	13486.46.5	Shakespeare, William. Merry wives. London, 1778.
	13486.46.9	Shakespeare, William. Merry wives. London, 1797.
	13486.46.10	Shakespeare, William. Merry wives. London, 18- ?
	13486.46.15	Shakespeare, William. Merry wives. London, 1804.
	13486.47	Shakespeare, William. Merry wives. London, 1804.
	13486.47.4	Shakespeare, William. Merry wives. N.Y., 1817. 2 pam.
Htn	13486.47.5*	Shakespeare, William. Merry wives. N.Y., 1817.
Htn	13486.47.6*	Shakespeare, William. Merry wives. N.Y., 1817.
Htn	13486.47.10*	Shakespeare, William. Merry wives. Boston, 1822.
	13486.47.15	Shakespeare, William. Merry wives. London, 1830?
Htn	13486.47.16*	Shakespeare, William. Merry wives. London, 1830? 2 pam.
	13486.48.5	Shakespeare, William. Merry wives of Windsor. N.Y., 1847.
Htn	13486.48.6F*	Shakespeare, William. Merry wives. N.Y., 1847.
	13486.49.10	Shakespeare, William. Merry wives. Boston, 1855.
	13486.50	Shakespeare, William. Merry wives. London, 1886.
	13486.50.5	Shakespeare, William. Merry wives. N.Y., 1886.
	13486.50.6	Shakespeare, William. Merry wives. N.Y., 1886.
NEDL	13486.50 12	Shakespeare, William. Merry wives of Windsor. London, 1896.
	13486.51	Shakespeare, William. Merry wives. London, 1910.
Htn	13486.51.5*	Shakespeare, William. Merry wives. London, 1910.
	13486.51.6	Shakespeare, William. The merry wives of Windsor. N.Y., 1910.
Htn	13486.51.25*	Shakespeare, William. Merry wives. N.Y., 1913.
13486.52	Individual authors, etc. - 1558-1660 - Shakespeare - Individual plays - Merry wives of Windsor - Criticism	
	13486.52	Perry, W. Treatise on the identity of Herne's Oak. London, 1867.
	13486.52.01	Pamphlet box. Shakespeare, William. Merry wives of Windsor.
	13486.52.5	Halliwell-Phillipps, J.O. Account of only known manuscript of Shakespeare's plays, comprising some important variations and corrections in the Merry wives of Windsor. London, 1843.
	13486.52.10	Robertson, J.M. The problem of "The merry wives of Windsor". London, 1917.
	13486.52.15	Grindon, R.L. In praise of Merry wives. 2d ed. Manchester, 1902.
	13486.52.20	Crofts, J.E.W. Shakespeare and the post horses. Bristol, Eng., 1937.
	13486.52.25	Green, William. Shakespeare: Merry wives of Windsor. Princeton, 1962.

FIG. 3-9. Shelflist, Widener Library, Harvard University.

would be more readily accessible, Harvard began in 1964 to convert the Widener shelflist to a printed classified catalog, with indexes by author and publication date, and with each class in a separate volume. The earliest volumes, published in 1965, used standard uppercase-only print-out typography; this was changed to printout using an upper and lower case chain in 1968, and to photocomposition in 1970 (see Fig. 3-9). All entries are brief, partly because the entries in the original sheet shelflist are brief, and partly to reduce cost. An early cost analysis indicated a figure of 22 cents per entry for conversion: 17 cents for keypunching and 5 cents for editing. Brief entries also take advantage of the space-saving feature of photocomposition: the print-out volumes averaged 70 entries per page, whereas the photocomposed volumes average 140 entries per page, allowing substantial savings in printing and binding. Harvard plans to issue new and enlarged editions when the basic volumes have become outdated, "generally after five or more years."[53]

One of the largest book catalog systems using photocomposition was implemented in 1966 at the National Library of Medicine as a by-product of MEDLARS (the Medical Literature Analysis and Retrieval System). The catalog is called the *National Library of Medicine Current Catalog* (or simply the *Current Catalog*) and is published monthly, with quarterly and annual cumulations. Copies are sold to medical libraries around the world. Page copy was for many years produced by a Photon photocomposer called GRACE (for Graphic Arts Composing Equipment), but in recent years has been produced on Linotron equipment at the Government Printing Office.[54]

NOTES

1. LARC Association, *A Survey of Automated Activities in the Libraries of the U.S. and Canada*, 2d ed., the Association, Tempe, Arizona, 1971, pp. 5-6.
2. Harry Dewey, "Punched Card Catalogs--Theory and Technique," *American Documentation*, 10, 36 (January 1959).
3. Dorothy Alvord, "King County Public Library Does It With IBM," *PNLA Quarterly*, 16, 123-131 (April 1952).
4. Phillis A. Richmond, "A Short-title Catalog Made with IBM Tabulating Equipment," *Library Resources & Technical Services*, 7, 81-90 (Winter 1963).
5. *Ibid.*, "Book Catalogs and Supplements to Card Catalogs," *Library Resources & Technical Services*, 8, 359-365 (Fall 1964).

3. Cataloging Systems Before MARC

6. Lorin R. Burns, "The Use of IBM Unit Record Equipment in the Lake County Public Library," in *IBM Library Mechanization Symposium, Endicott, New York, May 25, 1964*, International Business Machines, White Plains, New York [1965], pp. 15-35.
7. Catherine MacQuarrie, "IBM Book Catalog," *Library Journal*, 82, 630-634 (March 1, 1957).
8. George B. Moreland, "Montgomery County (Maryland) Book Catalog," in *IBM Library Mechanization Symposium, Endicott, New York, May 25, 1964*, International Business Machines, White Plains, New York [1965], pp. 43-60.
9. George B. Moreland, "An Unsophisticated Approach to Book Catalog and Circulation Control," in *Data Processing in Public and University Libraries*, Spartan Books, Washington, D.C., 1966, pp. 58-63. A brief chronology of some of the early book catalog projects appears on page 63.
10. George R. Luckett, "Partial Library Automation with the Flexowriter Automatic Writing Machine," *Library Resources & Technical Services*, 1, 207-210 (Fall 1957).
11. Noel W. Johnson, "Automated Catalog Card Reproduction," *Library Journal*, 85, 725-726 (February 15, 1960).
12. Stephen R. Salmon, "Automation of Library Procedures at Washington University," *Missouri Library Association Quarterly*, 27, 11-12 (March 1966).
13. News item, *Wilson Library Bulletin*, 39, 126 (October 1964).
14. *Recent Developments in Automation at British Columbia University Libraries*, number 1, p. 2 (November 1966).
15. Committee on Library Automation, *Minutes*, January 6 & 7, 1968, p. 2.
16. John P. Kennedy, "A Local MARC Project: the Georgia Tech Library," in *Proceedings of the 1968 Clinic on Library Applications of Data Processing*, University of Illinois Graduate School of Library Science, Urbana, 1969, pp. 206-212.
17. David O. Lane, "Automatic Catalog Card Production," *Library Resources & Technical Services*, 10, 383-386 (Summer 1966).
18. Letter from Page Ackerman, University of California at Los Angeles, December 1, 1966.
19. Mary Seely Dodendorf, "870 Document Writing System of International Business Machines Corporation in the Library Section, Los Angeles City Schools," in *Proceedings of the 1965 Clinic on Library Applications of Data Processing*, University of Illinois Graduate School of Library Science, Urbana, 1966, p. 57.
20. Robert I. Hirst, "Adapting the IBM MT/ST for Library Applications; Manual for Planning," *Special Libraries*, 59, 626-633 (October 1968).

21. M. M. Williamson, "MT/ST and MCRS at the University of Houston Libraries," in *RLMS Micro-File: Current State of Catalog Card Reproduction*, American Library Association, Chicago, 1974, pp. 74-88.

22. Paul J. Fasana, "Automating Cataloging Functions in Conventional Libraries," *Library Resources & Technical Services*, 7, 350-365 (Fall 1963).

23. Ben-Ami Lipetz, "Labor Costs, Conversion Costs, and Compatibility in Document Control Systems," *American Documentation*, 14, 117-122 (April 1963).

24. Kelley L. Cartwright, "Automated Production of Book Catalogs," in *Library Automation: a State of the Art Review*, American Library Association, Chicago, 1969, p. 57.

25. Margaret C. Brown, "A Book Catalog at Work," *Library Resources & Technical Services*, 8, 349-358 (Fall 1964).

26. John J. Nicolaus, *The Automated Approach to Technical Information Retrieval: Library Applications*, Bureau of Ships, Washington, 1964, pp. 19-22.

27. Donald P. Murrill, "Production of Library Catalog Cards and Bulletin Using an IBM 1620 Computer and an IBM 870 Document Writing System," *Journal of Library Automation*, 1, 199 (September 1968).

28. Frederick G. Kilgour, "Development of Computerization of Card Catalogs in Medical and Scientific Libraries," in *Proceedings of the 1964 Clinic on Library Applications of Data Processing*, University of Illinois Graduate School of Library Science, Urbana, 1965, pp. 30-33.

29. Kilgour, "Library Catalogue Production on Small Computers," *American Documentation*, 17, 124-131 (July 1966).

30. Conversation with David Weisbrod, Yale University, June 10, 1974.

31. Michael Reynolds, "Indiana University Regional Campus Libraries: Toward a System of Academic Libraries," in *Proceedings of the 1968 Clinic on Library Applications of Data Processing*, University of Illinois Graduate School of Library Science, Urbana, 1969, pp. 89-138.

32. Murrill, *op. cit.*, pp. 198-212.

33. Mildred Breiland, "Data Processing for Libraries in the Albuquerque Public Schools," *Drexel Library Quarterly*, 5, 92-100 (April 1969).

34. See Guenter A. Jansen, *Univac Electronic Data Processing in the Public Library Systems of Long Island*, Univac Division, Sperry Rand Corp., Washington, [1968?]; *Univac Data Processing Procedures for Library Systems*, Univac Division, Sperry Rand Corp., Washington, [1968?]; and *The Year We Pushed the Button*, Nassau Library System, Hempstead, N.Y., [1965?].

3. Cataloging Systems Before MARC

35. Ritvars Bregzis, "The Ontario New Universities Library Project--an Automated Bibliographic Data Control System," *College & Research Libraries*, 26, 495-508 (November 1965).
36. *Ibid.*, "The ONULP Bibliographic Control System; an Evaluation," in *Proceedings of the 1965 Clinic on Library Applications of Data Processing*, University of Illinois Graduate School of Library Science, Urbana, 1966, pp. 112-140.
37. Edward A. Weinstein and Joan Spry, "Boeing SLIP: Computer Produced and Maintained Printed Book Catalogs," *American Documentation*, 15, 185-190 (July 1964). Indexes prepared in this way, often called KWIC (for Keyword In Context) or KWOC (Keyword Out of Context) indexes, were and have been used frequently in information retrieval projects.
38. H. William Axford, "Florida Atlantic University Library," in *Encyclopedia of Library and Information Science*, Marcel Dekker, New York, v. 8, p. 552.
39. *Ibid.*, p. 554.
40. Estelle Brodman, *Catalog of Books, Plus a Complete Catalog of Reserve Books*, Washington University School of Medicine Library, St. Louis, 1965, p. iii.
41. *Ibid.*, pp. iii-iv.
42. Doris Bolef et al., "Mechanization of Library Procedures in the Medium-Sized Medical Library: VIII. Suspension of Computer Catalog," *Bulletin of the Medical Library Association*, 57, 265.
43. See Glyn Evans, *The Redesign of the Automated Acquisitions-Catalog System at Washington University School of Medicine Library*, the Library, 1969, p. 1.
44. Bolef, *op. cit.*
45. Paula Kieffer, "Book Catalog--To Have or Not to Have," *Library Resources & Technical Services*, 15, 292 (Summer 1971).
46. Charles W. Robinson, "The Book Catalog: Diving In," *Wilson Library Bulletin*, 40, 264 (November 1965).
47. Kieffer, *op. cit.*, p. 291.
48. Robert C. Jones, "A Book Catalog for Libraries--Prepared by Camera and Computer," *Library Resources & Technical Services*, 9, 205-206 (Spring 1965).
49. James S. Healey, "An Automated Library in New England," *Wilson Library Bulletin*, 41, 438-439 (December 1966).
50. Robert M. Hayes and Ralph M. Shoffner, *The Economics of Book Catalog Production*, Advanced Information Systems Division, Sherman Oaks, California, 1964.
51. Robert M. Hayes, Ralph M. Shoffner and David C. Weber, "The Economics of Book Catalog Production," *Library Resources & Technical Services*, 10, 57-90 (Winter 1966).

52. Richard D. Johnson, "A Book Catalog at Stanford," *Journal of Library Automation*, 1, 13-50 (March 1968).

53. See Richard De Gennaro, "A Computer Produced Shelflist," *College & Research Libraries*, 26, 311-315, 353 (July 1965); "Automation in the Harvard College Library," *Harvard Library Bulletin*, 16, 217-236 (July 1968); and "Harvard University's Widener Library Shelflist Conversion and Publication Program," *College & Research Libraries*, 31, 318-331 (September 1970).

54. Irvin J. Weiss and Emilie V. Wiggins, "Computer-Aided Centralized Cataloging at the National Library of Medicine," *Library Resources & Technical Services*, 11, 83-96 (Winter 1967).

Chapter 4

MARC
AND OFF-LINE SYSTEMS AFTER MARC

Real progress in automated cataloging systems beyond the point described in the previous chapter was impeded by the lack of any recognized standards for the format of cataloging information in machine-readable form. Each library initiating a cataloging project was faced with the necessity of keyboarding all of the data to be entered in the proposed catalog, and except for very small libraries this was an enormous, expensive barrier to overcome. As the realization of the dimensions of this problem grew, more and more libraries began to urge the Library of Congress to consider making its cataloging available in machine-readable form. Since 1901, libraries had been able to avoid original cataloging for many of their books, since standard printed catalog cards were available from the Library of Congress Card Division. What now seemed to be needed was a similar service, providing the same information in machine-readable and machine-manipulable form, arranged in a format that could be agreed upon nationally, and capable of being used by all of the different computers likely to be employed in library systems.

The MARC Pilot Project
As a preliminary step, the Council on Library Resources commissioned a feasibility study by Lawrence F. Buckland of Inforonics, Inc., which demonstrated the practicality of the idea and identified many

of the issues to be decided (whether additional data such as the
language of publication should be added, for example, and to what
extent future uses of the data could be predicted).[1] The Library of
Congress then invited representatives from universities, research
laboratories, Government agencies and private industry to consider
the report at the First Conference on Machine-Readable Catalog Copy,
held at LC on January 11, 1965. The conference concluded that the
Library should proceed with the development of a machine-readable
format for cataloging information, and three LC staff members were
assigned the task of analyzing cataloging data from a machine-pro-
cessing point of view.

Their report, issued in June 1965 as "Planning Memorandum No.
3," suggested both the bibliographical elements to be included in
the content of the record, and the manner of identifying the data
elements for processing purposes.[2] The proposal was widely distributed and reviewed by librarians and technicians around the country.
A second conference was held in November of 1965, the main conclusion of which was that LC should seek to initiate a pilot project
to distribute machine-readable cataloging data as soon as possible.
Only a month later, in December 1965, the Council on Library Resources awarded a grant to LC for this purpose, and the MARC (for
Machine-Readable Cataloging) Pilot Project was begun.

By February 1966, several contracts had been let for design and
development of the computer programs that would be required, design
of costing models, and plans for evaluation of the project. From
approximately forty libraries that had expressed interest in participating in the Pilot Project, sixteen were selected:

Argonne National Laboratory
Georgia Institute of Technology
Harvard University
Indiana University
Montgomery County (Maryland) Public Schools
Nassau County (New York) Library System
National Agricultural Library

4. MARC and Off-Line Systems After MARC

    Redstone Scientific Information Center
    Rice University
    University of California Institute of Library Research
    University of Chicago
    University of Florida
    University of Missouri
    University of Toronto
    Washington State Library
    Yale University

Those selected were chosen to represent so far as possible a wide variety of different types of libraries: research, public, school, special, and government.

Representatives of these participating libraries, the contractors, and LC staff members were brought together at a Third Conference on Machine-Readable Catalog Copy in February 1966, at which time it was announced that distribution of tapes would begin later the same year.

In the Pilot Project, the regular "manuscript card" (the form used by LC to prepare printed cards) was reproduced on an input worksheet (see Fig. 4-1). An editor then wrote numerical "tags" alongside each item of information, and both tags and data were typed on a Dura paper-tape typewriter. The paper tape was input to the computer, which then printed a "diagnostic listing" (see Fig. 4-2) for proofreading and correction. An editor compared the original data against the proofsheet and marked errors for correction. After these were edited, a new proofsheet was prepared by the computer, and the cycle was repeated until the record was determined to be error-free. A final check was then performed by a higher-level editor (called a "verifier"), after which the record was stored on the master tape. From this tape, copies were made and distributed to the sixteen participants, beginning with a test tape in October 1966 and regular weekly tapes starting in November 1966.

The project was originally planned to cover all English language monographs cataloged at LC, but the advent of the National Program

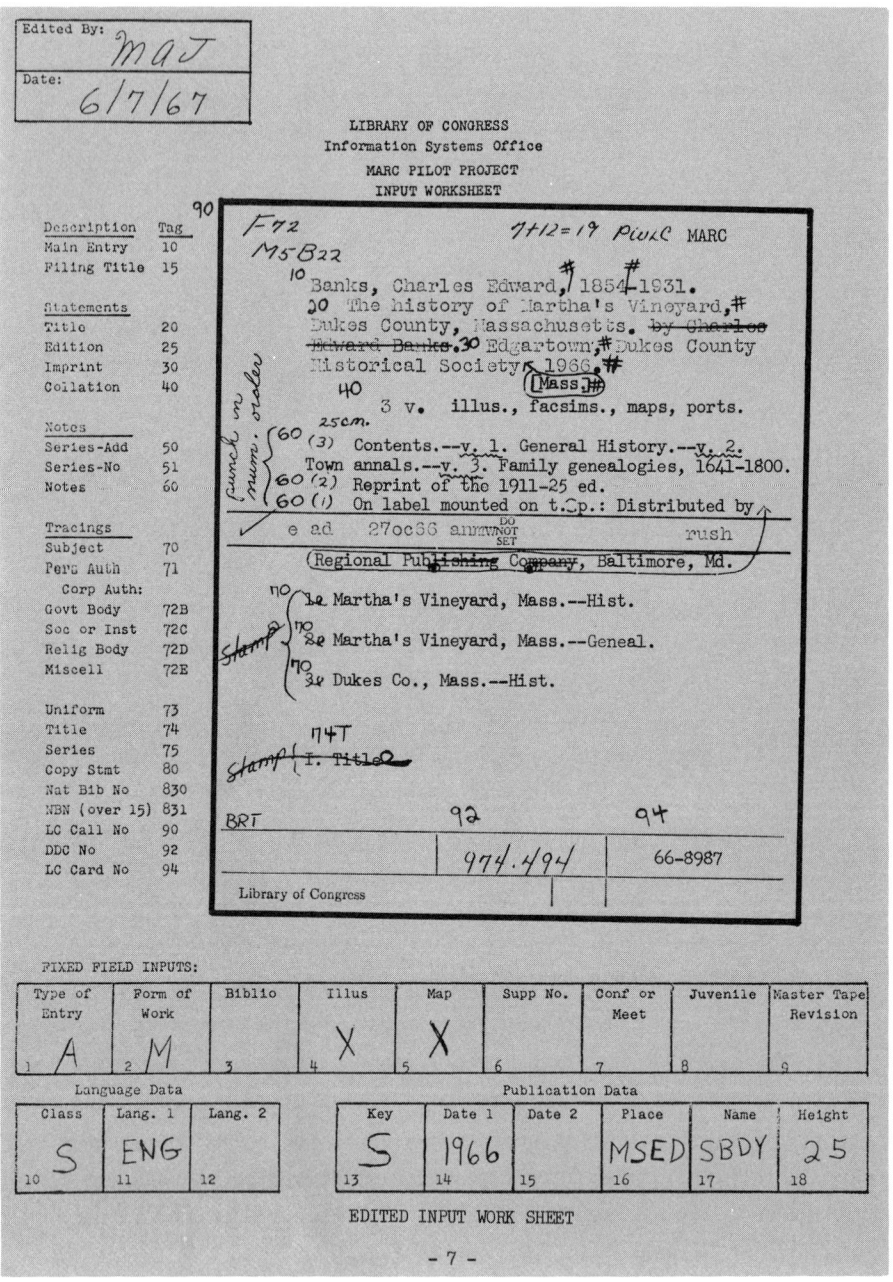

FIG. 4-1. Input worksheet, MARC Pilot Project.

4. MARC and Off-Line Systems After MARC 77

```
                          THE MARC PROJECT RECORD
                             DIAGNOSTIC LISTING                              RECORD         66-013024
                                                                             BATCH NO.      NM00012

TYPE OF          FORM OF                           SUPPLEMENT   CONFERENCE   JUVENILE       RECORD
ENTRY(1)         WORK(2)    BIBLIO(3)   ILLUS(4)   MAPS(5)      NUMBER(6)    OR MEETING(7)  WORK(8)        INDICATOR(9)
PERSONAL AUTHOR  MONOGRAPH  YES         NO         NO           NO           NO             NO             TWO WKS OLD

LANGUAGE DATA
CLASS(10)        LANG 1(11) LANG 2(12)  PUBLICATION DATA
                                        KEY(13)    DATE 1(14)   DATE 2(15)   PLACE(16)      NAME(17)       HEIGHT(18)
SINGLE           %                      SINGLE     1966                      HAHO           %              24 CM

TYPE OF SECONDARY ENTRY-
VARIABLE FIELDS-            GS          SERIES-NO              LENGTH OF RECORD-0381

L. C. CALL NUMBER       90  JQ1745.A1S5
DEWEY CLASS. NUMBER     92  354.59301
MAIN ENTRY              10  Siffin, William J.
TITLE STATEMENT         20  The Thai bureaucracy:# institutional change and development,# by William J. Siffin.
IMPRINT STATEMENT       30  Honolulu,# East-West Center Press# 1966 #
COLLATION STATEMENT     40  x, 291 p. 24 cm.
NOTES                   60  Bibliography: p. 282-286.
SUBJECT TRACING         70  Thailand--Pol. & govt.
TITLE TRACING           74  T
```

FIG. 4-2. Diagnostic listing, MARC Pilot Project.

for Acquisitions and Cataloging jumped the number of such works from 600 to over 1,000 titles per week, and made this goal temporarily impossible. Other problems were also uncovered. Cross-references were included at first, but were difficult for the participants to use because they were not linked in any way to the catalog records that generated them; they were dropped from the tapes in the spring of 1967. As a part of the project, LC also supplied programs to enable the participants to produce four items: catalog cards, cross-reference cards, an abbreviated author/title list (see Fig. 4-3), and a prooflist. The programs, prepared not by the Library of Congress but by a contractor, never worked properly and could be used only after some of the participants themselves made corrections.[3]

Despite these minor problems, the participants were able to put the tapes to an interesting variety of uses. Georgia Tech, Harvard, and Toronto produced catalog cards, and the Washington State Library produced a union book catalog for current acquisitions of three public library systems in the state. Harvard experimented with production of specialized listings, one for medical titles (as an acquisitions tool for the Countway Library of Medicine), one for titles in philosophy and religion (for the Andover-Harvard Theological Library), and one for books related to India (specifically, books published in India, or which had a classification number relating to India, or which had been given corporate author, title, or subject headings having to do with India--this one for the library's South Asia book selection specialist).[4] Rice University produced a list for acquisition purposes, and did significant research on the relative efficiency of machine searching using various items of data in combination.[5]

Other users searched and selected MARC records by subject headings and classification numbers for SDI (Selective Dissemination of Information) services to university faculty members; produced course outlines, syllabi and reading lists; and studied problems related to filing rules and reclassification projects.[6] The sixteen "primary" participants also redistributed tapes to some twenty "secondary" participants who made similar use of the records.

4. MARC and Off-Line Systems After MARC 79

```
LIBRARY OF CONGRESS              THE MARC PILOT PROJECT                  11/23/66         PAGE    3
ABBREVIATED AUTHOR/TITLE LISTING OF ALL RECORDS IN MARC MASTER FILE                   ISO EDITION 0001

** 66-077173   Dreyfus, Marie, comp.
               'Crimes against creation:' a compilation.

** 66-077174   Dumitriu, Petru.
               Westward lies heaven; translated by Peter Wiles.

** 66-077062   Durrell, Lawrence.
               Sauve qui peut. Nicolas Bentley drew the pictures.

** 66-077440   Egan, E. W.
               France in pictures; prepared by E. W. Egan.

** 66-008851   Eggleston, Edward, 1837
               The Hoosier school-boy.

** 66-077295   Evans, Benjamin Ifor, Sir, 1899
               The use of English [by] Ifor Evans.

** 66-077293   Fabricant, Isaac Nathan.
               Sermons and addresses [by] I. N. Fabricant.

** 66-077441   Feininger, Andreas, 1906
               Form in nature and life.

** 66-022346   Fisher, John H., ed.
               The medieval literature of western Europe; a review of research, mainly 1930-1960. General edito

** 66-077512   Frewin, Leslie Ronald, 1916
               The spy trade: an anthology of international espionage in fact and fiction, collected and

** 66-077297   Gilbert, Bentley B., 1924
               The evolution of national insurance in Great Britain: the origins of the welfare state [by]

** 66-027476   Gladwyn, Hubert Miles Gladwyn Jebb, baron, 1900
               Halfway to 1984, by Gladwyn Jebb, Lord Gladwyn.

** 66-021807   Glen, John Stanley, 1907
               Erich Fromm; a Protestant critique, by J. Stanley Glen.

** 66-077176   Glenavy, Patrick Gordon Campbell, baron, 1913
               All ways on Sundays, by Patrick Campbell.
```

FIG. 4-3. Author-title list, MARC project.

MARC II

Originally the Pilot Project was scheduled to end in June 1967, but the enthusiasm of the participants persuaded LC to continue while work proceeded on a revised format called MARC II. The new format embodies many changes recommended by the participants, other interested librarians, computer technicians, and special committees formed by the U.S.A. Standards Institute (now the American National Standards Institute) and the American Library Association. A major emphasis was placed on "generality and flexibility--i.e., a format that would be an efficient means of communicating bibliographic descriptions of all forms of materials (monographs, serials, maps, music, etc.) between library centers."[7] MARC II also provided more fields to allow for recording more types of data (see Fig. 4-4), more internal discrimination between data elements, a more complete incorporation of variable length fields, and coding of individual characters based on a new USASI (ANSI) standard, the latter designed to free the format from dependence on any particular make or brand of computer. Magnetic tapes in the new MARC II format were made available to all libraries on a subscription basis beginning in April 1969. In July of the same year, production was expanded to include all English language monographs, thus reaching the original objective.

Efforts have also been made to provide records in MARC format for retrospective titles. In 1969, the Council on Library Resources sponsored a feasibility study, the report of which recommended that retrospective conversion should be accomplished as a centralized project and tested in an operational situation.[8] CLR subsequently awarded a second grant to LC to conduct such a test over a 24-month period. Various input techniques were tested, and the relative merits of performing the necessary keyboarding in the Library or in a commercial firm were studied. Some 18,000 records were sent to a commercial keying firm, but the delays inherent in this approach caused it to be discarded as unfeasible. In all, some 85,000 English language monographs cataloged by the Library during 1968 and 1969 were converted.

4. MARC and Off-Line Systems After MARC

REVISED LIST OF MARC II TAGS

CONTROL FIELDS
0 0 1   Control Number
0 0 2   Sub-Record Directory
0 0 3   Reserved
0 0 4   Cataloging Source
0 0 8   Fixed Fields
0 0 9   Languages

CONTROL NUMBERS
0 1 0   LC Card Number
0 1 1   Linking LC Card Number
0 1 5   National Bibliography Number
0 1 6   Linking NBN
0 2 0   Standard Book Number
0 2 1   Linking SBN
0 2 5   Overseas Acquisitions Number
        (PL480, LACAP, etc.)
0 2 6   Linking OAN Number
0 3 5   Local System Number
0 3 6   Linking Local Number
0 3 9   Search Code

KNOWLEDGE NUMBERS
0 5 0   LC Call Number
0 5 1   Copy Statement
0 6 0   NLM Call Number
0 7 0   NAL Call Number
0 7 1   NAL Subject Category Number
0 8 0   UDC Number
0 8 1   BNB Classification Number
0 8 2   Dewey Decimal Classification No.
0 9 0   Local Call Number

MAIN ENTRY
1 0 0   Personal Name
1 1 0   Corporate Name
1 1 1   Conference or Meeting
1 3 0   Uniform Title Heading

SUPPLIED TITLES
2 4 0   Uniform Title
2 4 1   Romanized Title
2 4 2   Translated Title
2 4 3   Uniform Title (Collective works)
        (Reserved for British MARC)

TITLE PARAGRAPH
2 4 5   Title
2 5 0   Edition Statement
2 6 0   Imprint

COLLATION
3 0 0   Collation
3 5 0   Bibliographic Price
3 6 0   Converted Price

SERIES NOTES
4 0 0   Personal Name-Title (Traced Same)
4 1 0   Corporate Name-Title (Traced Same)
4 1 1   Conference-Title (Traced Same)
4 4 0   Title (Traced Same)
4 9 0   Series Untraced or Traced
        Differently

BIBLIOGRAPHIC NOTES
5 0 0   General Notes
5 0 1   "Bound with" Note
5 0 2   Dissertation Note
5 0 3   Bibliographic history Note
5 0 4   Bibliography Note
5 0 5   Contents Note (Formatted)
5 0 6   "Limited use" Note
5 2 0   Abstract

SUBJECT ADDED ENTRY
6 0 0   Personal Name
6 1 0   Corporate Name (excluding
        political jurisdiction alone)
6 1 1   Conference or Meeting
6 3 0   Uniform Title Heading

LC Subject Headings
6 5 0   Topical
6 5 1   Geographic Names
6 5 2   Political Jurisdiction Alone or
        with Subject Subdivisions
6 5 3   Proper Names Not Capable of
        Authorship
6 5 4   Headings Modified for Children

Other Subject Headings
6 6 0   NLM Subject Headings (MESH)
6 7 0   NAL Subject Headings (Agricultural/
        Biological Vocabulary)
6 9 0   Local Subject Heading Systems

OTHER ADDED ENTRIES
7 0 0   Personal Name
7 1 0   Corporate Name
7 1 1   Conference or Meeting
7 3 0   Uniform Title Heading
7 4 0   Title Traced Differently
7 5 3   Proper Name Not Capable of
        Authorship

SERIES ADDED ENTRIES
8 0 0   Personal Name-Title
8 1 0   Corporate Name-Title
8 1 1   Conference or Meeting-Title
8 4 0   Title

9 0 0   BLOCK OF 100 NUMBERS FOR LOCAL
        USE

FIG. 4-4. MARC fields.

Format recognition

Perhaps the most significant result of the "Recon Project," however, was not the number of records converted but the development of a new internal technique for inputting the cataloging information. The process of assigning all tags manually and then repetitively keyboarding and correcting, as described earlier, had proved slow, tedious, and expensive, and constituted a major obstacle to further expansion of service. The new process developed by the project, called "format recognition," uses the computer to examine unedited bibliographic data and assign tags, indicators, and subfield codes automatically. The LC "manuscript card" is typed without preliminary editing, and the typist uses two (or more) carriage returns to indicate the end of a paragraph, a single carriage return to indicate the end of a line within a paragraph. The carriage returns produce machine-readable codes, which then can be used by the machine to identify the boundaries of fields. The sequence of fields also indicates the nature of the data in those fields; for example, imprint always comes before the collation. (The reader will recall that an almost identical technique was used in the Air Force Cambridge Research Laboratory catalog card project described on p. 49.)

> The collation is located first, and by working back through the data an attempt is made to locate and identify the call number, main entry and title paragraph. Analysis then continues by examining the paragraphs following the collation paragraph, identifying fields when possible. The title paragraph is divided into title, edition, and imprint; the collation block into collation, series, and price. Tags are assigned to each field identified and the tags are recorded in the preliminary record directory.[9]

Various clues also assist the computer in determining the identification of data and assigning tags and delimiters in the proper places. For example, the call number usually consists of one to three capital letters, followed by one to four numbers, followed by a period, a capital letter, and more numbers (there are variations, but most of these are easily identified). A personal name main entry code is assigned if there are open dates (such as "1933- "), date ranges covering twenty years or more (such as "1921-1967"), or

4. MARC and Off-Line Systems After MARC

phrases suggesting persons rather than corporate bodies (such as "ed.," "tr.," or "comp."). The "biography indicator" is set automatically if the word "biography" appears in the title or the Dewey number contains a "B" or a 920. And so on. The techniques are not foolproof, but all machine-edited records are subjected to human review just as those edited initially by humans.[10] Format recognition has proved such a valuable improvement that it was incorporated as part of the regular processing procedures for MARC record production in January 1972.

Other changes have been made in both processing techniques and in content of the records. "Default indicators"--indicators for the most commonly occurring situation, assigned by the computer by "default" but capable of being overridden by manual input if necessary --have simplified editing and correction. Filing indicators, added to the content of the records starting in 1971, allow initial articles to be ignored when MARC records are used to produce book catalogs by computer. Fields which proved of little use (such as "653 --Political Jurisdiction as Subject" and "750--Proper Name Not Capable of Authorship") have been dropped, and others requested by subscribers (such as "043--Geographic Area Code" and "086--Superintendent of Documents Number") have been added.

Expansion of MARC

Conversion of so-called "popular titles" to the MARC format has also added to the usefulness of the records. The immediate impetus for this addition to the corpus of records available came from the Card Division Mechanization Project (see below, pp. 85-89), which needed the records to be able to produce catalog cards for titles in heavy demand. The Card Division project also provided a means of identifying "popular titles," since information on the number of orders received for each LC card number had been gathered on a daily basis and cumulated on a weekly basis since Phase I of the Card Division project began in September 1968. Data from this source on over 9 million orders for more than 1.2 million titles was analyzed, and titles for which thirty or more orders had been received were selected, copied on a separate tape, and compared against the existing MARC data base. Of the 50,000 card numbers selected, almost 28,000 were already in MARC form. Of the remaining 22,000 titles, 18,000 were English-language monographs, and conversion of these to machine-readable form began in July 1971. As work on them is completed, groups of titles are made available to subscribers, the first group of 7,831 titles having been distributed in August of 1973.[11]

In 1971, Cataloging-In-Publication records (preliminary bibliographic descriptions) were also added to the distribution service. Records for other types of materials, such as audiovisual presentations, maps, and serials, were added in 1972 and 1973, and records for titles in languages other than English began to be added in 1973. By 1975, MARC records were being produced at a rate of approximately 127,000 titles per year, including all current Library of Congress cataloging in English, French, German, Spanish, and Portuguese (some sixty percent of all current LC cataloging), and the total number of records available had passed half a million.[12] By this time also, MARC had become an international as well as a national standard, and was accepted almost universally as the basis for present and future planning of individual and cooperative cataloging projects. A new grant announced by the Council on Library Resources in December 1974 will fund a project that promises to make the use of MARC even more widespread: LC will accept machine-readable records produced in MARC format by other libraries, compare them with LC's Official Catalog, update them for consistency as required, "identify" them, and redistribute them through the MARC distribution service.[13] If successful (and there appear to be no inherent difficulties), the goal of a true national standard for machine-readable cataloging will at last have been reached, both in theory and in practice.

Small wonder, then, that the MARC Project has been widely acclaimed as the most significant development in the history of library automation!

4. MARC and Off-Line Systems After MARC   85

Post-MARC cataloging systems.

Most of the automated cataloging projects initiated since 1969 have naturally attempted to utilize MARC records to a greater or lesser extent in order to avoid the time and expense of local conversion. If MARC records are available, input techniques need only add local information such as call number, location symbols, and any necessary changes in the data to conform to the item at hand. For those titles not available on MARC, input devices such as those described in the previous chapter (keypunches, paper-tape typewriters, or keyboard-to-magnetic tape devices) may be used. For some cataloging projects involving large-scale conversion (usually book catalog projects) ordinary typewriters with special type fonts have been employed, and the resulting output fed through optical scanners designed to read the special fonts and convert the data to machine-readable form.

Subsequent processing by computer in off-line systems is the same as for systems which do not use MARC, except that a considerable amount of computer processing may be necessary to convert MARC records from the "communications" format in which they are received to a format suitable for production of cards and book catalogs.

Final output may be in any of the forms previously discussed: computer print-out, photocomposed printing plates, or computer-output-microfilm (COM).

Off-line catalog card systems

One of the earliest and largest users of MARC for catalog card production was not unnaturally the Library of Congress' own Card Division, which began a system known as CARDS (for Card Automated Reproduction and Distribution Service) or, more simply, as the Card Division Mechanization Project, in 1968. The Card Division, which each year supplies millions of printed catalog cards to some 25,000 libraries around the world, had for years experienced growing difficulties in operating with an almost completely manual system. Delays of several months in filling catalog card orders had become common. Rising labor costs contributed to the problem, as did the difficulties in filling literally hundreds of routine jobs; under the old system, for example, sixty-one people were required merely for manual arrangement of orders in alphabetical or numerical sequence, and thirty-seven people were employed in manual preparation of bills.

The new mechanized system began where the entire process of filling catalog card orders began, with the receipt of the orders themselves. This posed some unusual system design constraints, because the orders were in many cases simply a single part of a multipart, three-by-five-inch book order form. Unless the acquisition systems of all libraries using the Card Division's services were to be changed, these orders would have to remain the same size and approximately the same thickness. Many libraries also required the return of the form. Most of the common methods of input were therefore ruled out: keypunching or rekeying the information in machine-readable form was eliminated because of the high potential rate of errors that would be introduced; mark-sense cards were impractical because of insufficient space for the information; 51-column "stub" cards could not be used because they could not be incorporated in libraries' multipart forms; and MICR (magnetic-ink character recognition) documents (such as bank checks) were undesirable because the cost of including them in multipart forms would have been too expensive.

In the end, LC contracted with Recognition Equipment Inc. of Dallas, Texas to develop and install an optical character recognition device for input of the orders. An analysis was made of over 500,000 order slips, and the typewriter fonts used to produce them were laboriously identified. The results showed that some twenty-five commonly used typewriter fonts, together with handprinting, accounted for all but 1.8 percent of the sample. The input device was therefore specially built to read these twenty-five fonts and handprinting.

In actual operation, the machinery reads virtually all other fonts as well, with the exception of unusual fonts such as script type. After an initial period of experimentation and adjustment, the handprinting reader incorporated in the device also worked well, and became, so far as is known, the first handprinting reader in the

4. MARC and Off-Line Systems After MARC 87

country to be used routinely in production.

Catalog card orders are placed in the optical reading device as they arrive, and pass through the machine at a rate of 1,200 per minute. The numerical information from the orders is recorded on magnetic tape, and also on the back of each order form itself in a pattern of small, orange fluorescent bars, just as on most gasoline credit-card receipts.

The information recorded on tape is then used to select from a large random access storage device the machine-readable version of the catalog cards ordered. An RCA Videocomp photocomposition device composes photographic paper masters, each containing ten catalog card images, almost identical in appearance to the cards printed by traditional means (see Fig. 4-5). After development in a continuous processor, the printing masters are placed (either manually or automatically) on high-speed offset presses which print the required number of catalog cards. In assembly-line fashion, the cards then pass through a series of special machines which cut the cards apart, stack them with each customer's order in a separate stack with an address label (also printed by the computer-driven photocomposition device) on top, wrap them in shrink-wrap polyethylene film, and drop them in the mail bag. The total process is thus almost completely automated, from the receipt of the order in the incoming mail to the shipment of the order in the outgoing mail.

As with all automated catalog card systems, the cards can only be produced if the information on them has first been converted to machine-readable and machine-processable form. As indicated earlier, the MARC project has done this for several hundred thousand titles, including those titles most frequently ordered by the Card Division's customers, but the Card Division supplies cards for over five million titles, and some means is therefore required to expedite orders for cards not yet in machine-readable form. Here the tiny orange bars traced on the back of the order form during the initial input stage are employed more fully. Special sorting machines read the information thus encoded, and sort the order slips into sequence by Library of Congress card (stock) number. The orders must then be

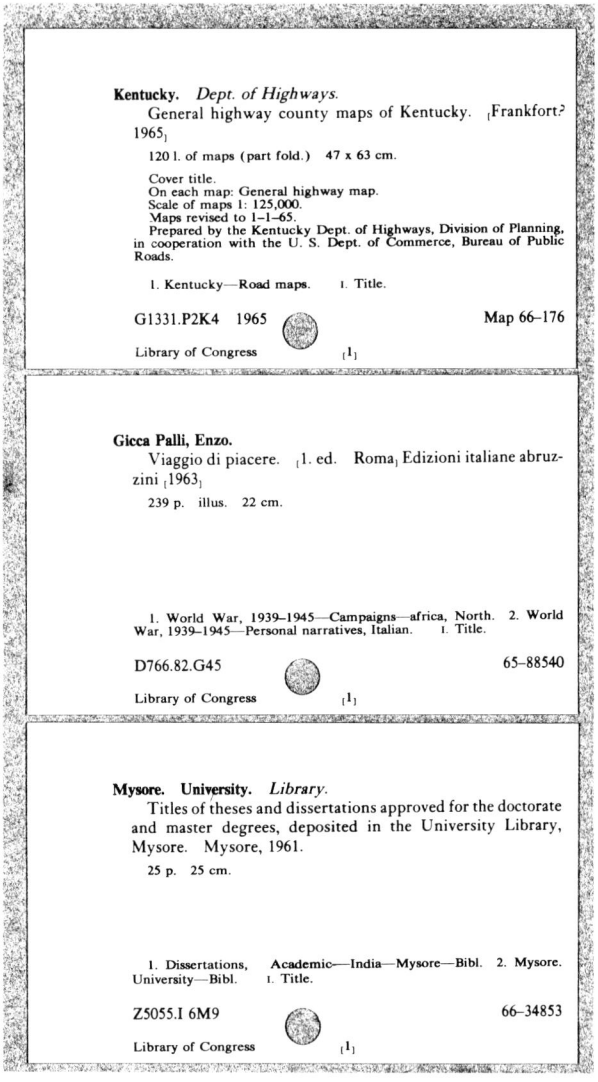

FIG. 4-5. Photocomposed catalog cards, Library of Congress CARDS project.

manually filled from stock, but this process is expedited by the fact that all orders for a single stock number are together. The catalog cards are placed behind each order form as the orders are filled, and the same special sorting machines then arrange both the

4. MARC and Off-Line Systems After MARC

orders and the catalog cards in sequence by customer (library) number, and simultaneously compute and print an invoice and prepare an address label. Completed orders are then ready for wrapping and mailing.[14]

One of the earliest off-line computer systems for catalog card production using MARC data was instituted at the Georgia Institute of Technology Library in Atlanta in 1967. Georgia Tech was one of the participants in the original MARC Pilot Project, and has continued to use MARC for both catalog card and book catalog production. In the Pilot Project, a Burroughs B5500 computer was used to select and process MARC records, print the catalog cards, and produce punched cards that were then converted to paper tape and used to produce such additional items as book cards, book pockets, and spine labels on a Flexowriter. Costs were calculated at eighty cents per title, or ten cents per card. The poor quality of printed output from the Burroughs line printers caused serious problems, and the difficulties with Flexowriters mentioned in the previous chapter (see p. 47) led to their eventual abandonment for output purposes. When the university decided to change from the Burroughs computer to a Univac 1108 a new on-line system was developed (see Chapter 5, p. 105) and the earlier system was discontinued.[15]

One of the largest post-MARC catalog card systems to be implemented to date is the BCL (for Books for College Libraries) Project at the Massachusetts Central Library Processing Center, located at the University of Massachusetts in Amherst. The Project began in 1969 with a special appropriation by the Massachusetts legislature to the Massachusetts Board of Higher Education for the purchase and processing of library materials for twenty-eight state-supported institutions which collectively were below ALA standards by more than three million volumes. The initial grant of $2 million for books and $250,000 for processing was followed by an identical one the following year, and in both cases the University of Massachusetts library was asked to do both the purchasing and processing, based on the library's own estimate that the money saved by such centralized processing, as compared with the use of a commercial processor, would pay for an additional 80,000 volumes.

MARC was not used for the initial project; instead, 22,400 different titles representing 260,000 volumes were selected from *Books for College Libraries*, using data supplied on magnetic tape by Richard Abel & Co. After this first effort, however, MARC tapes were incorporated; the second project used the 1969 and 1970 MARC tapes and a list of serial backfiles to print out selection lists, combine the selections from the twenty-eight libraries into one master list, place the orders, and produce both catalog cards and book labels.[16]

Savings were estimated by the Board of Higher Education, which oversees the project, as "in the millions of dollars" through handling the books centrally, through larger discounts and more reliable filling of orders, and by assembly-line procedures. A study in 1972 found that 70 percent of the items were being processed within one day after being received, and the rest (with a few exceptions) within three.[17] This success encouraged the legislature to continue support of the project with additional annual appropriations, and by 1973 the center had processed almost 800,000 volumes and produced almost four million catalog cards. The cost of processing was less than a dollar per volume, including purchasing, cataloging, shipping to the participating libraries, overhead, and developmental costs. The system has also been improved and augmented, so that it now produces book catalogs and specialized listings as well as financial reports, and participants may order material not listed on the MARC tapes, including foreign publications, audiovisual material, back runs of serials, and microforms.[18]

Unfortunately, the expansion to provide for all types of materials and items not on the MARC tapes has led to some difficulties. As might be expected, costs have risen, and the efficiency of cataloging procedures has dropped. From an average of twelve copies per book and a corresponding discount of 20 percent in the first year, the respective averages dropped to 1.6 and 11.7 percent in the fourth year. Despite these problems, a poll of participants indicated continued support for the project and continuing savings, estimated at over $350,000 for the 1972-1973 fiscal year alone.[19]

4. MARC and Off-Line Systems After MARC 91

The University of Massachusetts is also the home of BOSS (the Book Order and Selection System) described in Chapter 2 (see pp. 30-31). Catalog cards and labels for the university library itself have been produced by this system since August of 1970. A study in 1972 by Buckland and others noted that "the clerical staff in the acquisitions and catalog departments have been reduced by 14, catalogers have been reduced from 12 to 8, and file clerks have been reduced from 8 or 9 to 4 or 5. It takes about 3-5 days for most of the material ordered to get through the catalog department."[20]

Approximately 35 percent of the cataloging data comes from MARC, the rest from conventional Library of Congress printed sources or elsewhere. Palmer notes that the speed of computer operations in the system "tends to forestall delays and backlogs," and "the capacity of the computer to handle clerical routines that humans find boring and tedious fosters better staff morale. ... The system, especially in view of its contribution toward savings in cataloging costs, is surprisingly economical to operate. It provides library management with a flexibility and efficiency that should characterize library computerization efforts."[21]

Other catalog card systems using off-line computer production have been implemented at Trinity University in San Antonio, Texas and at Guelph University in Ontario, Canada. The system at Guelph (called SCOPE, for Systematic Computerized Processing) produces not only catalog cards but spine labels, book pocket labels, and book cards for the circulation system. Approximately 1,000 titles are processed per week at an estimated eighty cents per title, not including of course the cost of the actual cataloging. All programs are written in COBOL and run on an IBM Model 50 computer.[22]

The Trinity system is called MARCIVE,* and began in 1969

---

*Like many library automation project acronyms, this one is a bit obscure, but apparently resulted when the programmer involved remarked facetiously that his format was so "advanced" that he would call it MARC IV. The space was later ignored and the "E" was added for ease of pronunciation.

when Trinity decided to create a data base compatible with MARC II
records. The format used for MARCIVE records is described as being
the same as MARC so far as variable tags are concerned, but without
certain fixed fields and without the record "directory" which locates
data elements within each MARC record, these features having been
deemed unnecessary for the MARCIVE system's purposes. The first catalog cards were produced in 1970, but further progress was delayed
by changes in hardware and programming staff in the Trinity computer
center. In 1972, the university's two IBM 360 computers (a Model 40
and a Model 44) were exchanged for a 370 Model 155, which forced rewriting of all programs. In the process, programs were completed
to convert MARC records to the MARCIVE format, and the system now
uses both locally generated records and converted MARC II records.
Access to the combined data base is by LC card number only.[23] By
1975, the MARCIVE system was producing over one million cards per
year for some 120 Texas libraries. Costs are estimated at seven to
ten cents per card, depending on specifications and the number of
card sets ordered, with the average cost per set being about sixty-
six cents. The system also produces accession lists, book pockets,
spine labels, and book catalogs of three types.[24]

Off-line book catalog systems

Book catalogs after MARC have varied markedly in size and format. One early and interesting departure from the usual arrangement
of entries into author, subject and title groupings, for example,
was the book catalog produced as part of the MARC Pilot Project by
the Washington State Library. Covering the titles acquired by the
Timberland, North Central, and King County public library systems in
Washington State during 1967 and produced only as a one-time demonstration project, the full entries were arranged in a "register"
volume by unique numbers assigned to titles as they came into the
system. Accompanying the register were three additional volumes,
which were indexes or "finding lists" by author, title, and subject,
containing only very brief information: enough to find the item on
the shelf, to request it on interlibrary loan, or to find fuller

4. MARC and Off-Line Systems After MARC

bibliographic information in the register. The advantage of this arrangement is that only the indexes need be cumulated, and the register volumes remain unchanged.[25] Similar catalogs have since been offered by the Bro-Dart Company.

Photocomposed book catalogs as opposed to those produced directly from computer print-out were discussed in the previous chapter (see pp. 65-68). One of the largest such catalogs produced to date was the University of California *Union Catalog Supplement*. The *Supplement* included all monographs cataloged by the nine campuses of the University of California during the period from 1963 through 1967, and its forty-seven volumes (thirty-one for the author-title portion and sixteen in the subject section) contained 2,600,000 entries for about 750,000 titles. The machine-readable format used was MARC-like, but simplified in order to reduce costs; for example, all main entries other than titles were assigned MARC tag 100, which in MARC itself is reserved for personal name main entries. As another means of reducing costs, the Institute of Library Research at the University of California in Berkeley developed a technique called AFR (for Automatic Field Recognition), which, although less sophisticated and specific than the format recognition techniques developed by the Library of Congress for the MARC project, was sufficiently specific for the UC book catalog project, and apparently did reduce input costs. As a final cost-cutting measure, an error rate of one in every five entries was considered acceptable; as a result, the catalog has far more errors than might normally be expected of a research library catalog, and the large data base created by the project also has less value to other libraries than if it had been more carefully edited; apparently, however, the budget of the project required such concessions. Approximately 250 sets were produced at a total cost of $1,250,000, or about $1.66 per title.[26]

The system used for the UC *Union Catalog Supplement* was later revised, supplemented, fully documented and used by the California State Library for production of several book catalogs for public libraries in the state.[27] A report produced for the State Library,[28] analyzing catalog sampling techniques, costs, input methods and conversion of MARC records, has been called "the finest study of its type to date."[29]

It is also possible to design a book catalog system so that the method of output may be either computer printout or photocomposition, depending on the use to be made of the catalog and the funds available. Some commercial photocomposing firms work with the data as it is read onto tapes, without special characters or controls, whereas others require preprogramming, but it is possible to produce tapes that can be used on virtually any machine. One such system, called BIBLIOS, has been implemented at the Orange County Public Library in California. The first edition of the Orange County book catalog was produced in 1971 by photocomposition, and later catalogs have been done by conventional print-out techniques.

An unusual feature of the Orange County catalog is that the holdings of the individual libraries are not included, but are displayed separately in a "locator guide." This list is arranged according to item numbers, each of which is followed by the code number for each branch having the item, and the number of copies if more than one copy is held. The locator guide is kept current with cumulative supplements (see Fig. 4-6).

> This approach, rather than displaying holdings in the book catalog, was chosen for a variety of reasons. First, it makes little sense to display strictly numeric data which lend themselves to tightly packed typography in a format designed for text and for which a premium page rate is being paid. Second, inventory data are volatile for a multibranch library. The holdings of any given branch vary significantly from month to month due to patron losses, acquisitions, gifts, etc. In addition, holdings (inventory) shifts are fostered by a standing policy that titles not being used extensively at one branch be reassigned to another branch to fill a known requirement.
>
> While the locator guide tracks the holdings for all titles in the collection, BIBLIOS also creates holdings lists for each branch. These lists display, in shelf-list sequence, the materials in each branch's collections. In use, they replace the traditional shelf list (and related filing) at the individual branch as well as facilitating periodic full branch inventory to maintain the accuracy of the inventory file.[30]

4. MARC and Off-Line Systems After MARC   95

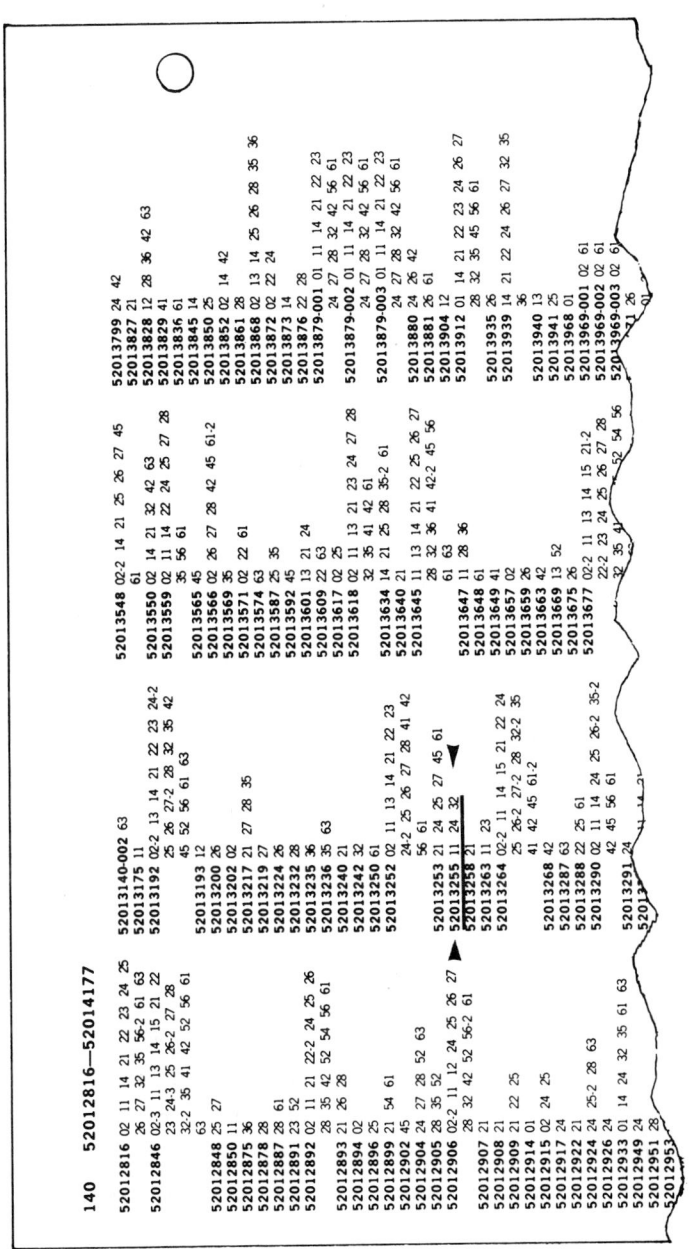

FIG. 4-6 "Locator Guide," Orange County (California) Public Library.

Total costs for the first edition of the catalog were $237,000, including conversion, programming, and publication of 500 copies of the book catalog, plus 100 copies of the locator guide. The use of MARC has been abandoned for cost reasons; according to its developer, in this system "it costs $0.32 to manually place a bibliographic description on file ... vs. $2.96 to process the same entry from MARC."[31] Despite such simplifications, "the system requirements on library personnel have led to some difficulty. Future implementation will be planned to reduce the degree of difficulty primarily by simplifying input to the system and extending in-house training courses."[32]

Difficulties notwithstanding, Orange County has recently "gone commercial" by arranging for the sale of both the BIBLIOS programs and the data base through a firm called Inovar Corporation. The State Library of Hawaii is the first purchaser of the BIBLIOS programs, reportedly for $58,000. The State Library does the processing for all of the forty-two public and school libraries in the state, and hopes to speed up both acquisitions and cataloging by use of the system.[33] According to one report, Inovar pays a "significant" portion of its BIBLIOS sales to Orange County, which hopes to recoup some of the $450,000 invested in development of the system. Inovar has priced the use of the data base, consisting of about 170,000 titles, at twenty cents per title for the first 50,000 items and sixteen cents thereafter. Among the first customers are the six members of the Raisin Valley (Michigan) library consortium, using a $30,000 Federal grant.[34]

Mention was made earlier of a recent variation in the form and method of book catalog production called COM (for computer-output microfilm or microfiche). In this technique, data are read from magnetic tape by the computer and reproduced, character by character, on a cathode-ray tube as in photocomposition devices; the difference is that the characters are then captured photographically not on photographic paper, in full size, but on microfilm or microfiche in reduced size. According to a recent estimate,[35] at least two dozen libraries are now using COM, many of them for book

4. MARC and Off-Line Systems After MARC

catalogs in microfiche form. Perhaps the best example and one which illustrates a possible transition from photocomposition to COM is the book catalog of the Hennepin County (Minnesota) Public Library. The first edition of this catalog, some 2,800 pages, was printed using an RCA Videocomp photocomposition device. Conversion was facilitated by the use of two systems developed for other projects, one at the New York Public Library and one at the University of California. The New York Public Library contributed an "authority control" system and file developed for its own book catalog project. Terms used by Hennepin County were checked against the file by the system, and if present were automatically accepted; if a cross-reference led to another term, the other term was used; and if neither was the case the term was sent back to the cataloging department for alteration or approval. The system also accepted automatically all terms used on MARC records. The Institute of Library Research at the University of California contributed the conversion system used for the University of California's Union Catalog Supplement described earlier. After the production of the first edition was completed, Hennepin County switched to COM, and the first supplement was produced on microfiche by a service bureau in Minneapolis.

One library with long experience in the use of COM is the Price Gilbert Memorial Library at the Georgia Institute of Technology. As noted earlier, the library was one of the participants in the MARC Pilot Project, and began computerized catalog card production in 1967. More recently, the library has microfilmed its card catalog, converted new cataloging data to machine-readable form, and produced quarterly catalog supplements on microfiche using COM. The catalog and catalog supplements are part of a program called LENDS (for Library Extended Catalog Access and New Delivery Service), which is intended to provide centralized bibliographic service to widely scattered departments on campus, hopefully avoiding the necessity of creating separate branch libraries. Quality control of the microfiche catalog supplements has been a problem, however, and the university has changed service bureaus and COM units three times "in an attempt to get the appearance and clarity it's after."[36] Matters have been complicated by the fact that Georgia Tech, as noted earlier, uses a Univac 1108 for library data processing, whereas most COM service bureaus are geared to IBM output.

Other libraries utilizing COM for catalogs include those at El Centro College in Dallas, Texas; the University of Texas of the Permian Basin (Odessa, Texas); and the Washington University School of Medicine. A variation from the usual catalog format that should also be noted is the Louisiana Numerical Register; this publication records the locations of 1,100,000 books in twenty-one Louisiana libraries in a COM catalog consisting not of bibliographic data but the Library of Congress card number and letter codes for the libraries holding each book. Costs are reported as 2.8 cents per volume.[37] A similar publication for Texas libraries now records over three million locations for over 1.2 million titles.

Combined book catalog and catalog card systems

Although several of the catalog card systems discussed earlier can also produce book catalogs, and vice versa, most are designed for regular production of either one or the other. A few systems, however, have been designed for regular and simultaneous production of both. At Lorain County (Ohio) Community College, the public catalog and shelflist have been retained in card form to allow them to be kept current economically, but book catalogs are also produced "to extend and facilitate use of the collection." Flexowriters are used to produce book orders and catalog cards, and an IBM 1440 computer is used to produce eight copies of author, title, and classified catalogs, which are cumulated semiannually.[38] At the other end of the scale in size is the CAIN (for Cataloging and Indexing) system at the National Agricultural Library in Washington, D. C. Originated in 1970, this system uses data from a single keyboarding to produce catalog cards, book catalogs, bibliographies, and "related internal reports." In the course of preparing such publications as the *Bibliography of Agriculture* and the *Pesticides Documentation Bulletin* as well as its regular catalogs, the library handles some 600,000 publications per year through the system. CAIN also provides service

4. MARC and Off-Line Systems After MARC

for the herbicides data base of the Agricultural Research Service and the International Tree Disease data base of the Forest Service. Cards are printed in upper- and lowercase format by a chain printer, and the book catalogs are printed either by the same method or with a computer-driven photocomposer (the Linotron in the Government Printing Office). Periodic multiple-year cumulations of the book catalog are printed by a commercial firm under contract. Bibliographies, both scheduled and special, are normally produced on the Linotron, but may also be produced on the computer's chain printer.[39]

NOTES

1. Lawrence F. Buckland, *The Recording of Library of Congress Bibliographical Data in Machine Form*, Inforonics, Inc., Maynard, Mass., 1964.
2. H. D. Avram, R. S. Freitag, and K. D. Guiles, *Planning Memorandum No. 3: a Proposed Format for a Standardized Machine-Readable Catalog Record*, Library of Congress, Washington, D.C., 1965.
3. Hillis L. Griffin, "Automation of Technical Processes in Libraries," in *Annual Review of Information Science and Technology*, v. 3, Encyclopedia Brittanica, Chicago, 1968, p. 245.
4. Library of Congress Information Systems Office, *The MARC Pilot Experience: an Informal Summary*, Library of Congress, Washington, D.C., 1968, pp. 9-13.
5. See Frederick H. Ruecking, Jr., "MARC at Rice University," in *Proceedings of the 1970 Clinic on Library Applications of Data Processing: MARC Uses and Users*, University of Illinois Graduate School of Library Science, Urbana, 1971, pp. 66-77; Ruecking, *MARC Pilot Project Progress Report No. 3*, Rice University, Houston, Texas, 1967; and Ruecking, "Bibliographic Retrieval from Bibliographic Input: The Hypothesis and Construction of a Test," *Journal of Library Automation*, 1, 227-238 (December 1968).
6. See Henriette D. Avram, "MARC Is A Four-Letter Word," *Library Journal*, 93, 2604 (July 1968); and Avram, "Implications of Project MARC," in *Library Automation: A State of the Art Review*, American Library Association, Chicago, 1969, pp. 83, 86.
7. Avram, "MARC Is A Four-Letter Word," p. 2605.
8. Library of Congress RECON Working Task Force, *Conversion of Retrospective Catalog Records to Machine-Readable Form: A Study of the Feasibility of a National Bibliographic Service*, Library of Congress, Washington, D. C., 1969. For a discussion of the

various problems involved in retrospective conversion on a national scale, see also *National Aspects of Creating and Using MARC/RECON Records,* Library of Congress, Washington, D.C., 1973.

9. Henriette D. Avram, "The Evolving MARC System: The Concept of a Data Utility," in *Proceedings of the 1970 Clinic on Library Applications of Data Processing: MARC Uses and Users,* University of Illinois Graduate School of Library Science, Urbana, 1971, pp. 16-17.

10. See Henriette D. Avram et al., "MARC Program Research and Development: a Progress Report," *Journal of Library Automation,* 2, 250-253 (December 1969); Library of Congress Information Systems Office, *Format Recognition Process for MARC Records: A Logical Design,* American Library Association, Chicago, 1970; and Brett Butler, "Automatic Format Recognition of MARC Bibliographic Elements: a Review and Projection," *Journal of Library Automation,* 7, 27-42 (March 1974).

11. *Library of Congress Information Bulletin,* 32, 273-274, 279 (August 3, 1973).

12. *Library of Congress Information Bulletin,* 34, Appendix A, pp. 9, 11, 14 (January 10, 1974).

13. *Library of Congress Information Bulletin,* 33, 416-417 (December 20, 1974).

14. Stephen R. Salmon, "Development of the Card Automated Reproduction and Distribution System (CARDS) at the Library of Congress," in *Proceedings of the 1969 Clinic on Library Applications of Data Processing,* University of Illinois Graduate School of Library Science, Urbana, 1970, pp. 98-113.

15. John P. Kennedy, "A Local MARC Project: The Georgia Tech Library," in *Proceedings of the 1968 Clinic on Library Applications of Data Processing,* University of Illinois Graduate School of Library Science, Urbana, 1969, pp. 206-212.

16. "Massachusetts Central Book Processing Center Effects Savings for State-Supported Institutions," *College & Research Libraries News,* no. 4, 89-90 (April 1971).

17. Lawrence F. Buckland et al., *Final Report, Phase I: Survey of Automated Library Systems,* Prepared for the California State University and Colleges, Infloronics, Inc., Maynard, Mass., 1973, Appendix A, p. D-E 4.

18. "Massachusetts Central Library Processing Center Report," *JOLA Technical Communications,* 3, 5-6 (May/June 1972).

19. "Hammer Outlines Central Processing Difficulties," *Advanced Technology/Libraries,* 2, 1-2 (June 1973).

20. Buckland, *op. cit.,* p. D-E 5.

21. Richard Phillips Palmer, *Case Studies in Library Computer Systems,* R. R. Bowker, New York, 1973, p. 147.

4. MARC and Off-Line Systems After MARC

22. Ellen Tom and Sue Reed, *SCOPE in Cataloging*, Guelph University Library, Guelph, Ontario, 1970 (ED 045108).

23. See Ruby B. Miller and Robert A. Houze, "New Horizons in Computer Applications at Trinity University Library," *Texas Library Journal*, 48, 227-229, 254-255 (November 1972), and Virginia M. Bowden and Ruby B. Miller, "MARCIVE: A Cooperative Automated Library System," *Journal of Library Automation*, 7, 183-200 (September 1974).

24. Letter from Robert A. Houze, January 16, 1975.

25. Josephine S. Pulsifer, "MARC Book Catalog Production in Washington State," in *Proceedings of the 1970 Clinic on Library Applications of Data Processing: MARC Uses and Users*, University of Illinois Graduate School of Library Science, Urbana, 1971, pp. 59-61.

26. "U. Cal. Book Catalog Now Available," *JOLA Technical Communications*, 3, 7-8 (July-August 1972).

27. Buckland et al., *op. cit.*, Appendix A, p. S-1. See also Liz Gibson, "BIBCON--A General Purpose Software System for MARC-Based Book Catalog Production," *Journal of Library Automation*, 6, 237-256 (December 1973).

28. Kelley L. Cartwright and Ralph M. Shoffner, *Catalogs in Book Form: a Research Study of Their Implication for the California State Union Catalog, with a Design for Their Implementation*, Institute of Library Research, Berkeley, California, 1967.

29. Barbara Evans Markuson, "Automation in Libraries and Information Centers," in *Annual Review of Information Science and Technology*, v. 2, Wiley, New York, 1967, p. 270.

30. John C. Kountz, "BIBLIOS Revisited," *Journal of Library Automation*, 5, 73 (June 1972).

31. *Ibid.*, p. 85.

32. Buckland, *op. cit.*, Appendix A, p. Y-2.

33. "Hawaii State Library System to Automate Processing," *Journal of Library Automation*, 7, 145 (June 1974).

34. "Inovar Takes on Orange County's BIBLIOS: Hawaii a User," *Advanced Technology/Libraries*, 4, 7 (January 1975).

35. "COM, Low in Price, High in Sophistication, Enters the Library," *Advanced Technology/Libraries*, 2, 104 (August 1973).

36. *Ibid.*

37. William E. McGrath and Donald Simon, "Regional Numerical Union Catalog on Computer Output Microfiche," *Journal of Library Automation*, 5, 217-229 (December 1972).

38. Jack W. Scott, "An Integrated Computer Based Technical Processing System in a Small College Library," *Journal of Library Automation*, 1, 149-158 (September 1968).

39. Vern J. Van Dyke, "Multipurpose Cataloging and Indexing System (CAIN) at the National Agricultural Library," *Journal of Library Automation*, 5, 21-29 (March 1972).

Chapter 5

ON-LINE CATALOGING SYSTEMS

As noted in Chapter 3, the development of cataloging systems has roughly followed the development of acquisition systems, and this holds true in the progression from off-line to on-line systems. In the case of cataloging systems, however, the end products are normally produced off-line in a "batch" mode--that is, all at one time, rather than as the data are entered--and only the functions of inputting data and searching the data files are performed on-line and in "real time." With rare exceptions, this tends to be true whether the products are catalog cards, book catalogs, or both. Typewriters and typewriter-like devices have been used as terminals connected to the computer, as well as visual display (cathode-ray tube) units, the advantage of the latter being principally the increased speed with which the information is displayed. The capability of continuous interaction with the computer is particularly valuable in cataloging systems because of the nature of cataloging. There is a greater need for precision and typographical accuracy in cataloging records as opposed to acquisition records, so the ability to perform editing on-line and see the results of the editing action immediately is helpful. Further, the files to be searched in cataloging are much larger, so the ability to modify search strategies as one sees the results of the search is also highly advantageous.

On-line input, off-line catalog cards

Perhaps the earliest on-line cataloging system used routinely for production of catalog cards began in 1970 at the Shawnee Mission Public School system in suburban Kansas City. IBM 2740 and 2741 typewriter terminals were used to input bibliographic data, and an IBM 360 Model 40 computer to do the processing and print catalog cards. A generalized package of programs called FASTER was obtained from IBM, thus avoiding much of the programming effort (and expense) such a system normally requires. Unit costs to create and key data, print cards and labels, and prepare items for delivery were estimated at $2.50 per item, based on an estimated 100,000 items to be processed in 1971.[1] In 1972, the cost of cards and labels was calculated at $2.25 per item, or $2.53 if the various listings, reports and other printed products were included.[2] The developers of the system write that "the librarians are satisfied that direct access to master library disk files is an efficient, accurate, and economical method of creating and updating bibliographic and holdings information. Terminals provide an easy way to add to and change files instantly ... the system has worked dependably since its first days ... and the work flow has been stripped of time-consuming steps."[3]

The public schools of Oregon were also early users of an on-line system using the same terminals (IBM 2740s). A large, generalized computer system located in Eugene was already available. This system, called OTIS (for Oregon Total Information System), utilized an IBM 360 Model 50 computer with 77 keyboard terminals located in various buildings around the state. Three of these terminals were placed in the Springfield School District's Library Processing Center, and approximately 43,000 titles, representing the complete holdings of the district's libraries, were then entered and edited on-line.[4] By 1971, catalog cards were being supplied for several other libraries.[5]

University systems also began to be implemented in 1971. At Northwestern University, 2470s were connected to a small IBM 370 Model 135 computer in the Administrative Data Processing Center. The system as implemented is a "total" system in that it provides information on titles in process as well as those cataloged, plus

5. On-Line Cataloging Systems

bibliographic and holdings information for approximately 35,000 serial titles. "The greatest immediate impact," however, has been in catalog card production.

> Cards are produced once a week at the rate of over 6,000 in two hours, thereby equalling the production of the original typing pool for approximately seven-and-a-half work days. Cards are printed in correct filing order, sorted to the eighth character, and grouped for each of the various catalogs.[6]

MARC records are converted for use in the system whenever possible, and original cataloging may also be done using the terminals.

The machine-readable files were originally on a data cell (a large and relatively inexpensive form of computer storage), but when this became operationally inconvenient the records were transferred to portable disk packs. Lack of tape drives in the Data Processing Center created another inconvenience, necessitating transfer of MARC records from tape to disk at another institution; tape drives were later added for this reason. The most serious equipment limitation, however, was the "display" rate of the typewriter terminals, which is only 14 characters per second, "far from ideal when long bibliographic records are involved."[7] This difficulty in communication has been the chief reason for the use in later on-line systems of cathode-ray tube terminals, with their much faster and often almost instantaneous response.

Georgia Tech, whose work on other methods of catalog card and book catalog production was noted in earlier chapters, began inputting data in 1971 with Model 33ASR teletype terminals on-line to their Univac 1108,[8] and the University of Toronto began the same year, using Model KSR37 teletype terminals on-line to a Xerox Sigma 7 computer. The Toronto teletypes were modified to include a large number of characters--seven more, in fact, than the MARC character set. The Toronto system also uses a Xerox Graphic Printer which provides upper and lower case type fonts and various type sizes, thus allowing more characters to be placed on a single card and reducing the number of second (continuation) cards needed. Several hundred thousand records have been input at Toronto using the on-line system, and another 700,000 by a separate keypunch activity. Commendably, the university offers the services of the system (including batch searching of the files) to other libraries in the area.[9]

OCLC

The largest, best-known, and most influential cataloging system--the Ohio College Library Center in Columbus, Ohio, known universally as OCLC--also began its on-line operations in 1971. Perhaps no other system has had as much effect on library practice in this country; indeed, if the development of MARC is the most significant accomplishment to date in library automation, the development and operation of the Ohio College Library Center is probably the second most significant. This is not primarily because of the technological expertise employed in the development of the system (although that is great), but because it is the largest and most efficient shared cataloging system yet implemented. OCLC produces catalog cards economically, as do many of the other systems already described, but its importance lies in the fact that it provides a common cataloging data base for searching and consultation by almost 350 libraries. The margin of savings achievable by any system of catalog card production is small in relation to the total budget of most libraries, but the cost of performing the intellectual task of original cataloging is much larger; the OCLC system provides significant savings because both MARC records and the cataloging records prepared by all member libraries can be displayed on the terminal screens in any one member's library, thus obviating the need for any library but the first to catalog it. Catalog cards can then be ordered from Columbus and arrive in a few days, formatted to a member library's specifications and arranged in rough filing sequence.

The Center was founded by the Ohio College Association in 1967 with over fifty members "to operate a computerized, regional library center to serve the academic libraries of Ohio."[10] From the beginning, it was agreed that records compatible with the MARC II format would be used in the Center's cataloging system so that the Center could play a part in any future national system. By 1970, the first

5. On-Line Cataloging Systems

OCLC operation, an off-line card production system, was functioning. Members submitted IBM punched cards containing the LC card numbers of books for which they wished catalog cards, along with their own call numbers if they were unwilling to accept LC's, and OCLC then ran these requests against the MARC II data base. If the titles were in MARC, catalog cards were then produced on computers at Ohio State University using programs modified from the Yale project described earlier (OCLC's first and only director, and its principal designer, Frederick Kilgour, had been intimately associated with the Yale project before coming to OCLC). By 1971, little over a year later, a sophisticated on-line system had been implemented, using the Center's own Xerox Sigma 5 computer.[11]

Two technical developments associated with this effort should be noted in particular. Visual display terminals were abundantly available by 1971, but most of them were unsatisfactory for library use; typically only uppercase characters could be displayed, and the number of characters that could be displayed at any one time on the screen was far too low. After beginning with Spiras LTE terminals, the Center contracted for production of a visual display terminal specifically designed for the OCLC application, manufactured by Beehive Medical Electronics, Inc. (see Fig. 5-1). Called the "OCLC 100," the terminal has been enthusiastically received in those libraries employing it. The second development of interest is the design of an efficient searching mechanism. OCLC files could be accessed from the beginning by a Library of Congress card number, but a method was also needed to allow searching by authors and titles. After some interesting experiments at OCLC and elsewhere, a search "key" technique was devised which requires the terminal operator to input only six characters: either the first three characters of the author and the first three characters of the first word of the title not an article, or the first three letters of the first word of the title not an article and the first letter of the next three words. This technique and the programs written to accommodate it reportedly retrieve five or fewer titles 99 percent of the time for 80 percent

FIG. 5-1. OCLC terminal.

of the member libraries; additional standardized procedures reduce the number of replies in the remaining one percent to less than eighteen with very few exceptions.[12] Keyboarding of complete author and title information in order to obtain cataloging copy is thus made unnecessary.*

By September 1974, the number of titles in the on-line file had passed the one million mark, and was growing by over 25,000 titles

---

*It should be pointed out that this technique is effective only for on-line techniques, not for batch processing, and is also less effective for works by corporate authors than works by personal authors.

5. On-Line Cataloging Systems 109

monthly. Approximately half of the titles were from MARC records, the other half from participating libraries. And the number of participating libraries was growing rapidly, following a decision in 1973 to allow other regional networks to connect to the system. As of this writing, the following regional networks have contractual arrangements with OCLC:

> The AMIGOS Bibliographic Network in the Southwest
>
> The Cooperative College Library Center, Atlanta, Georgia
>
> The Federal Library Experiment in Cooperative Cataloging (FLECC)
>
> The Five Associated University Libraries (FAUL) of Upstate New York
>
> The Higher Education Coordinating Council (HECC) of Metropolitan St. Louis
>
> The Illinois Research and Reference Center Libraries (IRRN)
>
> The New England Library Information Network (NELINET)
>
> The Pittsburgh Regional Library Center
>
> The Pennsylvania Area Library Network (PALINET)
>
> The State University of New York (SUNY)
>
> The Southeastern Library Network (SOLINET)

The libraries in these networks and several independent connections cover 33 states plus the District of Columbia, and more libraries in the U. S. and Canada are negotiating for affiliation.

For many of these customers, as for Ohio members, the economic justification for participation in the system is more than the saving on cataloging costs. As the price of library materials has risen, the need to share regional library resources has become increasingly urgent, and the OCLC system provides a convenient and effective means of doing so; precise statistics are difficult to come by, but it is clear that more and more participating libraries are using the OCLC system to find and request a copy of a book owned by another library, rather than to catalog a copy already owned.[13] Indeed, the implications of the system for resource sharing have often been felt to be as significant as the implications for savings in cataloging costs.

The open-handedness of OCLC in allowing other networks to connect has not been without its concomitant problems, of course. On more than one occasion, such connections have interrupted service, sometimes seriously, and as the number of terminals connected to the system increases, the response time decreases. At one point in 1974, with 240 terminals connected to the Xerox Sigma 5 computer, the response time for the simplest search (by LC card number) was 6.6 seconds[14] and many searches took much longer. A new Sigma 9 computer, Xerox's largest and most powerful, has recently been installed, however, and a second Sigma 9 will be added shortly. On the bright side, too, additional members mean additional revenue, and the Center expects the current charge of around $2.00 per title (counting searching, production of cards and arranging them for filing) to decline even further because of the economies of scale.

Chicago and Stanford

Two large university-based systems, each costing millions of dollars in grant and institutional funds to develop, have also used on-line techniques to initiate production of catalog cards as well as other products. The University of Chicago library automation project began in 1966. For several years, however, it was unclear to many in the profession precisely what the project was intended to accomplish; it was variously described as "an integrated, computer-based, bibliographical data system for a large university library,"[15] a "total integrated library system utilizing computer-based data-handling processes,"[16] and "a computerized system to handle large bibliographic data files,"[17] phrases which the principal investigator for the project and Chicago's library director, Herman Fussler, ruefully admitted were "somewhat awkward" and "perhaps ... obscure."[18] The design philosophy was "to be able to create a record and to update it at any point in the technical processing operations; to enter data, partial or complete, at any time and subsequently be able to use, amend, or correct these data; to signal desired output at any time and get it at the desired time in the proper format, and positioned in an array designed for easiest use."[19] As some of these

5. On-Line Cataloging Systems

phrases imply, much of the early design and development effort of the project was concentrated on techniques of file-handling rather than on products, and one of its goals was "to eliminate or decrease much of the manual record generation ... associated with library technical processing operation."[20] In 1970, however, another description by the same writer said that "the system emphasizes printed products,"[21] even though the system is on-line.

What does seem clear from the literature is that the system has produced catalog cards and other cataloging products almost from the beginning in 1966. At first, IBM 1050s were used for input and also for production of cards and labels,[22] but catalog card production was transferred in 1968 to a high-speed computer printer because of "the high incidence of inaccurate printing and frequent machine breakdowns" associated with the 1050 printers.[23] Since that time, the system has handled all Roman alphabet cataloging and ordering for the library, "allowed data to be input to an in-process file at the time either of ordering or cataloging, accepted input from either MARC tapes or keyboard terminals, and produced printed products for the Library."[24] These printed products include several hundred thousand catalog cards per year, as well as book cards and book pocket labels.

Despite this production success, the "experience at Chicago" has been that "a data processing system which merely prints products for use in library processing operations does not necessarily improve the way that operation is carried out or even affect the efficiency of it."[25] Apparently because of this, the library in 1975 was in the process of scrapping almost the entire system and replacing it with a completely new one.

Several factors were involved in this decision. For one thing, access to the files under the old system was based on a single key-- the internally generated order number--and the library wanted to have access by other keys as well, such as the Library of Congress card number and the International Standard Book Number. It was also desired to make the Chicago record format follow the MARC format more closely. Most importantly, the library wanted to improve communication with the system through the use of visual display terminals (the same Beehive terminals used by OCLC, in fact), which would allow catalog card information to be displayed on the screen and edited before being printed.[26]

One problem that plagued the old system may still be a problem with the new, although the library appears to be taking steps to avoid it. In the old system, the computer used was changed from a 360 Model 30 to a Model 40, then to a Model 50, then to a Model 65, and somewhat later to the present 370 Model 168, all with inevitable delays. For the new system, a Varian 73 minicomputer is being installed in the library itself and connected to the 370.

> It was the University policy that major computing be done at the Computation Center's central facility, and it was also reasonably clear from the beginning that the large data base and data management system would require a large computer for implementation. Later, as detailed library requirements and system design showed the extent to which on-line interaction was desired and the potential number of terminals needed, the advantages of a minicomputer became more apparent. ... A study showed that a minicomputer as part of the front end for the system had definite operational and economic advantages in the Chicago environment. Without a minicomputer, several dozen lines to the Computation Center would be needed. ... We therefore decided to incorporate a minicomputer ... as a data concentrator and high-speed interface to the Computation Center's IBM 370/168.

The Varian also provides backup if the main computer is down due to malfunction, for maintenance or for testing.[27]

Significantly, the new system is also designed so that eventually it can support other users, whereas the old system supported only the University of Chicago library. Perhaps ironically, the part of the system that makes it accessible to multiple users is called CHASM (for Chicago Access Support Module),[28] symbolizing the wide gap between a single-library system and a cooperative one. Whether Chicago will bridge this chasm in time to attract users away from such established and growing cooperative projects as OCLC remains an important question.

5. On-Line Cataloging Systems 113

As noted in Chapter 2, perhaps the most sophisticated technical processing system presently in operation is the BALLOTS system at Stanford University. Development of the system began in 1967, but its first production operations did not occur until 1972, when the capability of searching the MARC data base and using it to produce catalog cards became operational. A large IBM 360 Model 67 computer is used with a small PDP 11 computer as an intermediary and a number of Sanders 804 programmable display terminals. The searching capabilities of the system, developed for the most part under another program called SPIRES (for Stanford Physics Information Retrieval System) are its most impressive feature, with many files and indexes on-line and numerous automatic promptings and suggestions from the computer to the terminal user as a search proceeds.

For cataloging, the user consults one of eleven terminals located in a single area shared by Acquisitions and Cataloging, and following the instructions displayed progressively on the screen calls up the bibliographic information generated in the acquisition process, makes any necessary changes, and adds copy numbers and shelving location symbols. The end of this process signals production of cataloging products, including not only catalog cards and necessary cross-references in filing sequence, but also two kinds of labels, produced on an IBM 2741 terminal with a Se-Lin labeling device attached. One label is for the spine, the other for the inside of the book in connection with circulation use.

If the record used in acquisitions was not derived from MARC, the cataloging department may also search the on-line BALLOTS/MARC file to see if a MARC record is now available.[*] If so, the user may substitute the MARC record for the preliminary acquisitions record and add information as needed. If no MARC record is available, original cataloging does not necessarily have to be performed at this point, because the system is designed to continue searching for

---

[*]The BALLOTS/MARC file, however, contains only a portion of the total MARC data base.

MARC records automatically, at least in categories for which MARC data are expected. If the system later finds a MARC record, the library is notified automatically; if none is found within a specified period of time (up to eight months), the search is terminated and original cataloging is then performed.

In the event that no MARC record is found either on receipt of the item or after the automatic search period, the terminal presents a pretagged form to facilitate input. Editing of the input may be done directly on the terminal or by a "catalog data sheet" (see Fig. 5-2), which the cataloging personnel use for making handwritten changes that clerical staff then enter via the terminals. The catalog data sheet may appear redundant, but it has the advantage of providing a portable version of the proposed catalog information, which can be taken to official and public catalogs or other sources of information for checking. In this respect, the BALLOTS system has overcome a disadvantage noted for the OCLC system: the physical problem of checking information retrieved on a visual display terminal against information located elsewhere.[29]

Foundation support for the project has been used solely for development and Stanford has paid the operating costs, so when the grant funds eventually disappear the operation of the system presumably can continue. Nevertheless, certain operational aspects of the system are expensive (particularly the construction and maintenance of large data files), and Stanford shares with Chicago the danger of having a glorious white elephant on its hands unless these costs can be spread over a broader base--presumably by supporting the technical processing activities of other libraries as well. In Stanford's case, work along this line is well advanced. With a new grant from the Council on Library Resources of almost $350,000, announced in early 1975, Stanford will alter the system's software to develop BALLOTS as a California library automation network, and incidentally enable it to handle all of the diacritics in the MARC character set.[30] The California State Library has also arranged with Stanford to make BALLOTS available to seven public libraries as the first step toward a California Public Library Automation

5. On-Line Cataloging Systems

```
                              86S1
QE83.A25 no. 38               STK
                              SST:3S

Eakins, Gilbert R.
  Uranium in Alaska, by Gilbert R. Eakins.  College,
State of Alaska, Division of Mines and Geology, 1969.
  49 [1] p.  illus., col. maps (2 fold. in pocket)
29 cm.  (Geologic report no. 38)

  Bibliography: p. 47-[50]

  1.Uranium ores - Alaska.  I.Alaska. Division of
Mines and Geology.  II.TITLE.
CRD:72630996
LCA:TN490.U7    DC:553/.09798 s@ 553/.493

PRO:PO          BAC:NKC001        SNI:2
VENDOR:BRILL

1.1 MRI.04/19/73 LC.04/19/73
```

CP:AKU L:ENG REC:AM CI: MS:N	INPUT BY:
INST: ETC: PMI:	DATE: SUL-222

FIG. 5-2. Data Sheet, BALLOTS Project, Stanford University.

Network (PLAN).[31] If these trials are successful, a West Coast network of the OCLC type may emerge, with interesting and important consequences.

Commercial cataloging systems

Commercial firms have also become interested in the possibilities of on-line systems. As early as 1967, the System Development Corporation began development of a project called LISTS (for Library Information System Time-Sharing), which would allow libraries connected to the system to perform a variety of technical processing tasks, including not only production of catalog cards but also printing of orders and acquisition reports, maintaining outstanding order and in-process files, and even circulation control. The system began in 1968 with seven libraries (two public and four academic, plus the SDC library) connected by ASR33 teletype terminals to a 360 Model 67 located at SDC headquarters in Santa Monica, California, but it has never been seriously marketed.[32]

In 1973, the Information Dynamics Corporation announced a service called BIBNET, which uses Datapoint 2200 or Hazeltine 2000 terminals connected via regular telephone lines (through Tymshare's TymNet service) to a computer owned by System Development Corporation. The Datapoint terminals (Fig. 5-3) have not only a keyboard and a cathode-ray tube, but also a small computer memory and provision for insertion of two magnetic tape cassettes containing programs or data; in effect, therefore, they are minicomputers themselves. When a desired record or information is located by searching, it can be stored on one of the cassettes and then called up on the screen at a later time and edited without tying up expensive telephone lines. GE Terminet printer terminals are also available, with rated speeds of either 30 or 120 characters per second. The printers can be used for production of catalog cards, or printing of proof sheets to be checked against an existing card catalog.[33]

Searching may be done by the LC card number, the International Standard Book Number, by author, by title, or by use of a "Ruecking algorithm" (a code made up of several characters from the author

5. On-Line Cataloging Systems							117

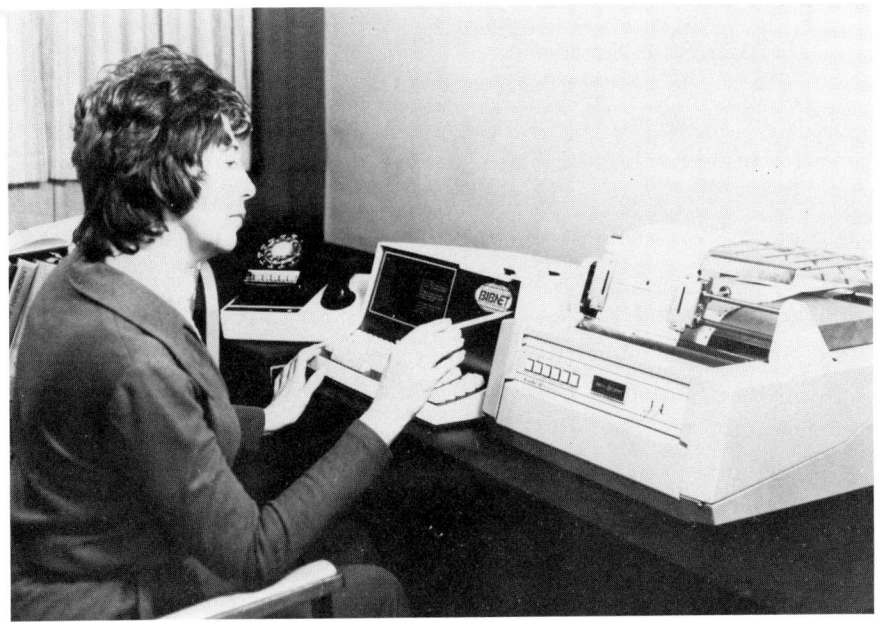

FIG. 5-3. BIBNET terminal.

and title, as in the OCLC system). In early 1975, the company was still in the process of loading MARC records into the system, but brief "index" entries for many records were already available, providing the full author, title and imprint, as well as the LC card number and ISBN. If the full bibliographic record is desired, a key on the terminal can be depressed to ask personnel at IDC headquarters to search manually for the full record, convert it to machine-readable form, and send it back, several days later.[34]

The New Mexico State Library has used the system and a Hazeltine terminal to add holding codes for eighteen libraries in the state, and then search for locations on request from interlibrary loan librarians around the state. SDC's ORBIT program is used for the searching operation. The costs, in addition to the cost of the terminal and its installation, are $45 per hour, plus 20 cents per location added and 90 cents per location retrieved.[35]

The New York Public Library book catalog system

All of the systems described above use on-line input and searching techniques in connection with the production of catalog cards; one other large on-line system, however, has book catalogs as its final product instead. This is the New York Public Library system, perhaps the best and certainly the biggest book catalog system in existence at this time. NYPL is really two libraries in one—a large research library, and a public library with eighty-six branches—so two book catalogs are produced, each containing records added since February 1972. The catalogs are produced on a schedule of so-called "continuous re-accumulation." The alphabet is divided into twelve sections, and each month one-twelfth of the alphabet is "re-accumulated," while the new records in the rest of the alphabet are added to a cumulative supplement. This means that in order to locate a particular title the user must consult only the cumulation for that portion of the alphabet, plus the cumulative supplement, plus the old card catalog for entries prior to February 1972.[36] To reduce printing costs, all added entries are condensed, omitting "title page extension," publisher, and bibliographic notes, "the assumption being that the user who is interested in such data will take the trouble to refer to the main entry."[37]

Input to the system is off-line, but three 2740 terminals are used for inquiry. An IBM 370 Model 145 computer is used for processing, and production of the book catalog pages is done by an RCA Videocomp photocomposer. In 1972, the cost of production was about $100,000 per year for 550 to 600 copies of the branch libraries' catalog, and about $90,000 per year for 200 copies of the Research Libraries' catalog, of which about forty are sold. The costs of development for the system have been estimated at anywhere from $2 million to $4 million, and the annual computer bill is around $360,000; of this latter amount, however, approximately $200,000 is paid for by renting out time to private industry.[38]

The project traces its origins to the work of a Columbia University doctoral candidate who found that at NYPL approximately 20

5. On-Line Cataloging Systems

percent of its nine million cards showed substantial deterioration.[39] This study led to a fuller report, which recommended that the library cease adding to the card catalog, attempt to restore the cards in question, and produce catalog cards for new titles using automated techniques.[40] By 1968, plans had been developed for new card catalogs which would grow for five years and then be converted to book form; by 1969, however, the idea of using catalog cards had been dropped, and a decision was reached to use book catalogs exclusively.

The largest program in the system and its strongest feature is its authority file control; a single machine-readable file includes all subjects, series titles, and names used in the system, and every new record is checked against this file before being entered in the system. This provides valuable assistance to the catalogers and avoids the problem of variant forms of entry, a problem that has plagued other similar systems, notably OCLC. This feature also makes it possible to change outdated terminology for new, readily and efficiently, both in catalog headings and in the cross-reference structure.[41]

Other products of the system include processing information lists, cataloging work sheets (which report the results of automatic authority file searches) and two shelflist cards for each book which are sent to the branches or divisions.[42] Several other book catalogs, including one of the Dance Collection of the Research Library of the Performing Arts, have also been published.

On-line input, off-line catalog cards and book catalogs

At least two systems have been designed to produce both catalog cards and book catalogs from on-line input. The Western Kentucky University library in Bowling Green originally began its project as a means of reclassifying from Dewey to the Library of Congress classification. Ten IBM ATS (2741) terminals were installed in 1971 on-line to an IBM 360 Model 40 computer, and temporary workers were used to enter data. The computer printed out proofsheets of the data daily, and these were then proofread and edited by catalogers, reinforced as needed by librarians from other parts of the library. Labels, pockets and book cards were produced for reprocessing of some 250,000 items, and both catalog cards for a divided card catalog and book catalogs were then printed. Since the reclassification project, catalog cards and book catalogs continue to be produced on a regular basis.[43]

The UCLA Biomedical Library's cataloging application differs from most others in that it makes no attempt to use MARC records, and is designed to accommodate only "original" cataloging. The majority of the records acquired by the Biomedical Library are not available on MARC in any case, since the Library of Congress (which produces MARC) by policy avoids adding works in clinical medicine or other areas covered by its sister institution, the National Library of Medicine. The cataloger for the Biomedical Library types information on a "cataloging coding sheet" which a clerk then rekeys on a terminal, the redundant keyboarding action apparently necessitated by the objections of the cataloger to using the terminal. The terminal itself is a Delta Data Systems device with a cassette section added; the information is recorded on the cassette, and periodically the computer (an IBM 360 Model 91) reads the information from the cassette into disk storage. A prooflisting is printed periodically, and is used by the cataloger to make editing changes. Corrections are then input by the typist. Catalog cards are produced once a week on a 360 Model 20, prearranged in filing sequence, and a list of new accessions is produced once a month. The same programs that arrange the cards are also used for the book catalog, which is produced primarily for regional interlibrary loan purposes. A three-year, $40,000 grant provided funds for development of the system, and operating costs are estimated at $1,000 per month.[44]

On-line catalog reference, without cards or book catalogs

A few libraries have taken what some regard as the ultimate step and devised systems that use on-line terminals not only for input and searching but also for regular consultation of the catalog file, thereby eliminating the use of catalog cards and book catalogs altogether. Perhaps the first such system was the Experimental Library

5. On-Line Cataloging Systems   121

Management System (ELMS) at the IBM Advanced System Development
Division library in Los Gatos, California, parts of which have been
in operation since 1965. Catalog information is input via IBM 2741
terminals, and is consulted by both library staff and patrons using
IBM 2260 display terminals. There are four of these--two in the
processing area, one at the reference desk, and one in a carrel.
Public use appears to be successful, but since this is a small,
specialized library it is difficult to estimate the problems (such
as queuing) that might result if the same techniques were used in a
large research library.[45] Before the on-line reference function was
implemented, the system produced nine separate book catalogs or listings, and apparently this capability is still used. Spine labels
and book pocket labels are also produced.[46]

On-line reference to machine-readable catalog files was also
the subject of much intensive study during Project Intrex (for Information Transfer Experiments) at the Massachusetts Institute of
Technology. Intrex was a multimillion-dollar research project, which
began in 1965 and was finally terminated in 1973. One idea that received much experimental study during the life of the project was the
concept of an "augmented catalog," which would be consulted on-line
and would contain not only the usual bibliographical information, but
such additional data as the "author's purpose," the "level of approach," excerpts from the text, and "user comments."[47] The most
helpful fields, as determined by the Intrex experiments, were the
abstracts, the title, subject terms, the author, the table of contents, and excerpts from the text, all except the author being what
the project staff referred to as "content-indicating" fields. Main
entry and publisher were deemed helpful only 9 percent of the time,
and such fields as edition, place of publication, and physical dimensions were ignored completely by the users.[48] A variety of terminals was used, some of them designed by the project and some
commercially available. Not surprisingly, those terminals with full
screen displays were preferred to those that had only a typewriter
for communication from the computer to the user.[49]

The other major effort of Project Intrex that is pertinent here was the attempt to store and retrieve, via on-line terminals, the full text of documents. Storage of the text was in microform, scanned and transmitted electrically, on demand, to the same terminals used for searching and other purposes.[50] Permanent copies could also be obtained, either in microform or in full-size hardcopy. A summary of use during the project indicated that

1. Over 80 percent of the experimental sessions involved use of the text-access subsystem. Most users said they found rapid access to full text a crucial element in a fully satisfactory system and that the text-access system, as implemented, was more than fast enough for them.
2. The system operated reliably; over 90 percent of the commands initiated by the user resulted in the specified output.
3. Although most users seem satisfied by the quality of the image when text access is used for the purpose for which it was originally intended (the preliminary examination of the document), most users prefer higher resolution and express the desire to eventually obtain hard copy.
4. Users in this experiment employed the text-access system primarily to judge the relevance of documents after preliminary judgements have been made on the basis of the catalog data. Users employed text access only to a small extent to <u>read</u> document text for information contained ...
5. Relevance judgments with the full-text system are made primarily on the basis of document text, as such, rather than associated parts such as illustrations, or the abstract. If we assume that academic level (by year of study) is a reasonable measure of a student's depth of knowledge about the subject of his search, then this

5. On-Line Cataloging Systems

depth of knowledge is negatively correlated with the utility of full text for the relevance judging function. The more a user knows about a subject, the more he is willing to rely solely on catalog information.

6. The average user spends somewhat more time looking at catalog data than he does looking at text, but since he looks at catalog data on more documents, he spends more time, per document, looking at text.[51]

Although the Intrex Project has been formally discontinued, it seems likely that the results of its extensive experimentation, especially with the augmented catalog and full-text access, will be important to designers of similar systems in future years.

NOTES

1. Ellen Wasby Miller and B. J. Hodges, "Shawnee Mission's On-Line Cataloging System" *Journal of Library Automation*, 4, 13-26 (March 1971).

2. *Ibid.*, "Shawnee Mission's On-Line Cataloging System: the First Two Years," in *Proceedings of the 1972 Clinic on Library Applications of Data Processing*, University of Illinois Graduate School of Library Science, Urbana, Illinois, 1973, p. 100.

3. Miller and Hodges, 1971, p. 24.

4. John R. Blair and Ruby Snyder, "An Automated Library System: Project LEEDS," *American Libraries*, 5, 172-173 (February 1970).

5. Caryl McAllister, "On-Line Library Housekeeping Systems," *Special Libraries*, 62, 466 (November 1971).

6. Karen Horny, "Automation of Technical Services: Northwestern's Experience," *College & Research Libraries*, 35, 368 (September 1974).

7. *Ibid.*, p. 365.

8. Lawrence R. Buckland, James Dolby and Mary Madden, *Final Report, Phase I: Survey of Automated Library Systems*, Inforonics, Inc., Maynard, Mass., 1973, Appendix A, p. Z 1-2.

9. *Ibid.*, Appendix A, p. T 1-2.

10. Frederick G. Kilgour, "Initial System Design for the Ohio College Library Center: a Case History," in *Proceedings of the 1968 Clinic on Library Applications of Data Processing*, University of Illinois Graduate School of Library Science, Urbana, 1969, p. 79.

11. Judith Hopkins, "The Ohio College Library Center," *Library Resources & Technical Services*, 17, 308-318 (Summer 1973).
12. Frederick Kilgour, "Evolving, Computerizing, Personalizing," *American Libraries*, 3, 145 (February 1972).
13. Hopkins, *op. cit.*, p. 318.
14. "OCLC Adds Numbers--Dollars, Books, Members--to its New Budget," *Advanced Technology/Libraries*, 3, 6 (June 1974).
15. Herman H. Fussler and Charles T. Payne, *Annual Report, 1967/68, to the National Science Foundation from the University of Chicago Library*, University of Chicago, Chicago, 1968. PB 179 426, available from the Clearinghouse for Federal Scientific and Technical Information.
16. "University of Chicago to Set Up Total Integrated Library System, Utilizing Computer-Based Data-Handling Processes," *Scientific Information Notes*, 9, 1-2 (June-July 1967).
17. "University of Chicago Library Grant," *JOLA Technical Communications*, 2, 1 (June 1971).
18. Herman H. Fussler, "Statement to ARL (Association of Research Libraries) on the University of Chicago Library Automation Project," January 8, 1967.
19. Charles T. Payne, "The University of Chicago's Book Processing System," in *Stanford Conference on Collaborative Library Systems Development; Proceedings of a Conference Held at Stanford University Libraries, October 4-5, 1968*, Stanford University Libraries, Stanford, California, 1969, p. 120.
20. *Ibid.*
21. Charles T. Payne, "What Can We Discern from Present Activities and Where Are We Going in the Immediate Future," in *Collaborative Library Systems Development*, M.I.T. Press, Cambridge, Mass., 1961, p. 122.
22. *Ibid.*, "An Integrated Computer-Based Bibliographic Data System for a Large University Library: Problems and Progress at the University of Chicago," *Proceedings of the 1967 Clinic on Library Applications of Data Processing*, University of Illinois Graduate School of Library Science, Urbana, 1967, p. 32.
23. *Annual Report*, 1967/68, p.9.
24. Charles T. Payne, "The University of Chicago Library Data Management System," in *Proceedings of the 1974 Clinic on Library Applications of Data Processing: Applications of Minicomputers to Library and Related Problems*, University of Illinois Graduate School of Library Science, Urbana, 1975, pp. 105-106.
25. *Ibid.*, p. 106.
26. Remarks by University of Chicago staff members at a meeting of the COLA (Committee on Library Automation) Discussion Group during the ALA Midwinter Conference in Chicago, January 19, 1975.

5. On-Line Cataloging Systems

27. Payne, "The University of Chicago Library Data Management System," pp. 114, 116.
28. *Ibid.*, p. 112.
29. Frances Ohmes and J. F. Jones, "The Other Half of Cataloging," *Library Resources & Technical Services*, 17, 320-329 (Summer 1973).
30. "Chicago, Stanford Systems Receive New CLR Grants Toward Further Development," *CLR Recent Developments*, 3, 1 (May 1975).
31. "BALLOTS Being Used by California Public Libraries," *Advanced Technology/Libraries*, 4, 3 (May 1975).
32. Donald V. Black, "Library Information System Time-Sharing on a Large, General-Purpose Computer," in *Proceedings of the 1968 Clinic on Library Applications of Data Processing*, University of Illinois Graduate School of Library Science, Urbana, 1969, pp. 139-154.
33. David P. Waite, "The Minicomputer: Its Role in a Nationwide Bibliographic and Information Network," in *Proceedings of the 1974 Clinic on Library Applications of Data Processing: Applications of Minicomputers to Library and Related Problems*, University of Illinois Graduate School of Library Science, Urbana, 1975, pp. 140-142, 147, 152-153.
34. Telephone conversation with James Flanagan, Vice President, Information Dynamics Corporation, January 30, 1975.
35. Comments by Bill Scholls, New Mexico State Library, at a meeting of the COLA (Committee on Library Automation) Discussion Group during the ALA Midwinter Conference in Chicago, January 19, 1975.
36. S. Michael Malinconico and James A. Rizzolo, "The New York Public Library Automated Book Catalog Subsystem," *Journal of Library Automation*, 6, 15 (March 1973).
37. *Ibid.*, p. 16.
38. Buckland, *op. cit.*, Appendix A, p. U 5.
39. Seoud Makram Matta, *The Card Catalog in a Large Research Library: Present Conditions and Future Possibilities in the New York Public Library*, Columbia University School of Library Service, New York, 1965.
40. James W. Henderson and Joseph A. Rosenthal, *Library Catalogs: Their Preservation and Maintenance by Photographic and Automated Techniques*, M.I.T. Press, Cambridge, Mass., 1968.
41. Malinconico and Rizzolo, *op. cit.*, 5-11.
42. *Ibid.*, 33-34.
43. See Buckland, *op. cit.*, Appendix A, pp. L 1-2; Simon P. J. Chen, "On-Line and Real-Time Cataloging," *American Libraries*, 3, 117-119 (February 1972); and "On-Line Cataloging and Circulation at Western Kentucky University: an Approach to Automated Instructional Resources Management," *The LARC Reports*, 6, no. 1 (1973).

44. Information from a personal visit by the author, November 27, 1973.
45. See Ruth Winik, "Reference Function in an On-Line Catalog," *Special Libraries*, 63, 217-221 (May/June 1972); and Caryl McAllister and John M. Bell, "Human Factors in the Design of an Interactive Library System," *Journal of the American Society for Information Science*, 22, 96-104 (March-April 1971).
46. Robert M. Hayes, "The Concept of an On-Line, Total Library System," *Library Technology Reports*, 1, 1-13 (May 1965).
47. Alan R. Benefeld, "Generation and Encoding of the Project Intrex Augmented Catalog Data Base," in *Proceedings of the 1968 Clinic on Library Applications of Data Processing*, University of Illinois Graduate School of Library Science, Urbana, 1969, pp. 155-198.
48. Massachussets Institute of Technology, Project Intrex, *Semiannual Activity Report, 15 September 1971-15 March 1972*, Cambridge, Mass., 1972, pp. 1-43.
49. *Ibid.*, pp. 6-7.
50. *Semiannual Activity Report, 15 March 1970-15 September 1970*, Cambridge, Mass., 1970, pp. 73-74.
51. *Semiannual Activity Report, 15 September 1971-15 March 1972*, Cambridge, Mass., 1972, pp. 8-9.

Chapter 6

THE EFFECT OF AUTOMATION
ON CATALOGING PRACTICE

Automation has affected most library processes to some extent, and in many cases has influenced the development of library policy. In the chapters that discuss acquisitions, serials, and circulation systems, the most significant changes are noted in passing. In the area of cataloging, however, the effects of library automation have been so far-reaching and profound that a separate discussion of their impact seems warranted.

The effects may be seen in four general areas:

1. Extent of cataloging information presented to the users
2. Choice of information given
3. Arrangement of information
4. Typographical presentation of such information

Typographical presentation of cataloging information

The last of these areas is one of the most interesting from a mechanical point of view, but certainly the least significant so far as cataloging policy is concerned. Librarians, however, have bemoaned the "uppercase mentality" of computers and related machines since their use in library work began. At the "Airlie Conference"--more properly, the Conference on Libraries and Automation held at Airlie Foundation, Warrenton, Virginia, May 26-30, 1963--

Verner W. Clapp, President of the Council on Library Resources, reminisced about his personal attempts to deal with the problem:

> I am one of those who, back in the thirties, looked at EAM equipment and fancied that it certainly ought to be put to library work. We were fascinated by the great speed of that equipment at that time; this was its great attractiveness to us. How little we knew of speed in those good old days! What impressed us was the ability to do clerical operations such as sorting and printing. What bothered us, however, was the font of type which was available. So we used to travel up to New York every so often, and visit Thomas B. Watson in his office, and we would say to him, "Mr. Watson, we know you're interested in library work, we know what you've been doing out there at Montclair, New Jersey. Won't you please make us a machine that will print upper and lowercase? Then we can really do some useful things in bibliography!" Then Mr. Watson would lean back in his chair and look benevolent, as indeed he was, and he would say, "Well, you boys know that I am interested in library work, I'll see what we can do." Then we'd go away feeling warm around the cockles of our hearts, and think we would get a printer in the next couple of weeks that would print upper and lowercase. How naive we were! We did not realize that it would have cost International Business Machines a couple of million dollars just to develop this one machine for us. We thought it was just a matter of putting on a little longer type bar with a few characters on it.
>
> If I may say so, the whole picture of automation in libraries from the thirties right down to the present date has been controlled by that uppercase limitation. The reason library files do not exist in machine-readable form is that nobody wants to go to the expense of converting files when the output can only be printed in capital letters without even decent punctuation.[1]

Although conversion to machine-readable form was actually delayed for different reasons, Clapp was of course right on other points. As the chapters on cataloging systems mentioned, early cataloging systems were produced with unit-record machines, which had only uppercase characters and a few symbols, and early computer systems used similar typography. The resulting catalogs were certainly less attractive and less readable than the printed or typed cards with which most people were familiar.

6. Effect of Automation 129

Within a few months of Clapp's talk, however, the situation began to change. Toronto, Florida Atlantic, and Yale universities did indeed acquire a "machine" (actually a special printing chain) to print upper and lower case, and fortunately it did not cost "a couple of million dollars." It did cost a substantial amount in computer processing time, however, which led to its abandonment by Florida Atlantic University. Photocomposition machines, which did not share this handicap, later became available, and in some cases offered the additional advantage of a wider variety of type faces and images than older printing techniques (the Videocomp and similar machines, for example, can compose and print Oriental text, symbols of all types, and in fact any image that has first been converted to electronic form using a special process).

Microform catalogs and computer terminal displays have encountered the same problem, but both have now advanced at least to the stage that acceptable upper and lower case characters in the Roman alphabet are available. Non-Roman alphabets and nonalphabetic characters are still a problem, but the capacity for providing these exists if the demand becomes sufficient.

Extent of information given

Changes in the extent of cataloging information presented to the user under each entry have been mainly deletions rather than additions, and such changes are most frequently seen in book catalog projects. Virtually every descriptive element has been eliminated or abbreviated in one project or another. The Boeing SLIP catalog restricts authors' forenames to one and represents the others by initials; other catalogs give only initials, with no forenames. The University of Rochester catalogs limit the main entry to twenty-one spaces, which necessitates a substantial amount of abbreviation in corporate authors.

Many catalogs delete subtitles entirely, or include them only if necessary to distinguish the work from others with the same title. Omission of the author statement and statements regarding editors and illustrators is common. Place of publication and publisher are also frequently omitted; the Harvard University shelflists, for example, omit publisher, and the Stanford Undergraduate catalog deletes place. Rochester and others show only the final two digits of the date.

Collation is perhaps the most frequently abridged set of elements. Stanford and Florida Atlantic give pagination only, and many catalogs give no collation at all. Notes and tracings are also frequently omitted, with the exception of series and contents notes in a few cases. The ONULP (Ontario New University Libraries Project) catalogs, however, give full tracings under main entries, as does the National Library of Medicine *Current Catalog*, the latter because other medical libraries use the catalog as a source of cataloging information.

In many catalogs the amount and type of abridgement varies according to the type of entry involved. Normally the main entry is reasonably full, and most abbreviation or abridgement takes place in added entries. In the Los Angeles County catalog, however, the subject entries are more complete than the author entries, because the subject entries include an annotation. As noted in Chapters 3 and 4, some libraries also use a "register" system, which presents a fairly full entry in the register volume and only index entries under author, title, and elsewhere.

The practice of abridging entries has been justified on several grounds. Undoubtedly it began, especially in catalogs produced with unit record equipment such as the University of Rochester listings, because of the eighty-column limitation of punched cards and the printing limitations of tabulators. As Weinstein and George have noted, "the one-to-one, punched card/printed line relationship, and line-length/field-length compromises, all encourage brevity of entry."[2]

At least in part, however, the elimination of data elements also reflects a desire to cut costs. Simonton has viewed it "as a reflection of the traditional policy of many of these libraries of shortening the bibliographical record for more economical processing."[3]

6. Effect of Automation 131

Another justification is based on the shorter life expectancy of the book catalog as compared to the traditional card catalog:

> As [card] catalogs serve as the basis for the permanent record and their cost can be prorated over several decades the need for a careful description of the many facets of a book is quite properly justified. In the case of catalog supplements, however, where the record will serve quite likely for only a few months, any attempt at detailed description of the book cannot be justified.[4]

As might perhaps be expected, the old argument over whether the catalog serves as a bibliographical tool or a "finding list" has also been revived. Robinson, for example, writes about the planning for the Baltimore County book catalog project:

> We also agreed on the concept that this catalog was to be a finding list, not a bibliographical tool. We had always done fairly simplified cataloging anyway, and frankly, we were convinced that, as bibliographical tools, catalogs are vastly overrated and underused anyway. Taking an educated guess, we estimated that only 50 percent of the people who come into our libraries use the catalog at all, and 98 percent of those use it as a finding list.[5]

Not all changes in the extent of cataloging information presented have been abridgements or deletions, however; some writers and projects, in fact, have seen automation as a means of increasing the amount of information made available. At the Brasenose Conference on the Automation of Libraries in 1966, Avram and Markuson identified a number of important questions which automation posed for bibliographical management, among them the following:

> Should certain data, now implicitly stated in the bibliographic entry, be made specific? For example, should the language of the title and the text, the kind of author (corporate, personal, etc.) and other attributes of a particular work be described explicitly?
>
> How many access points to the bibliographic data should be provided in a machine system? Should these include increased depth of subject indexing, more name entries, chapter headings, place of publication, etc?[6]

In the MARC project, which was developed soon after (and in which both Avram and Markuson were involved), the items mentioned in the first paragraph above were indeed made explicit. MARC has also provided additional "access points," as Fig. 4-4 indicates, although not chapter headings or additional name and subject entries as Avram and Markuson suggested. Many catalogs of special libraries have provided additional subject headings, however, taking advantage of the ease with which machines can reproduce entries under various headings. Most book catalogs also reproduce title entries for all items in the catalog, not just those with "distinctive" titles, and as mentioned in the discussion of the Boeing SLIP catalog some also "permute" the titles so that they appear several times for each work, under each significant word in each title.

Choice of information given

The choice of main entry has long been a critical issue in cataloging policy and in the development of cataloging rules, but with the advent of machine-produced book catalogs the need for the concept of "main entry" may be questioned. When catalog cards were printed or typed by hand, it made economic sense to produce only one card, with the data arranged in a standard format under a "main entry," and then to reproduce other cards as needed, typing only the added headings required after the "unit cards" had been duplicated. Computers, however, can rearrange data in any fashion deemed appropriate, so this rationale is no longer applicable. Despite this fact, many book catalogs continue to follow the unit card and main entry concepts. The ONULP catalogs, for example, print the author under each title entry, and then repeat the title (see Fig. 6-1), a practice that would appear to have no justification except for mechanically reproduced catalog cards. A few book catalog projects have abandoned this anachronistic practice and reproduce entries under various headings without any attempt to designate one as the "main" entry (see Fig. 6-2), even though the entries under each heading are still "unit" (i.e., identical) entries. Abandonment of the main entry concept, it should be pointed out, also means abandoning any attempt to designate the person or body primarily responsible for the intellectual content of a work, but clearly it makes the choice of entry less critical, particularly in difficult cases

6. Effect of Automation

FIG. 6-1. Title entries, ONULP book catalog.

Angell, Robert Cooley
  The use of personal documents in
  history, anthropology, and sociology.
  By Louis Gottschalk, Clyde Kluckhohn
  and Robert Angell. Prepared for the
  Committee on Appraisal of Research.
  Social Science Research Council, 1945.
  243 p.   H61.G6

Gottschalk, Louis
  The use of personal documents in
  history, anthropology, and sociology.
  By Louis Gottschalk, Clyde Kluckhohn
  and Robert Angell. Prepared for the
  Committee on Appraisal of Research.
  Social Science Research Council, 1945.
  243 p.   H61.G6

Social Science Research Council.
  Committee on Appraisal of Research.
  The use of personal documents in
  history, anthropology, and sociology.
  By Louis Gottschalk, Clyde Kluckhohn
  and Robert Angell. Prepared for the
  Committee on Appraisal of Research.
  Social Science Research Council, 1945.
  243 p.   H61.G6

The use of personal documents in history,
  anthropology, and sociology. By Louis
  Gottschalk, Clyde Kluckhohn and Robert
  Angell. Prepared for the Committee
  on Appraisal of Research. Social
  Science Research Council, 1945.
  243 p.   H61.G6

FIG. 6-2. "No main entry" entries, Stanford University book catalog.

such as conference proceedings, where the choice between conference title, sponsoring body or editor may be little more than arbitrary. A related effect of automation on choice of entry is that choosing the authorized or established _form_ of entry may be facilitated, either through the use of standard decks of subject heading cards, as in the Los Angeles County and Baltimore County projects, or through a fully automated authority control system as in the New York Public Library book catalog project.

Arrangement of catalog information

One of the greatest effects of automation on cataloging practice to date has been in the arrangement of entries in relation to each other. Virtually all book catalogs are divided catalogs, abandoning the so-called dictionary arrangement that interfiles all types of entries in a single sequence.

The type of division is not consistent from one catalog to another. Some have separate author, title, and subject sections; some combine author and title entries in one catalog with a separate subject section; and at least one (the Boeing SLIP catalog) combines titles and subjects, with the author entries separate. Regardless of the method of division, however, two principal reasons are usually given for the arrangement: users make different uses of

6. Effect of Automation 135

subject entries as opposed to author and title entries, according to a number of user studies, and the filing or sequencing of entries can be simplified if all types of entries are not interfiled.

The latter reason is normally the more urgent when automation is involved. Catalogs can be divided without being automated, and if ease of use were the only justification for division there would be no reason to attribute the popularity of the practice to automation. Filing, however, is another matter, and simplification of filing for automation purposes is undoubtedly the main reason for the predominance of the practice.

Computers can sequence and arrange data with extreme speed and accuracy if given explicit rules for doing so, but traditional library filing arrangements are a mixture of alphabetical, chronological and other sequences presumed to be "logical," with numerous general and specific exceptions. In addition to the complexity of the rules, many of them are based on the ability of human filers to recognize information that is only implicit, not explicitly stated, and computers can work only with explicit data.

The problems are not trivial, and the solutions arrived at are important. As Rather has pointed out:

> Filing arrangement is the capstone of the system of bibliographic control that begins with descriptive cataloging and includes subject analysis and classification. The entire effort to achieve bibliographic control necessarily reaches its fulfillment in the means of displaying catalog information to users.[7]

At least five categories of difficulty may be identified:

1. *Information in the headings must be ignored or removed* in order for computers to sort it acceptably. The obvious example is initial articles in the nominative case. "The European discovery of America" is liable to be found more easily under "European" than "The," and "L'enfance du Christ" under "enfance." But practice is not always consistent: "Los Angeles," for example, normally files under "Los."

Honorific titles such as "Sir" in proper names are also commonly disregarded, so that "Drake, Sir Francis" files as "Drake, Francis."

2. *Information that is implicit must be made explicit.* A common example is "U.S.--History--Civil War," which as a subdivision of "U.S.--History" files not alphabetically under "C" but chronologically, as if it were "U.S.--History--1861-1865." This category of problems is perhaps the most difficult for computers to deal with because there are no clues for most such instances, and the number of "as if" situations in most current filing practices is large. It is also the least defensible. "Dr." is filed as if it were spelled "Doctor" or "Doktor," depending on the language of the text, but if the reader does not know the rule, or has only a title such as "Dr. Jacob Dubs" to go on, he may miss the entry entirely. "Mrs.," (and presumably "Ms." but not "Miss") is filed as if it were spelled "Mistress." "St." if filed as if it were "Saint" or "Street." "Mc" is filed as "Mac," although McKenzies insist they are not Mackenzies. Numbers are a special example of the "as if" problem; they file as if spelled out (again depending on the language of the text) at the beginning of titles, but file as numbers, in numerical sequence, in headings for numbered conferences, series and so forth.

3. *Information in headings must be rearranged* in order for machines to sort it into the desired sequence. "Charles II, King of England" must be read as "Charles, King of England, II"--or actually, since there is also a numeral in this case and the second category of difficulty comes into play, as "Charles, King of England, 2."

4. *Exceptions must be made to alphabetic order.* Some rules require that entries beginning with the same word or phrase be sub-arranged not alphabetically by the next filing element but by bibliographic function (authors, then subjects, then titles, for example), or according to the type of entity the heading describes (persons, then places, then things).

5. *Punctuation is even a problem,* because of complications introduced both by the machines and by filing rules. Computers regard punctuation marks as characters just as letters and numerals, and sort them into a certain order (differing to some extent by brand of machine) unless programmed to do otherwise. Extra spaces inadvertently inserted by humans will affect machine filing

6. Effect of Automation 137

order as well. Existing rules differ on the treatment of certain marks, for example, whether "Brewer's Dictionary of Phrase and Fable" should be filed as "Brewers" or "Brewer s," and "Mott-Smith" as "Mott Smith" or "MottSmith."

The ideal solution to these various problems is unclear, but attempts to solve them in automated catalogs have produced a significant amount of change as compared with manually filed catalogs. Most projects have used a combination of four basic approaches:[8]

1. Continue to follow present filing rules, using people to assign additional codes to headings as necessary to allow computers to arrange the headings as desired.
2. Abandon present filing rules, and use the arrangements produced by the computer's sorting sequences with a minimum amount of change.
3. Change the headings themselves as necessary so that computers can arrange them in accordance with very simple filing rules.
4. Attempt to program computers so that they will arrange headings automatically, either by present filing rules or by modifications of them.

Florida Atlantic University used the first approach in its book catalog, the first edition of which was published in 1964. "Nonfile" symbols were used to indicate to the computer that portions of an entry were to be ignored in filing. Determination of when the symbols were to be added and actually adding them were of course operations performed by human beings. Use of the symbols was limited to initial articles, qualifying phrases such as "jt. author," and titles of honor; for example, "Churchill, Sir Winston," was input as "Churchill, <Sir> Winston," to enable it to sort as "Churchill, Winston." Umlauted letters were converted to letters without the umlaut, but followed by an "e." Unfortunately, this also meant that "coöperate" became "cooeperate," and "Brontë" became "Brontee." Abbreviations were filed as written, not as if spelled out, and "Mc" was filed as "Mc."[9]

A more thoroughgoing example of the first approach is the Stanford Undergraduate Library book catalog published first in 1966. A considerable amount of manual coding was performed in order to follow as closely as possible the filing rules used in the University's main card catalog. Entries were sorted not on the text of the entries themselves but on separate "sort keys" composed of a total of 100 characters, 80 from the filing element (the author, added entries or subject headings) and 20 additional characters from the title, which was used throughout the catalog for subarrangement of entries under each heading. "Nonfile" symbols were used as in the Florida Atlantic catalog, but more extensively. For example, "Van Buren" was input as "Van<>Buren" so that it would file as "VanBuren" but print as "Van Buren." The "nonfile" symbol was also used to make chronological sequences. For example

    GT. BRIT.--HISTORY--<EDWARD, THE CONFESSOR,>1042-1066
    GT. BRIT.--HISTORY--<NORMAN PERIOD,>1066-1154
    GT. BRIT.--HISTORY--<MEDIEVAL PERIOD,>1066-1485
    GT. BRIT.--HISTORY--<STEPHEN,>1135-1154
    GT. BRIT.--HISTORY--<HENRY II,>1154-1189
    GT. BRIT.--HISTORY--<ANGEVIN PERIOD,>1154-1216

In addition to the "nonfile" symbol Stanford also used a non-printing "file symbol," the @ sign; information between two @ signs filed but did not print. For the title *1848: Chapters of German History* the input was "@eighteen forty-eight@<1848>: chapters of German history." This technique was used in an ingenious way to arrange periods before the Christian era in chronological form. In effect, the year in question was subtracted from "Z9999" and placed between @ signs. For years in the Christian era, the "Z" was omitted. The resulting input looked like this:

    ROME--HISTORY--<REPUBLIC, 510-30 B.C.>@Z9489-Z9969@
    ROME--HISTORY--<REPUBLIC, 365-30 B.C.>@Z9734-Z9969@
    ROME--HISTORY--<AUGUSTUS, 30 B.C.-14 A.D.>@Z9969-0014@

An obvious disadvantage of extended use of sorting and filing codes was noted at Stanford: the technique requires manual maintenance of authority files, very careful inputting, and very careful editing and proofreading.[10]

6. Effect of Automation

Few projects have attempted the second alternative (following the computer's own sequencing arrangements), because of the radical differences from traditional filing that would result, but a number of catalogs have used the third approach--changing the headings so the computer would arrange them in accordance with simplified but more or less traditional filing rules. Usually such projects have taken a strictly pragmatic approach, solving the simplest problems and ignoring the others. The Baltimore County book catalog, first published in 1965, is an example. Initial articles, titles of honor and such designations as "ed." or "comp." were omitted from headings during input, which of course meant that they were ignored not only in filing but also in printing. Abbreviations, numerals, and symbols such as the ampersand were written out. Some titles were rearranged, e.g., titles of annual reports were input as "annual report," followed by the date. In all other cases, the computer sequencing was accepted as it came.[11]

The foremost advocates of changing headings to produce the desired sequence have been Theodore Hines and Jessica Harris. In 1963, Hines urged that "filing should be a purely mechanical operation which can be reduced to a straightforward arrangement of sorts and nuls. The filer or program should not be expected to expand or interpret entries for filing purposes. These functions should be shifted to the formation of entries."[12] In 1966, he and Harris published a work entitled *Computer Filing of Index, Bibliographic, and Catalog Entries*.[13] Actually, the work is not so much a filing code as a proposal for rewriting headings as Hines suggested in 1963--so that they would automatically be arranged in a sequence deemed to be acceptable. "Charles II, le Chauve, King of France," for example, was to be written "Charles 2, King of France, le Chauve," and "Scott, Sir Walter," as "Scott, Walter, Sir." "Bibliothèque d'art" was to be written as if it were "Bibliothèque dart" and "Saint'Ange" as if it were "Saintange."

Publication of the Hines-Harris code created a storm of protest. One reviewer warned, "This little book seems likely to do more harm than good. The end it proposes may be laudable, but the means are not. The book rests on the proposition that what is awkward for the machines must be eliminated and the simplicities of the machine system imposed on non-machine processes."[14] Another criticized the proposal for failing to make efficient use of the computer: "Entries are arranged only after the format has been decided by a human. ... If we must spend professional time in this manner, what, then, is the advantage of using the computer?"[15]

The fourth approach, which is the extreme--attempting to program the computer to follow traditional rules as closely as possible--was taken by William R. Nugent of Inforonics, Inc., in a study commissioned by the Council on Library Resources. Unlike most proposals which advocated sorting abbreviations and similar exceptional cases "as is" rather than "as if," Nugent proposed a system of "substitution notes" which would continue traditional "as if" filing. Extensive rules to permit arrangements by category (under Bible entries, anonymous classics, and corporate authors, for example) were also suggested. In not every case, however, was Nugent happy with his assignment to propose ways of "programming the LC Filing Rules."

> If one set out deliberately to destroy the simple precision of numerical hierarchy, little worse could be done than to insist that numbers be ordered by the spelled out equivalents of their spoken sound. In this writer's view, the present filing rule should be quickly replaced by one in which all cardinal or ordinal numbers, whether in alphabetic or numeric form, would be ordered by their elementary numeric form. ... As this is unlikely to occur with any haste, it will probably be necessary to write programs to convert the numeric portions of entries to alphabetic form.[16]

He then pointed out that it would be necessary to devise further rules to ensure consistency, because "1810" could be written out as "eighteen ten," "one thousand eight hundred ten" or "one eight one (zero? oh? naught?)," and the existing LC Rules convert such numbers "to differing forms by application of some unspecified and doubtless unprogrammable subtlety." This kind of problem of necessity led Nugent to propose various types of manual coding as well as elaborate programming.

6. Effect of Automation

Perhaps the most thoroughgoing and thoughtful consideration of the entire range of automated filing problems is in a series of papers by John C. Rather, Chief of the Technical Processes Research Office in the Library of Congress. In February 1970 Rather distributed a working paper entitled *Filing Arrangement in the Library of Congress Catalogs* within LC and to a limited extent outside it, setting forth a series of principles and basic approaches. Consensus within the Library led to public distribution of a full set of rules with the same title the following year. In 1972, the principles and basic approaches were elaborated in print,[17] accompanied by an abridged version of the rules. They have since been used as the basis for a computer program to arrange MARC records and produce a variety of book catalogs for LC. Since they are also being considered for use in automatic preparation of the *National Union Catalog*, their significance is obvious.

Rather is eloquent on the dangers of changing headings merely because of the filing difficulties they present in automated systems.

> The complexities of catalog headings and their arrangement are not attributable primarily to the rules that govern them; they arise from the varieties of materials being cataloged and the size of the catalog being maintained. The need to differentiate names in the catalog while still conveying intelligible information about the name results in forms of heading that indubitably present difficulties of arrangement. The fundamental conflict between the function of headings as units of intelligence and their function as filing guides cannot be underestimated, but the integrity of the heading (in its role of conveyer of intelligence) must necessarily take precedence over any attempt to structure it so that it files "automatically." Or, to put the matter succinctly, headings do not exist merely to be filed.

Rather thus eschews revision of headings for the sake of filing convenience, but he also advocates abandonment of the "as if" or "file as spoken" tradition, and for essentially the same reasons.

> Variations in form among name and subject headings are an essential part of the structure of a file arrangement; they should not be ignored in filing. It is illogical to construct a heading one way and then to file it as if it were constructed another way.

The three basic principles of his code are

1. Elements in a heading should be taken in exactly the form and order in which they appear.
2. Related entries should be kept together if they would be difficult to find when a user did not know their precise form.
3. A standard set of fields should be established for each major type of filing entry.

The first principle "emphasizes the way a heading looks, not how it sounds," the second "preserves important values offered by the present arrangement of the LC catalogs," and the third "applies the legal precept 'De minimis non curat lex' (the law cannot take care of trifles) as a way of preventing the proliferation of special rules."

Since Rather's rules have already met with general acceptance at LC and been used to produce several book catalogs, and since a computer program already exists to arrange MARC entries following these rules, their influence is likely to be evident in cataloging practice for some time to come.

On-line techniques

Another important influence on the arrangement of cataloging information has been the use of on-line techniques. By 1968, Stanford University's on-line BALLOTS project had evolved a technique of filing machine-readable catalog entires not by any of the usual rules, but in an arbitrarily arranged file with indexes by various bibliographic elements, such as author, title, topical subjects, and so forth. By itself, this was not new. The significant and important aspect of the technique, however, was that the position of each entry in the author and title indexes was computed directly from the data itself, using the first three letters from the author's last name and the words of the title.[18] The computer, of course, followed the same procedure in retrieving the index entries on command. In effect, the actual filing arrangement of the "catalog" was transparent to the user.

6. Effect of Automation   143

This technique of "derived keys" was being studied by several researchers at about this time. Nugent described four different "compression coding" techniques,[19] and Kilgour and Ruecking reported the results of separate tests using various combinations of characters from author and title entries for retrieval purposes.[20-21]

In 1970, Kilgour and two associates analyzed the effectiveness of derived keys varying from four to eight characters in length for retrieval of name and title entries taken from a sample of 132,808 entries. They concluded that a "3,3" key--that is, the first three characters of the author's last name and the first three characters of the title--would retrieve five or fewer entries 99 percent of the time.[22] Further experiments with titles only (using the first three letters of the first two words, or the first three characters of the following three words) produced similar results.[23]

The results of this research led to the use of 3,3 keys for name and title searches and 3,1,1,1 keys for title-only searches in the design of the Ohio College Library Center (OCLC) system,[24] and the technique has been one of the major factors in OCLC's success.

The implications of this practice, while perhaps not immediately obvious, are nevertheless enormous. In effect, when the user names a key of six characters, he designates what Kilgour has called a "microcatalog" of five or fewer entries, on average, or twenty or fewer entries 95 percent of the time. Because ten entries can be displayed on the screen of the on-line terminal used by OCLC participants, and twenty entries require only two screen displays, the desired entry is easily chosen. "Such a catalog," comments Kilgour, "makes it unnecessary to include bibliographical embellishments required for entries in huge card or book-form catalogs,"[25] and of course it also makes unnecessary the solution of the filing rule problems discussed earlier.

Nor are the implications of such on-line techniques necessarily limited to OCLC participants, at least not for long. At a meeting in 1975 of the Association of Research Libraries, Rather reviewed the difficulties of improving existing card files or converting them to machine-readable form, and proposed a "radical solution": "What if the MARC data base were considered to be complete for cataloging purposes?" This would enable LC to begin on-line cataloging on a production basis, and close its existing card catalogs, as several other research libraries already have, or have proposed to do. But it would also have widespread effects on cataloging practice throughout this country and abroad. The name and subject authority files used by LC to establish the headings which appear on cards and in its book catalogs, as well as in the MARC tapes, would be limited to names and subjects already on MARC records, and the call numbers would be formed with reference only to a "shelflist" composed of call numbers on MARC records. But, again quoting Rather, "the future would no longer be constrained by the past."[26]

It is characteristic of technical revolutions that we are unaware of them while they are in progress. It is also characteristic that it is not so much the technology that makes the revolution but an idea. Someone must see that the use of a technology in a particular way can change fundamental concepts of perception and action. In this sense, Kilgour's concept of "microcatalogs," and the use--now predominantly by library staff members but increasingly by the public--of on-line terminals, may revolutionize the heart of library science, cataloging.

NOTES

1. Verner W. Clapp, "Libraries and the 'Uppercase Limitation,'" in *Libraries and Automation*, Library of Congress, Washington, D.C., 1964, p. 54-55.
2. Edward A. Weinstein and Virginia George, "Notes Toward a Code for Computer-Produced Printed Book Catalogs," *Library Resources & Technical Services*, 9, 320 (Summer 1965).
3. Wesley Simonton, "Automation of Cataloging Procedures," in *Library Automation: A State of the Art Review*, American Library Association, Chicago, 1969, p. 45.
4. Dana Roth, "The Caltech Science Library Catalog Supplement," *Journal of Library Automation*, 7, 145 (June 1974).
5. Charles W. Robinson, "The Book Catalog: Diving In," *Wilson Library Bulletin*, 40, 264 (November 1965).

6. Henriette D. Avram and Barbara Evans Markuson, "Library Automation and Project MARC: An Experiment in the Distribution of Machine-Readable Cataloging Data," in *Brasenose Conference on the Automation of Libraries*, Mansell, London, 1967, pp. 98-99.

7. John C. Rather, "Filing Arrrangement in the Library of Congress Catalogs," *Library Resources & Technical Services*, 16, 240 (Spring 1972).

8. This classification of methods is suggested by Robert K. Hayes and Joseph Becker in their *Handbook of Data Processing for Libraries*, Becker and Hayes, New York, 1970, pp. 610-611.

9. Description and examples are given by Kelley L. Cartwright in his "Mechanization and Library Filing Rules," in *Advances in Librarianship*, vol. 1, Academic Press, New York, 1970, p. 87.

10. Richard D. Johnson, "A Book Catalog at Stanford," *Journal of Library Automation*, 1, 34-37 (March 1968).

11. See Paula Kieffer, "The Baltimore Country Public Library Book Catalog," *Library Resources & Technical Services*, 10, 135-137 (Spring 1966).

12. Theodore C. Hines, "Machine Arrangement of Alphanumeric Concordance, Thesaurus, and Index Entries: The Need for Compatible Standard Rules," in *Automation and Scientific Communication; Short Papers Contributed to the Theme Sessions of the 26th Annual Meeting of the American Documentation Institute*, the Institute, Washington, D.C., 1963, v. 1, p. 7-8.

13. Theodore C. Hines and Jessica L. Harris, *Computer Filing of Index, Bibliographic, and Catalog Entries*, Bro-Dart Foundation, Newark, N.J., 1966.

14. J. W. Jolliffe, review in *Journal of Documentation*, 22, 338, (December 1966).

15. Donald S. Culbertson, "Filing Rule Modifications," *Library Journal*, 91, 6060 (December 15, 1966).

16. William R. Nugent, "The Mechanization of the Filing Rules of the Dictionary Catalogs of the Library of Congress," *Library Resources & Technical Services*, 11, 161 (Spring 1967).

17. John C. Rather, "Filing Arrangement in the Library of Congress Catalogs," *Library Resources & Technical Services*, 16, 240-261 (Spring 1972).

18. Edwin B. Parker, "Developing a Campus Information Retrieval System," in *Collaborative Library Systems Development*, M.I.T. Press, Cambridge, Mass., 1971, pp. 213-225.

19. William R. Nugent, "Compression Word Coding Techniques for Information Retrieval," *Journal of Library Automation*, 1, 250-260 (December 1968).

20. Frederick G. Kilgour, "Retrieval of Single Entries from a Computerized Library Catalog File," *Proceedings of the American Society for Information Science*, vol. 5, *Information Transfer*, Greenwood, New York, 1968, pp. 133-136.

21. Frederick H. Ruecking, Jr., "Bibliographic Retrieval from Bibliographic Input: The Hypothesis and Construction of a Test," *Journal of Library Automation*, 1, 227-238 (December 1968).

22. Frederick G. Kilgour, Philip L. Long, and Eugene B. Leiderman, "Retrieval of Bibliographic Entries from a Name-Title Catalog by Use of Truncated Search Keys," in *Proceedings of the American Society for Information Science*, vol. 7, *The Information Conscious Society*, the Society, Washington, D.C., 1970, pp. 79-82.

23. Frederick G. Kilgour et al., "Title-Only Entries Retrieved by Use of Truncated Search Keys," *Journal of Library Automation*, 4, 207-210 (December 1971); and Philip L. Long and Frederick G. Kilgour, "A Truncated Search Key Title Index," *Journal of Library Automation*, 5, 17-20 (March 1972).

24. Frederick G. Kilgour et al., "The Shared Cataloging System of the Ohio College Library Center," *Journal of Library Automation*, 5, 171-176 (September 1972).

25. Frederick G. Kilgour, "Concept of an On-Line Computerized Library Catalog," *Journal of Library Automation*, 3, 5-6 (March 1970).

26. John C. Rather, *The Future of Catalog Control in the Library of Congress*, a paper presented at a meeting of the Association of Research Libraries, Chicago, Illinois, January 18, 1975, p. 7.

Chapter 7

SERIALS SYSTEMS

Many of the acquisition and cataloging systems described earlier include provision for handling serials, but a great number of separate systems have also been devised with the sole purpose of handling this type of material. Such separate serial systems are encouraged by the nature of the material itself. Monographs are received, paid for, cataloged, bound if necessary, and there (except for circulation) the matter normally ends. Serials, on the other hand, continue to be received; they have to be ordered and paid for repetitively; their cataloging data must include additional information, such as the frequency of publication, and all too often the cataloging information must be changed; information on the library's holdings must be constantly updated; and even binding must take place repeatedly and consistently. In all but the very smallest libraries, therefore, special controls are usually needed to handle these procedures.

The lure of controlling all these complexities by machine is not the only attraction of automated serials systems. Traditional library serial records are difficult to consult, but if the information is in machine form it can be printed out in an easily-readable format, and in multiple copies for display and consultation at various places. Since such lists merely supplement rather than replace the catalog records for serials, the typographical limitation of computer printout is also more easily accepted. In scientific libraries, where serials may account for as much as 75 percent of the total budget, personnel and time of the staff, any method which makes it possible to handle them more easily, more quickly or less expensively will be particularly attractive.

Unfortunately, most of the serials systems so far devised make the handling of serials neither easier, faster, nor cheaper. This is not true of straightforward periodical holdings lists, which are relatively easy to punch up and print out. But systems which attempt to provide mechanical means for checking in serial issues, issuing claims, handling binding, and other such functions have had a sad history. For the most part the problems are due simply to poor system design. An explicit or implicit assumption is made that serials are regular and predictable, and systems are then designed around this assumption. As serials librarians know all too well, however, the reverse is far too often the case; almost inevitably, some aspect of a serial--its title, its frequency, its issuing agency or publisher, its editor, its format, its indexing, its numbering, or what have you--will change at some time in its life, and it is these exceptions which kill most serials systems. Not uncommonly, 20 percent of the transactions attempted have some exceptional circumstance which must be taken into account, and for systems designed with regularity as a basis, a 20 percent exception ratio is likely to be disastrous. In many such systems, handling the exceptions becomes in fact more costly than handling the cases which are not.

Types of serials systems

The simplest type of serials system is the straight listing of information regarding each title. The information is keypunched, and then printed out by title, by subject, by library (if more than one library's holdings are included), or in any other arrangement provided for by the design of the system. The advantages of doing this by machine are that the list can be readily updated for subsequent editions, without rekeying information which is unchanged.

7. Serials Systems 149

Multiple copies may also be produced easily, and information on the library's holdings can thus be made readily available to users of the library and to potential users at remote points, an especially attractive feature for special libraries. The ability to produce such lists, one writer has pointed out, "more than once has become the sole justification for keeping an otherwise unsatisfactory system" alive.[1]

Systems which go beyond this function and attempt to automate other clerical procedures involved with the handling of serials usually start with the receiving or checking-in procedure. The most popular technique uses a pre-punched card--a so-called "arrival card"--for each issue of each serial expected during a given period of time, usually a month. The frequency of publication for each title is coded, and the computer then uses this code to punch an arrival card for each issue to be received during the period before the next computer run. Normally the arrival cards contain a brief title, information about the particular issue expected--volume, number and date--plus any other information required in the receiving process, such as routing. The cards are placed in a manual file, and as serial issues are received an attempt is made to match the issues against the corresponding arrival cards. These cards are then pulled and kept in a separate file. At the end of the month (assuming a monthly cycle) the cards for the issues received are fed into the computer, the holdings information is updated accordingly, and the computer punches another set of arrival cards for the next period. Any cards remaining in the file at the end of a period presumably represent issues that should have been received but were not, and are therefore potential claims. Most such systems also attempt to predict the arrival of title pages and indexes for bound volumes, and produce arrival cards for them as well, along with a binding slip and binding instructions. "Irregular" serials--those with no assumed predictability--are normally handled by generating a new arrival card only when the previous one is processed.

Such a system commonly has various listings as its principal product. New editions of a complete holdings list can be printed when funds permit, or lists of new issues received can be printed on a regular basis, and then cumulated whenever possible. Lists can also be printed for issues which were expected to arrive and did not.

Other functions

Claiming, binding, and routing may be handled as part of the receiving and accessioning system just described, or separately, utilizing the readily updated characteristic of machine files. In separate claiming systems the particular information regarding missing issues is usually punched into cards, which are used to print claim letters.. The cards can then be retained to print follow-up letters as required. Separate binding systems operate in much the same way. Cards are punched with binding information, pulled when binding for particular volumes is required, used to print binding lists, and then retained as a record of material at the bindery. When the volumes are returned the cards can be used to update the holdings record. Separate routing systems use computers to match names of personnel or offices with the titles of periodicals to be routed and then print multiple copies of routing slips. The rationale is that when routing is extensive, or when a large number of titles is involved and personnel are frequently changing, such a system may produce revised routing slips less expensively than a manual system.

Renewal of subscriptions is also handled separately by many libraries. Using either computers or unit record equipment, a regular cyclical run produces either a listing of titles to be renewed or the actual purchase orders to renew them. Such a system may also be broadened to keep complete financial records of serial purchases, and reports can be produced indicating expenditures by department or subject, as well as by year or fund.

The evolution of automated serials systems differs from that of acquisition and cataloging systems in that almost all serial systems have been computer-based and off-line. Very few unit record systems have been reported, and even fewer on-line computer systems have been developed.

7. Serials Systems

Unit record systems

One of the earliest punched-card systems used in libraries was developed in the 1940s for control of serial acquisitions at the University of Texas. For each serial, the title, expiration date, departmental account, dealer, country of publication, and location in the library were punched in separate cards, which were then used to prepare annual bidding lists, renewal orders, analyses of serial costs by department, annual records of all serial and continuation acquisitions, alphabetical location lists for all currently received serials and continuations, and lists of serials received by dealer and by country. The latter feature was particularly useful in preparing lists of serial subscriptions from Germany and German-occupied nations after World War II, when the Joint Committee on Importations announced a plan for allotments in securing serials from those nations.[2]

Special libraries also made significant use of unit record equipment for serial control prior to 1960. In a paper delivered to the Special Libraries Association that year, McCann described nine periodical systems in five different libraries (at the Linde Company in Tonawanda, N.Y., the IBM Research Laboratory in San Jose, California, the Diamond Ordnance Fuze Laboratories in Washington, the Abbott Laboratories in Chicago, and the General Motors Research Laboratories in Warren, Michigan). Included were systems for subscription renewal, routing, and even two arrival card systems for check-in and claiming, long before these became popular in university libraries. In one of these early arrival card systems, the cards were keypunched in advance using an "issue code" based on each serial's frequency, and the cards were then used for receiving by pulling each card when its matching issue arrived, as described earlier; in the other system, receipt was indicated by electrographic pencil marks on the cards, which were then passed through a machine that sensed the marking and punched the information regarding each issue into the cards. Cards not removed after a period of time were used for claiming.[3]

In the early 1960s, the library of the University of Illinois at Chicago Circle implemented a unit record system designed primarily to produce various lists of periodical holdings. Punched cards were prepared for each title and coded with bibliographic, financial, binding and shelf location information as well as subject codes. Using a mechanical sorter, the cards could be arranged in twelve different sequences:

1. by title
2. by method of acquisition
3. by source of acquisition
4. by month of volume change
5. by month of index arrival
6. by month of binding pickup
7. by year of binding
8. by type of index
9. by shelf location
10. by type of binding
11. by subject
12. by special categories, such as dead titles, changed titles, discontinued subscriptions, and so forth

Lists were then printed from the arranged decks of cards. Subject lists appear to have been the most frequently prepared, and for them subject headings and cross-references were added by mechanically merging a separate deck of cards before printing.[4]

More recent examples of small, noncomputerized serial control systems are the ones at the South Dakota School of Mines and Technology,[5] which produces various listings for a reported cost of 1.5 cents per title, and at the IBM Watson Research Center in Yorktown Heights, New York, which uses "decklets" of six to ten cards to provide holdings lists and subscription renewals.[6]

Off-line computer listings

Computer-produced listings of serials are numbered in the hundreds, and only a few examples of the most important or interesting need be given. The library of Lincoln Laboratory in Lexington,

7. Serials Systems 153

Massachusetts (operated by M.I.T. for the Air Force) began a listing of its government technical reports and documents, including serials, as early as 1960. From a small IBM 1401 computer, the system has been transferred successively to a 360 Model 40 and then to a 360 Model 67. Some eighteen different reports are produced from the data, including such things as a Contract Number list, a DDC Number list, a Post Office Registry list, and even a Documents Not Used list. Computer costs for the time used by the documents section of the library are estimated at $175 per month, and both the system's operators and outside observers report that it saves the library money as well as being faster and more accurate than a comparable manual system.[7]

Many university libraries began producing large serials lists by computer around 1964; in fact, 1964 began a short but very intensive period in the development of automated serials systems. At the University of Michigan, punched cards were used that year to print the *Union List of Scientific and Technical Serials in the University of Michigan Library* on a 1401 computer, and the listing was then photographically reduced for publication. In 1965 the University of Kansas produced a large regional union list of serials for the libraries of Kansas State University, Kansas State Teachers College at Emporia, Ft. Hays State College, Kansas State College at Pittsburg, and Wichita State University, as well as for the various libraries of the University of Kansas. The 22,000 entries involved were arranged in alphabetical sequence by a 1401 computer using "sort numbers" assigned manually. The same year, a *Current Periodical Holdings List* of approximately 16,000 titles was produced at the University of Illinois' Urbana campus, and was republished in revised format the following year. Sorting was done by IBM 7010 and 1460 computers without manual intervention, using up to 200 characters of the title if necessary. By 1968, the list had been expanded to 60,000 records, including 18,000 periodicals (defined by Illinois as publications appearing three or more times per year) and 27,000 other serials, plus 15,000 cross-references. An IBM 360 Model 50 computer was used for this larger list. The input and editing methods are of interest: manual files in the Library's Serials Department were photographed on a "photoclerk" machine, the photographic reproductions were edited and keypunched, the keypunched cards were listed on an IBM 407 tabulator and edited a second time, and the cards were then read into the 360 which transcribed the records to magnetic tape. Sorting and filing was again done by computer, this time using 150 characters of the title, but the resulting arrangement was judged unsatisfactory by the librarians and a combination of manual and machine methods was used to produce the final arrangement.[8]

In 1964 and 1965, a computer-produced listing of serials was used to facilitate the moving and merging of the holdings of the Boston Medical Library and the Harvard Medical Library to form the Francis A. Countway Library of Medicine. The two libraries had used different schemes for alphabetization, shelving, cataloging and recording of holdings, all of which had to be reconciled. The existing records of the two libraries were reproduced using a Xerox Copyflo, interfiled, verified, transcribed to worksheets, keypunched, listed several times on a 1401 computer, edited, and then used to produce various printed lists, new check-in forms for the Boston Medical titles, and labels to guide in the placement of volumes as they were moved.[9]

Off-line computerized accessioning systems

A myth persists that the University of California at San Diego invented the "arrival card" system. As noted above, such systems were already in use in special libraries as early as 1960, but the UCSD system is perhaps the best known of several computerized serials systems based on the arrival card concept and developed in the early 1960s. Work was begun on a pilot project at UCSD in 1961. The pilot system began operation in 1962 with several hundred titles, and the full system began operation in 1964. It has been operating ever since, although with numerous revisions and reprogrammings along the way. Part of the reason for development of the system was the prediction that the library's holdings would grow rapidly, and this

7. Serials Systems 155

has certainly been the case; from 45,000 volumes in 1961 the library grew to over 600,000 volumes in 1969, and the number of serial titles grew in the same period from 700 to almost 20,000.[10]

For the initial conversion, a worksheet called an "intermediate serial record" was used, since keypunching from existing serial record cards was judged impossible. Data were accumulated on these intermediate records, then keypunched and input. From this point, operation of the system was as described earlier; cards were punched each month by the computer for the issues expected to be received, these were manually withdrawn from the resulting file as the issues were checked in, and served to update the magnetic tape files during the next month's computer run. The updating run produced a new list of current holdings (see Fig. 7-1) and arrival cards for issues expected the following month. In the UCSD system, these new arrival cards had to be manually interfiled into the remaining arrival cards each month. Costs were determined to be only slightly more than the manual system, which was felt to be acceptable because of the increased accuracy of records.[11-12]

Two CDC computers, a 1604 and a 160-A were used for the initial system. Later the system was transferred to a CDC 3600, and still later to an RCA Spectra 70 Model 45. In a major redesign of the system in 1968, the arrival card feature was eliminated because of the increasingly difficult problem of providing recognizable and unique titles in the twenty-four columns alloted for the purpose on the cards. In the new system, a check-in list is produced, issues are checked off the list as they arrive, and once a day transaction cards, with transaction numbers matching the lines on the check-in list, are pulled and used to update the computerized records. Among the advantages of the check-in list are additional space for titles, ease of scanning as compared with the card files (the "finding time" of a title on the list was found to be nearly half the time required with the card files) and the capability of decentralizing the check-in process for branch libraries. The new system also employs a "12-month prediction calendar," which adds an estimated 40 percent to the number of titles with "predictable publication patterns;"

Z675 L24112	A.A.A.L.PUBLICATIONS SERIES U3,(1962- 1962)	SSE COLLECTION
M1 A275	A.H.I.L. QUARTERLY U3N3,U4N1-2,(1963-JAN1964)	BIO-MED LIBRARY
	A.I.B.S.BULLETIN.SEE AMERICAN INSTITUTE OF BIOLOGICAL SCIENCES.BULLETIN	SIO LIBRARY
TP1 A104	A.I.CH.E.JOURNAL U8-9,U10N1,(1962-JAN1964)	SSE COLLECTION
	A.M.A.AMERICAN JOURNAL OF DISEASES OF CHILDREN.SEE AMERICAN JOURNAL OF DISEASES OF CHILDREN	BIO-MED LIBRARY
	A.M.A.ARCHIVES NOW ENTERED AS ARCHIVES...	BIO-MED LIBRARY
REFZW1 A63	A.P.C.A.ABSTRACTS U8N8-12,U9N1-10,(1963-MAR1964)	BIO-MED LIBRARY
QC1 A645	A.P.L.TECHNICAL DIGEST U1-2,U3N1-2,(1961-DEC1963)	SSE COLLECTION
Q1 A154A	ABO,FINLAND.AKADEMI.ACTA ACADEMIAE ABOENSIS.MATHEMATICA ET PHYSICA B1-22,U23N1-9,U23N12,(1922-NOV1963)	SSE COLLECTION
REFZW1 A144	ABSTRACTS OF BACTERIOLOGY B1-9,(1917- 1925),UNITED WITH BOTANICAL ABSTRACTS TO FORM BIOLOGICAL ABSTRACTS	BIO-MED LIBRARY
QH1 A163	ABSTRACTS OF HUMAN DEVELOPMENTAL BIOLOGY B1,U2,U3N1,U3N3-12,(1961-DEC1963),1963 AS HUMAN DEVELOPMENTAL BIOLOGY	SSE COLLECTION
E51 A164	ABSTRACTS OF NEW WORLD ARCHAEOLOGY U1-2,(1959- 1960)	SIO LIBRARY
E51 A164 C.2	ABSTRACTS OF NEW WORLD ARCHAEOLOGY U1-2,(1959- 1960)	SIO LIBRARY
REFZW1 A165	ABSTRACTS OF SOVIET MEDICINE B5,(1961- 1961),CONTINUES ABSTRACTS OF SOVIET MEDICINE,PARTS A AND B	BIO-MED LIBRARY

FIG. 7-1. Serials holdings list, University of California at San Diego.

7. Serials Systems

the total of "predictable regulars" is now estimated at 80 percent.[12] In 1973, the output of the system was converted to computer-output microfiche, with considerable savings. A large number of microfiche readers were purchased, and the savings through use of COM output rather than large printouts more than paid for the readers.[13]

In late 1960--apparently just days after UCSD began its work--the Washington University School of Medicine library began the design of a remarkably similar serials system, complete with prepunched arrival cards, periodic listings, and binding and claiming routines. Its first listings were produced in 1963, and the system began full operation in 1964. IBM 1401 and 7072 computers were used, and a seven-digit code was used for alphabetizing. An intriguing "frequency code" used to predict the arrival of issues allowed for variations in publication patterns by dividing the year into quarters, treating each month in a quarter as one digit in a three-digit binary number, then converting the resulting binary number for each quarter to a decimal digit. For a periodical published in February, March, April, June, August, October, and November, for example, the binary code would be 011, 101, 010, 110, and the decimal code would be 3526. With such devices WUSM was able almost from the beginning to predict the arrival of a relatively large percentage of its titles.[14]

The UCSD and Washington University Medical School systems became the models for dozens of other serial check-in systems developed in the 1960s. Many of these were designed for special libraries, and some are still in operation. Examples reported in the literature are those at the Atomic Energy Commission Headquarters Library,[15] the Baker Library of the Harvard Graduate School of Business Administration,[16] and the Technical Information Department of Pfizer, Inc.[17] Another at the University of California's Lawrence Radiation Laboratory differed in two interesting respects: the master holdings record was updated and the complete holdings list printed on a daily basis, rather than monthly, and a remarkable 30,000-line-per-minute printer was used, permitting what would normally be a three-hour job to be completed in just over five minutes.[18]

Most of the arrival card systems designed for university libraries were never implemented, or were later abandoned, largely because of the problems already discussed. Ohio State University and Purdue reported months and even years of effort on design; Purdue began operating its system in 1964, but without producing print-outs or lists, merely for experiment and study, and discontinued it in 1965, having earlier cited the "baffling bibliographic instability" of serials.[19]

One of the most persistent problems--the difficulty of recording many serial titles in the restricted space available on an eighty-column card--has let to some interesting variations on the arrival card theme. Texas A&M University proposed to use either a special printer (the IBM 1404) or IBM's Multi-Function Card Machine to print several lines of information directly on the arrival cards, as well as punching information into them. A special programming language was devised for handling serials and serial control functions, perhaps the only instance of a special programming language constructed solely for library purposes.[20] Like many others, however, this serials system was never actually implemented.

One that was implemented, and that may have been based on the Texas A&M proposals, is at the San Francisco Public Library. Only a six-digit number is prepunched in the card, but up to 2,000 characters of identifying information are printed on the face of the card. The system designers note familiar difficulties in predicting arrival, but have continued to use the arrival card feature nevertheless. Similar cards are used to trigger binding.[21]

Another alternative has been tried at the Miami-Dade Junior College in Miami, Florida. Instead of ordinary punched cards, the Miami-Dade system uses edge-punched cards of the type readable (and prepared) by paper-tape typewriters. A gummed label is typed on the typewriter, which simultaneously punches the same information into the edge of a card, and the label is then affixed to the face of the card. The card now becomes a permanent record, rather than being prepared anew periodically. When an issue is received, the card is placed in the reader of the punched-tape typewriter, which reproduces

7. Serials Systems

the information in coded form in paper tape. The machine then stops, and the operator enters variable information, such as volume number, issue number, and date. The paper-tape records of issues received accumulate on a reel until the end of each week, when the tape is read by an IBM 1620 computer, and an updated periodical listing produced. Other reports listing the issues not received, the periodicals due to be renewed four months later, and those due to be bound the next month, are also produced by the system.[22]

A third alternative to the use of arrival cards is an arrival list, already mentioned above as part of the new system at the University of California at San Diego. The University of Minnesota Biomedical Library[23] and the New York State Library have described similar systems.

At the University of Kansas, the UKASE (for University of Kansas Automated Serials) system uses a computer print-out of the serials information attached by a perforated edge to a fanfold marking strip 3¼ inches wide. As issues are received, spaces ("channels") on the strip are marked opposite the appropriate title, using ordinary No. 2 pencils. Every two weeks, an Automata Optical Mark Reader processes the detached strips and transfers the information to magnetic tape for further processing. This method has the advantage that both the strips and the Optical Mark Readers may be at remote locations (such as branch libraries, or other libraries in a regional system) and the data may be transmitted over telephone lines or cables from the Optical Mark Readers to a central receiver. A Honeywell-GE 635 computer uses the tapes to update the master file regularly and produce lists of holdings, as well as the list of expected issues for the next processing cycle.[24]

Other off-line computerized serials systems

A number of systems have been implemented which automate one or another aspect of serials control without the use of an automated accessioning or check-in feature. The Information Center of the Monsanto Company in St. Louis, Missouri has established a simple system which can be run on either unit record equipment or a small

(1401) computer. It provides for check-in (on standard 5-by-8-inch check-in cards that are printed by computer), renewals, and various listings.[25] A claiming system has lately been added, using a simple log sheet to record the issue information, the record number and an action code. At the end of each month, this information is punched and generates the appropriate claim letters. Provision is made for deleting or changing claims as needed, and follow-up letters are produced each month for issues not received. The claiming programs are run on an IBM 360 Model 50 or 65, however, not the 1401.[26]

The library of the Moraine Valley Community College in southwestern Cook County, Illinois has used the college's IBM 370 Model 135 computer for an off-line serials system which is of interest primarily because of the unusually small size of the files handled: only 715 titles. Its developers have justified the system in terms of the benefits derived, but feel that "any automated system would be wasted on holdings of under 150 periodicals."[27]

Swarthmore College has installed a system, utilizing a small IBM computer, that provides for listings, renewals, and a binding routine that has eliminated two typings of lists by clerks. A deck of cards is punched each year with one card for every periodical volume to be bound. Every month, cards for the volumes to be bound that month are pulled from the deck, the volume number and dates are punched into them, and a binding list is produced. The list goes to the binder, the cards are retained by the library as its record of materials at the bindery, and when the bound volumes are returned the cards are used for manually updating the shelflist.[28]

Separate systems have also been established simply for renewal of subscriptions and for routing. Seventeen renewal systems are listed in the second LARC survey and thirteen routing systems are reported.[29]

On-line computerized serials systems

The problems associated with difficulties in communication between man and machine are particularly noticeable in off-line serial systems. The complexities and irregularities of serial publication demand efficient communication, and without it system

7. Serials Systems

problems and disruptions become particularly vexatious. Attempts to have the computer tell its operators what it expects in the way of serial receipts and holdings, and for the operators to tell the system what actually has happened--particularly when what has happened involves such circumstances as combined issues, special issues, changes or errors in numbering, and so forth--all by the use of punched cards, tape or listings, appear to be too slow and inflexible. The increased availability of on-line systems with provisions for interaction and "conversation" with the computer therefore offers a special degree of hope for dealing effectively with this area of library management.

Unfortunately very few on-line systems have yet been developed for serials control. As Bierman notes, it is curious that most systems are still batch-processing, since "it would appear that with the dynamic and unpredictable nature of serials control, on-line technology would be an absolute requirement for effective and efficient automated serials systems."[30] Presumably the designers of on-line systems have preferred first to tackle more straightforward problems, such as circulation.

One of the first on-line serials systems was begun in 1968 at the library of the Universitè Laval in Quebec, Canada, using three IBM 2260 display terminals on-line to an IBM 360 Model 50 computer. Instead of updating the master file immediately after new information is input as in most on-line systems, however, the Laval system accumulates the updating information in a special temporary working space on the disk, and processes it every two or three days. If an inquiry is made regarding one of these titles before the updating is processed, the system retrieves the modifying information from the working space, processes it, and presents the updated record to the user. The system thus responds to the user as if it were a completely "real-time" system--that is, a system which processes all information as it receives it--while avoiding much of the expense of real-time processing. On-line access is only by a seven-digit accession number at present, but additional searching capabilities are planned.[31] An earlier off-line system at Laval has also been reported in the literature.[32]

The most efficient, comprehensive and responsive serials system developed to date is the on-line system at the UCLA Biomedical Library. UCLA began with a batch system in 1963 on an IBM 1410; reprogrammed it in 1967 for an IBM 360; then, in 1969, with a grant from the National Library of Medicine, began work on an on-line system which finally became operational in 1971.

At first the on-line system used IBM 2260 display terminals, but these have now been replaced by three Delta Data terminals, plus one manufactured by Lear Sigler which is used for administrative purposes. Approximately 12,000 serial titles are on file, of which about 6,500 are currently received.

To check in receipts, one or two distinctive words of the title are keyed into the terminal, and in response all information needed for check-in is displayed by the computer on the screen. If more than ten titles have the words used, the system simply gives the number of titles with those words and the operator adds other words to narrow the search and recall the desired record. For obscure journals, the language or country of publication may also be used as search elements. In practice, the operators soon remember the most efficient words to retrieve frequently received titles; for example, to check in an issue of *Tropical Fish Hobbyist*, the operator keys "Hobbyist," knowing from experience that it is the only journal received with that word in the title.

The information displayed is for the predicted next issue, and gives that issue's expected volume number, issue number, date, binding information, and so forth; in most cases, therefore, the operator need only press a single key ("Send") and the computer responds by showing the updated holdings record for confirmation. While this is happening, the operator writes on the issue its call number and any routing instructions from information given on the screen. If the information displayed is not correct, an "xx" message cancels it and permits the recording of the correct information.

A separate program permits changes to a record or addition of new records. In the latter case, information is keyed and transmitted one line at a time, and when the keyboard input is finished

7. Serials Systems 163

the computer displays the full resulting record for confirmation. After the operator has checked it for accuracy, an "OK" message records the information on disk.

For reference purposes, searches of the file can be made by a variety of aspects--title words, subject, language, country of publication, and so on--resulting in a total of 381 different search options. The results of the search may either be displayed on the screen or printed in list form. Only brief information is normally displayed on the screen, but a further command results in display of the entire record if desired. The reactions of the public to the display terminal at the reference desk have been mixed; some patrons have apparently looked on it as a toy and have played with it extensively, while others have refused to use it at all. The need to teach patrons how to use the terminal and then to monitor its use placed such a burden on the reference librarians that printed copies of the list of holdings are now used instead for public consultation.

Searching for claiming purposes is done in three different ways: (1) by displaying particular records (if a request for a particular missing issue has been received, for example); (2) by displaying all titles for which the most recent issue is overdue by a designated period of time; (3) by displaying all "skipped" issues, i.e., all records for which a gap in the holdings record exists, and for which no claim has yet been issued. Under the first option, keying either the record number or the title displays the full record, and the volume number, issue number, date, and number of the claim (first claim, second claim, etc.) are entered; the complete claims history is displayed to facilitate matters. The second and third methods of claiming are performed one or two hours per day on a monthly cycle; the program automatically displays each overdue issue in turn, and depending on what information is displayed the operator decides whether or not to instigate a claim.

Binding routines are triggered by the check-in operation. Every three days, a "pickup" list is generated (see Fig. 7-2). Issues to be bound are then picked up, and any discrepancies noted are entered as corrections to the record, again using the terminals.

		VOLUMES COMPLETED AND READY TO BE BOUND AS RESULT OF COMPUTER RUN ON NOV. 20, 1973						PAGE 10
DATE PICKED UP			YEAR	VOL.	ISSUE	SER NUM	PTS/VOL	FREQUENCY	LOCATION
	151.	PISCATOR. W1 P1697						IRREGULAR	INCOMPLETES
	152.	PLANTA. W1 PL133	73	113	1-4	6104100	01	28 ISSUES/YR	RDNG ROOM
	153.	REFERATIVNYI ZHURNAL. BIOLOGICHESKAIA KHIMIIA. ZQU 4 R259	73		19-24	6116700	01	SEMI-MONTHLY	REF STACK
	154.	REFERATIVNYI ZHURNAL. FARMAKOLGIIA. KHIMIOTERAPEVTICHESKIE SREDSTVA. TOKSIKOLOGIIA. ZQV 4 R259	73		7-12	6413700	02	MONTHLY	REF STACK
	155.	REFERATIVNYI ZHURNAL. FARMAKOLGIIA. KHIMIOTERAPEVTICHESKIE SREDSTVA. TOKSIKOLOGIIA. ZQV 4 R259	73		7-12	6413700	02	MONTHLY	REF STACK
	156.	REFERATIVNYI ZHURNAL. KIBERNETIKA. Z T405 C9 R261	73		7-12	6416100	02	MONTHLY	REF STACK
	157.	REFERATIVNYI ZHURNAL. RASTENIEVODSTVO. Z 5353 R261	73		7-12	6418500	02	MONTHLY	REF STACK
	158.	RESEARCH IN VETERINARY SCIENCE. W1 RE220	73	14	1-6	6455700	01	BI-MONTHLY	RDNG ROOM
	159.	REVIEW OF EXISTENTIAL PSYCHOLOGY AND PSYCHIATRY. W1 RE257	72	11	1-3	6477300	01	3 ISSUES/YR	INCOMPLETES
	160.	REVISTA ARGENTINA DE UROLOGIA Y NEFROLOGIA. W1 RE308	71	40	1-12	6487500	01	MONTHLY	INCOMPLETES
	161.	REVISTA BRASILEIRA DE CIRURGIA. W1 RE313	73	NJA	1-	6488700	01	IRREGULAR	INCOMPLETES
	162.	REVISTA BRASILEIRA DE CIRURGIA. M1 RE313	72	62	1-	6488700	01	IRREGULAR	INCOMPLETES
	163.	REVISTA CUBANA DE CIRUGIA. W1 RE359H	72	11		6501300	01	BI-MONTHLY	INCOMPLETES
	164.	REVISTA CUBANA DE MEDICINA. W1 RE362	72	11		6503100	01	BI-MONTHLY	INCOMPLETES

FIG. 7-2. Binding pick-up list, UCLA Biomedical Library.

7. Serials Systems 165

Multiple-part binding slips are then produced by the computer, one part for the bindery, one part for a binding file in the library and one part for the circulation desk. A two-part packing list for each shipment is also produced, one part for the bindery and one part for the binding department. When the bound volumes are returned, student assistants use the terminals to change the holdings statements for each title, indicating those volumes as now bound. Binding slips are then sent to the circulation department to correct their records.[33]

Cost studies by the system's developers indicate savings of $18,229 per year for the on-line system, largely in personnel costs. These figures do not include development costs of $74,000, but a further analysis has indicated that the net present value of the system exceeds the value of a hypothetical alternative investment of the funds at 10 percent interest.[34]

The system is a sophisticated and powerful one which appears to have potential usefulness to other libraries of many types, and fortunately work is under way to put the system's programs and documentation into a form that may be used by other libraries.

MEDLARS

The largest system for searching serial citations is also a medical one, the MEDLARS system of the National Library of Medicine and its related service, MEDLINE. Work on MEDLARS (for Medical Literature Analysis and Retrieval System) began in 1960, and the system has since gone through several major revisions. The principal products are *Index Medicus*, a comprehensive index to the periodical literature of medicine; the *Current Catalog*, which is a supplement to the published National Library of Medicine catalog containing both monographic and serial citations; "Recurring Bibliographies," which are published lists of periodical citations in specialized medical areas; and "Demand Bibliographies," which are the printed results of specific, one-time computer searches using keywords in response to requests submitted by individuals. *Index Medicus* and the *Current Catalog* are produced on a photocomposition device, the others by print-out.

The first major change in MEDLARS occurred in 1964, when the project was decentralized and some ten regional centers (two in foreign countries and eight in the United States, in addition to NLM) were given responsibility for providing services in their geographic areas, particularly the demand bibliography services. This change was made, at least in part, to help cope with the increasing demands being made on the system, and the increasingly serious problems caused by the system's design. All of the data were stored on magnetic tapes, so that searches had to be conducted serially; that is, starting at the beginning of a tape or tapes, proceeding sequentially, selecting appropriate citations until the end of the body of data was reached. For individual searches, this became more and more expensive and time-consuming as the amount of data grew. Searches were "batched"--that is, grouped together, and processed together, in one serial search--but this, of course, delayed searches to some extent, and in any event did not solve the fundamental design problem. Similar systems by this time were using magnetic disks and other devices which provided so-called "random access"--meaning that positions in the store of data could be reached more or less directly instead of sequentially, much as a phonograph needle can be placed in the middle of a record. Use of random access devices meant that brief indexes could be constructed by the terms (or "keywords") which were used to construct the searches, the "addresses" of those citations which contained data indexed by those terms could be ascertained, and the appropriate citations could then be withdrawn and reproduced. MEDLARS, however, was to remain dependent on magnetic tapes for storage and retrieval long after this technique became commonplace.

By 1968, the problems were serious enough that a major redesign of the system, dubbed MEDLARS II, was initiated. Unfortunately MEDLARS II seemed starcrossed from the beginning. The contract for its development, issued in June 1968 to Computer Sciences Corporation (CSC), specified that the "initial capabilities" were to be operational by July 1, 1969, only a year later, but budget problems at NLM delayed certain key decisions (such as whether the new computer

7. Serials Systems   167

involved should be leased or purchased) and the "objectives became blurred and divergent as the project went along."[35] In 1969, instead of becoming operational, the project underwent a "major review," the entire management of the project was changed, the contract with CSC was renegotiated, and an agreement was signed that "redefined the description of the work, amended the delivery schedule, and increased the estimated cost of the contract."[36]

None of these measures seemed to help very much, and by 1970, it was clear that the project was in deep trouble. The Comptroller General of the United States issued a report criticizing the effort, and pointing out that several million dollars had been spent with little to show for it.[37]

The change from sequential-access, batch processing of searches to random access, which was one of the major goals of MEDLARS II, had been delayed again, so the problem of reliance on magnetic tapes remained. An IBM 360 Model 50 had finally been chosen as the new computer, but new programs were not available and the old programs, written for Honeywell equipment, would not run on the 360; in order even to use the new computer, in fact, programs had to be acquired, not from the contractor, but from the Swedish MEDLARS center which "had made the necessary program adjustments for the IBM 360/50."[38] Critics analyzing the history of MEDLARS II have also pointed to "more basic intellectual problems" attributable to a "general lack of appreciation of the complexities of bibliographic information and of library functions;"[39] this in turn may be attributable to the fact that most of NLM's managers are not professional librarians, but doctors and other personnel drawn from the medical community. Finally, in 1971, citing "complexities of design" and "considerable 'slippage' by Computer Sciences Corporation," the MEDLARS II system was simply discontinued.[40]

In the meantime a more successful project had begun. A teletypewriter service on-line to a much reduced data base, was offered beginning in 1970 under a pilot project called AIM-TWX (for Abridged Index Medicus Teletypewriter Exchange), which used an IBM 360 Model 67 computer at the System Development Corporation in Santa Monica,

California. The response from users around the country was enthusiastic, encouraging NLM to establish a more permanent service named MEDLINE (for MEDlars-on-LINE). Beginning in December 1971, terminals with 200-word-per-minute printing devices could be used to access an IBM 370 Model 155 computer at NLM. Communications were largely through Western Union's Datacom service, supplemented by leased telephone lines. In February 1972, a second phase was begun using a commercial network operated by TYMSHARE, which provides users with toll-free access to the NLM computer from over thirty different cities. By 1973, the project had expanded to forty major cities (including Paris), and searches were routinely being made from over 120 institutions (mainly medical libraries) using over 200 terminals.[41]

The data base being searched originally consisted of citations from 1,000 major journals indexed in Index Medicus from January 1969 forward. In early 1974, the data base was revised to include citations from 1972 forward only, but with almost twice as many journals (the entire MEDLARS data base of approximately 2300 titles); the data base from 1970 to 1972 was divided into two, MEDFILE (1200 "major" journals) and COMPFILE (the 1100 other journals). In 1975, the file of citations from 1969 to 1972 was recombined, so that it now contains all MEDLARS titles, and is called BACKFILE. There are thus only two data bases again, and both contain all MEDLARS titles: BACKFILE from 1969 through 1971, and MEDLINE from 1972 forward.

Several related on-line services were also being made available by 1975. These include access to the following data bases:

SDILINE, the citations to be printed in the following month's *Index Medicus*

CATLINE, the bibliographic information used in the *Current Catalog* since 1965

SERLINE, serial records containing bibliographic and other information on some 5,600 current biomedical serial titles held by 117 medical libraries

TOXLINE, citations and abstracts in the fields of toxicology and pharmacology as they relate to medicine, health and safety

7. Serials Systems 169

> CHEMLINE, information on nomenclature and structural elements for 60,000 compounds
>
> CANCERLINE, a new service instituted with the cooperation of the National Cancer Institute

Two IBM 370 Model 158s are now used at NLM for most of these services, and three commercial companies provide the necessary communication linkages: Tymshare, Inc., supplies most of the network, backed up with Western Union's Datacom and American Telephone and Telegraph's leased lines. In operation, a user fills out a search request using keywords, or index terms. He may also indicate whether he wishes a "few, very relevant" citations or a broader search, and whether he wants to use the "new-user format" or the "experienced-user format." The "new-user format" prints out specific instructions for using the system, the "experienced-user format" uses abbreviated codes in the interests of saving time.

If the user encounters difficulty, he may use a "help" command, which causes the terminal to ask questions designed to determine the nature of the difficulty and then respond appropriately. Because of the popularity of the service, users have recently been restricted to twenty-five citations or less; if more are needed, the search request is mailed to NLM. Costs of the searches vary depending on the local library's policies (some absorb part or all of the costs charged by NLM, and others do not: NLM, however, absorbs most of the major costs). In one major center (the Texas Medical Center Library in Houston, Texas) costs per search are $4.00, recently lowered from $5.00 because of the changes in the data base made available and in NLM charges.

National Serials Data Program and CONSER

For some time efforts have been under way at the national level to gain control of serials, but without the success that characterized the MARC effort. Study at the Library of Congress began as early as 1965, concentrating on the development of a comprehensive format for recording bibliographic information about serials in machine-readable form. In 1969 the Association of Research Libraries was awarded a grant from the National Agricultural Library to administer a two-year National Serials Pilot Project, supported thereafter by the Library of Congress, the National Agricultural Library and the National Library of Medicine, with additional support from the Council on Library Resources. This second phase began a union list of serials for the three national libraries, gathered data about the characteristics of serials, and studied various techniques for handling serial information. In 1972, a third phase was announced, again supported by the three national libraries, and with the further goals of providing "a base record of serial titles to which the International Standard Serial Number can be permanently affixed, thus ending the confusion about precise identification of serials," and providing "a serial system which will constitute the U.S. segment of the developing International Serials Data System."[42]

Although it was not apparent to most observers at the time, those phrases introduced serious bibliographic problems. The International Serials Data System, a part of a larger system proposed by UNESCO for the international exchange of scientific information, contains the concept of "key title," a bibliographic device designed to make each title unique but which often does not agree with the main entry for a serial as determined by the *Anglo-American Cataloging Rules* and applied in the MARC serials format. The discrepancies between the two systems delayed progress for several years, until finally a group of users who had "been holding in abeyance the development of their automated serials systems, some for several years, waiting for sufficient development at the national level to provide a base and guidance for the development of their individual and developing systems," decided they could wait no longer for resolution. "Local pressures from their users, their administrators, and their own developing systems are forcing these librarians to act without waiting for the national effort," said a spokesman.[43] Calling themselves the "Ad Hoc Discussion Group on Serials Data Bases," the group met without advance publicity during the June 1973 ALA Annual Conference in Las Vegas, Nevada. They expressed concern about three problems:

7. Serials Systems

1. The lack of communication among the generators of machine-readable serials files
2. The incompatibility of format and bibliographic data among existing files
3. The apparent confusion about the existing and proposed bibliographic description and format "standards."[44]

They found a sympathetic ear at the Council on Library Resources. Fortified by a change in its tax status, which enabled it to function as an "operating foundation," the Council offered not only money but management by its own staff for new efforts at serials control. A second meeting financed by the Council was held at York University in Toronto, attended by an "arbitrarily selected" Steering Committee made up of representatives from the Council, the Association of Research Libraries (ARL), the Library of Congress, the National Library of Canada, the Ohio College Library Center, the National Serials Data Program, the Canadian Union Catalogue Taskgroup, the Joint Committee on the Union List of Serials, the University of California, Northwestern University, the State University of New York, and the Université Laval. Significantly (and as it turned out, unfortunately), although the group began at an ALA meeting apparently no representative from the American Library Association was invited or attended. The purposes of the September meeting were defined as twofold:

1. To establish a mechanism for creating a set of "agreed-upon practices for converting and communicating machine-readable serials data"
2. To establish a mechanism for cooperatively converting a comprehensive retrospective bibliographic data base of serials.[45]

On October 10, 1973, three subcommittees met briefly at the Library of Congress and recommended that a cooperative conversion project be initiated as soon as possible, using OCLC as a vehicle because of "its proven capability to produce network software and support that will work."[46] The Steering Committee met shortly thereafter (on October 22, 1973, during a meeting of the American Society for Information Science in Los Angeles) and accepted these proposals. The question of affiliation with an existing professional organization was raised at the time, but not resolved.

Related questions regarding the group's authority to take such actions were quickly raised in other quarters. An editorial in the June 1974 issue of the *Journal of Library Automation*, the official organ of ALA's Information Science and Automation Division (ISAD), chided the Council on Library Resources for alleged secrecy, for working through *ad hoc* groups rather than through established ALA committees, and for slanting the development efforts of the project toward one type of library only, the large research library.[47] Paul Fasana of the New York Public Library, at an institute jointly sponsored by ISAD and the American Society for Information Science (ASIS) in October 1974 on "Automated Serials Control--National and International Considerations," saw the conversion project (by now called "CONSER," for Conversion of Serials) as "verging on the chaotic" and an "alarming threat."

> By admission, CONSER would undertake in the area of serials to create a data base (perhaps "file" would be a more exact description) of serials according to standards which may or may not be acceptable or consistent with previous records or emerging standards. It would attempt to do this by setting up a legally complex entity, making use of bits and pieces of technology and files, and involving a number of librar-ies having widely differing objectives and standards. It might work, but then again it might not. A project as im-portant as the building of a national serials data base must have a firmer base if it is to be effective and win the confidence of librarians.[48]

Fasana was particularly concerned that no authority control system was proposed for the initial conversion project, which by that time had increased its goals from 200,000 to 300,000 titles, and that insufficient attention had been given to the conflicts between the Anglo-American Cataloging Rules for serials, the International Seri-als Data System (ISDS), the International Standard Bibliographic Description for Serials (ISBD(S)), and the International Standard Serial Number (ISSN). He understood that "the sense of urgency that

7. Serials Systems   173

has fired recent serials developments is a reaction to the long years of study, deliberation, and inactivity that went into the original National Serials Data Program" and that this was "perhaps understandable,"⁴⁹ but warned that "it is not only irresponsible but folly to insist that getting something done (translate that to mean converting 200,000 to 300,000 titles in two years) is reason enough to forge ahead regardless of the consequences."⁵⁰

At the same meeting, Lois Upham of the Minnesota Union List of Serials, one of the participants, revealed further developments:

1. The Minnesota Union List of Serials would be used as a base file, along with the serial records so far produced by MARC.
2. The initial group of participants would be limited to 10 institutions: the Library of Congress, the National Library of Canada, the National Library of Medicine, the National Agricultural Library, the Minnesota Union List of Serials, Yale University Library, Cornell University Library, the New York State Library, the State University of New York, and the University of California.
3. Records prepared under both the Anglo-American Cataloging Rules (AACR) and the older ALA rules would be input, although the problem of handling the conflicts between them was still "under consideration."
4. The data base would contain only the location symbols for libraries having holdings, not the specific holdings themselves.⁵¹

A spokesman for the Council on Library Resources provided further details at a meeting of the Association of Research Libraries on January 18, 1975:

1. The contract between OCLC and the Council had been signed on December 17, 1974, after protracted negotiations on the rights to use of the data base. The Council felt the data base should be available to all of the library comcommunity "at nominal cost and with no restrictions as to

use, while OCLC saw this as "giving unwarranted advantages to potential competitors, especially those in the commercial sector." In the final agreement, "ownership and distribution rights to the CONSER data base accrue to the Library of Congress and the National Library of Canada," both of which had indicated that they were considering distributing the records as an adjunct to the regular MARC distribution service. OCLC agreed not to charge for the use of its systems, since they had been developed with CLR's assistance, and CLR agreed to pay for the additional machine storage, programming and staff services. Communication and terminal costs will be shared by the participating institutions and CLR.

2. The Minnesota file will be merged with MARC serial records, then existing OCLC serial records, then Canadian MARC serial records.

3. The MARC format for serials will be used, and recommendations for changes in that format to accommodate such things as "the bilingual requirements of Canada or certain elements required by the International Serials Data System" are being submitted for consideration through "established channels."

4. "The participating libraries have divided up the alphabet among themselves, each agreeing to begin at its assigned point, putting in the records of serials currently received. When each has exhausted its assigned portion of the alphabet, each will proceed through the alphabet, converting the remainder of its currently published serials holdings."

5. Provision will be made for adding "key titles" and International Standard Serial Numbers to the CONSER records.

6. The decision is still "clear" to "put bibliographically inconsistent records in at first and then work them over as time and resources ... permit." Likewise, the decision still stands "not to hold up file-building pending the

7. Serials Systems 175

availability of an authority file, but a machine-readable authority file is a firm requirement for the future."[52]

By early 1975, conciliation was also in the air. The project had appointed an "advisory committee" with broad representation from various groups, ALA's Interdivisional Committee on Representation in Machine Readable Form of Bibliographic Information (otherwise known as MARBI) published assurances that any changes in the MARC serials format would be submitted to and reviewed by the committee before finding their way into the MARC distribution service, and articles explaining the project had appeared in most of the appropriate professional journals. Issues of concern still remained, but were balanced by widespread excitement over the obvious fact that something, at least, was happening. Observers on both sides of the controversy agreed on one point: that the CONSER project was the most significant and important development yet in automated serials systems, and is likely to remain so for several years to come.

NOTES

1. Bruce W. Stewart, "Automated Serials Systems in Perspective," in *Library Automation: a State of the Art Review*, American Library Association, Chicago, 1969, p. 133.

2. Alexander Moffit, "Punched Card Records in Serials Acquisition," *College & Research Libraries*, 7, 10-13 (January 1946).

3. Anne McCann, "Applications of Machines to Library Techniques: Periodicals," *American Documentation*, 12, 260-265 (October 1961).

4. Louis A. Schultheiss, "Two Serial Control Card Files Developed at the University of Illinois, Chicago," *Library Resources & Technical Services*, 9, 271-287 (Summer 1965).

5. William E. McGrath and Helen Kolbe, "A Simple, Mechanized, Non-Computerized System for Serials Control in Small Academic Libraries: a Primer," *Library Resources & Technical Services*, 10, 373-381 (Summer 1966).

6. G. E. Randall, "Unit Record System for Serial Control in a Special Library," *IBM Library Mechanization Symposium, Endicott, New York, May 25, 1964*, International Business Machines, Inc., White Plains, New York [1965?], pp. 237-245.

7. Richard Phillips Palmer, *Case Studies in Library Computer Systems*, R. R. Bowker, New York, 1973, pp. 81-89.

8. Robert D. Kozlow, "Genesis of a Serials List," *Proceedings of the 1968 Clinic on Library Applications of Data Processing,* University of Illinois Graduate School of Library Science, Urbana, 1969, pp. 219-220.

9. Ann T. Curran, "The Mechanization of the Serial Records for the Moving and Merging of the Boston Medical and Harvard Medical Serials," *Library Resources & Technical Services,* 10, 362-372 (Summer 1966).

10. Don L. Bosseau, "The University of California at San Diego Serials System--Revisited," *Program,* 4, 1-3 (January 1970).

11. George Vdovin et al., "Computer Processing of Serial Records," *Library Resources & Technical Services,* 7, 71-80 (Winter 1963), and *Final Report, Serials Computer Project, University Library and Computer Center,* University of California at San Diego, La Jolla, California, 1964.

12. Bosseau, *op. cit.,* p. 4-29. See also, Bosseau, "The Computer in Serials Processing and Control," in *Advances in Librarianship,* vol. 2, Seminar Press, New York, 1971, pp. 110-113, 127-130, 137-141, 142, 149.

13. Telephone conversation with Melvin Voigt, library director at UCSD.

14. Irwin H. Pizer et al., "Mechanization of Library Procedures in the Medium-Sized Medical Library: 1. The Serial Record," *Bulletin of the Medical Library Association,* 51, 313-338 (July 1963).

15. Abraham I. Lebowitz and Walter A. Kee, "Mechanized Serial Record at the Atomic Energy Commission Headquarters Library," *Documentation Progress,* 7, 4-5 (November 1964).

16. Palmer, *op. cit.,* pp. 90-100.

17. Michael E. D. Koenig et al., "SCOPE: a Cost Analysis of an Automated Serials Record System," *Journal of Library Automation,* 4, 129-140 (September 1971).

18. J. B. Verity and E. L. Crocker, "A Computer-Based System for Serials Records at Lawrence Radiation Laboratory," *Journal of the American Society for Information Science,* 21, 247-253 (July-August 1970).

19. Donald P. Hammer, "Reflections on the Development of an Automated Serials System," *Library Resources & Technical Services,* 9, 225-230 (Spring 1965).

20. Bruce Warren Stewart, *A Computerized Serials Record for the Texas A & M University Library,* the Library, Texas A & M University, College Station, Texas, 1965; Stewart, *The Serials Mechanization of the Texas A & M University Library,* a Paper Presented at the First Texas Conference on Library Mechanization, Austin, March 23-25, 1966, [n.p.] 1966; Stewart, "Data Processing in the

7. Serials Systems

Texas A & M University Library," *Proceedings of the 1966 Clinic on Library Applications of Data Processing*, University of Illinois Graduate School of Library Science, Urbana, 1966, pp. 167-181; and Stewart, "Data Processing in an Academic Library," *Wilson Library Bulletin*, 41, 388-395 (December 1966).

21. Linda F. Crismond and Sylvia B. Fatzer, "Automated Serials Check-In and Binding Procedures at the San Francisco Public Library," in *American Society for Information Science, Proceedings*, v. 6, *Cooperating Information Societies*, Greenwood, Westport, Conn., 1969, pp. 13-20; Crismond, "A Computer System for Periodicals," *Library Journal*, 94, 3619-3621 (October 15, 1969); and David E. Belch, "The Computer-Controlled Periodicals Systems at the San Francisco Public Library," *Library Resources & Technical Services*, 13, 531-532 (Fall 1969).

22. Eleanor G. Eyman et al., "Periodicals Automation at Miami-Dade Junior College," *Library Resources & Technical Services*, 10, 341-361 (Summer 1966).

23. Audrey N. Grosch, "University of Minnesota Bio-Medical Library Serials System," *Special Libraries*, 60, 349-360 (July-Aug. 1969), and Karen D. Strom, "Software Design for Bio-Medical Library Serials Control System," in *Proceedings of the American Society for Information Science*, v. 5: *Information Transfer*, Greenwood, New York, 1968, pp. 267-275.

24. News item, *College & Research Libraries News*, 6, 187-188 (June 1971), and Anna R. Condit, "Optical Mark Sensing of Serials Check-in Records: a New Approach to Serials Automation," *American Society for Information Science: Proceedings*, v. 8: *Communications for Decision-Makers*, Greenwood, Westport, Connecticut, 1971, pp. 287-290.

25. W. A. Wilkinson, "A System for Machine-Assisted Serials Control," *Special Libraries*, 58, 149-153 (March 1967).

26. W. A. Wilkinson and Loretta A. Stock, "Machine-Assisted Serials Control: Bindery Preparation and Claims Control," *Special Libraries*, 62, 529-534 (December 1971).

27. Vivian Harp and Gertrude Heard, "Automated Periodicals System at a Community College Library," *Journal of Library Automation*, 7, 83-96 (June 1974).

28. Palmer, *op. cit.*, pp. 62-67.

29. LARC Association, *A Survey of Automated Activities in the Libraries of the U.S. and Canada*, 2d ed., the Association, Tempe, Arizona, 1971, p. 23.

30. Kenneth J. Bierman, "Library Automation," in *Annual Review of Information Science and Technology*, vol. 9, 1974, p. 147.

31. Rosario de Varennes, "On-Line Serials System at Laval University Library," *Journal of Library Automation*, 3, 128-141 (June 1970).

32. Rosario de Varennes, "Computerized Serials Record at Laval University: a Progress Report," *Canadian Library*, 24, 122-123 (September 1967).

33. Information from a personal visit by the writer. See also three articles by James Fayollat in the *Journal of the American Society for Information Science:* "On-Line Serials Control System in a Large Biomedical Library: 1) Description of the System," 23, 318-322 (September-October 1972); "On-Line Serials Control System in a Large Biomedical Library, Part II: Evaluation of Retrieval Features," 23, 353-358 (November-December 1972); and "On-Line Serials Control System in a Large Biomedical Library, Part III: Comparison of On-Line and Batch Operations and Cost Analysis," 24, 80-86 (March-April 1973). For information on the batch system, see Fred W. Roper, "A Computer-Based Serials Control System for a Large Biomedical Library," *American Documentation*, 19, 151-157 (April 1968).

34. Fayollat, "On-Line Serials Control System in a Large Biomedical Library, Part III: Comparison of On-Line and Batch Operations Cost Analysis," *Journal of the American Society for Information Science*, 24, 80-86 (March-April 1973).

35. Linnea Sodergren, "MEDLARS II: A Review," *Bulletin of the Medical Library Association*, 61, 400 (October 1973).

36. U. S. Government Accounting Office, *Information Gathering and Dissemination Activities of the National Library of Medicine: Report to the Congress by the Comptroller General of the United States*, the Office, 1970, p. 20.

37. *Ibid.*, p. 20-21.

38. Sodergren, *op. cit.*, p. 403.

39. *Ibid.*, p. 405.

40. *MLA News*, August 1971, p. 3.

41. Davis B. McCarn and Joseph Leiter, "On-Line Services in Medicine and Beyond," *Science*, 181, 318-324 (27 July 1973).

42. *College & Research Libraries News*, 33, 163 (June 1972).

43. Lawrence Livingston, "A Composite Effort to Build an On-Line National Serials Data Base (A Paper for Presentation at the ARL Midwinter Meeting, Chicago, 19 January 1974)," *Journal of Library Automation*, 7, 61 (March 1974).

44. Richard Anable, "The Ad Hoc Discussion Group on Serials Data Bases: Its History, Current Position, and Future," *Journal of Library Automation*, 6, 207 (December 1973).

45. *Ibid.*. p. 208.

46. Livingston, *op. cit.*, p. 62-63.

47. Susan K. Martin, "Who Will Steer the Ship?" *Journal of Library Automation*, 7, 71-72 (June 1974).

7. Serials Systems 179

48. Paul J. Fasana, "Impact of National Developments on Library Technical Services and Public Services," *Journal of Library Automation*, 7, 250-251 (December 1974).
49. *Ibid.*, p. 257.
50. *Ibid.*, p. 262.
51. Lois Upham, "CONSER: Cooperative Conversion of Serials Project," *Library of Congress Information Bulletin*, 33, A-247-A-248 (November 29, 1974).
52. Lawrence Livingston, *The CONSER Project: Current Status and Plans*, a paper presented to the Association of Research Libraries, January 18, 1975.

Chapter 8

CIRCULATION SYSTEMS

Automated systems for circulation control have been more successful than any other type of library system. There are obvious reasons for this: the operations to be performed are repetitive; the procedures to be followed can be described systematically; and circulation can be separated fairly easily from other library activities. Most importantly, the bibliographic information used in such systems need not be extensive or complex; the severe equipment and programming problems which arise from dealing with complex bibliographic entries, and which have impeded the development of serials, cataloging, and even acquisition systems, are therefore largely avoided. Uppercase typography is acceptable, and equipment and programming systems that otherwise could not be used are thus available.

Circulation systems are designed to capture and manipulate three kinds of information:

1. Information about the borrower (such as name, address, telephone number, identification number, and borrower category)
2. Information about the material being borrowed (such as call number, identification number, author, title, and date)
3. Information about the loan itself (such as date due or date of loan and, in some cases, time of loan)

This information may be gathered in a variety of ways. It may all be written out by the borrower or by a library clerk, and then keypunched for entry into the system. Alternatively, information on the borrower may be obtained automatically from a machine-readable identification card (or "badge" as it is sometimes called in industrial parlance), and information on the material borrowed may be read automatically from a previously punched book card placed in the book. Information on the loan transaction may be keypunched at the time the loan is made, or shortly thereafter; it may be keypunched in advance in the form of a "transaction number" to be assigned in sequence to loans as they are made; or it may be entered into remote terminals using a keyboard or various types of slide devices, cartridges, and dials.

After the three basic categories of information have been entered, circulation systems perform some or all of the following functions:

1. Provision of information on the location of circulating items--either all items, or only those items on loan or elsewhere than on the shelf (e.g., at the bindery, on reserve, being recataloged, or in storage)
2. Identification of items on loan to a particular borrower or class of borrowers (such as off-campus users)
3. Recording of "holds" or "personal reserves" for items on loan but desired by another borrower, often with additional provision for notifying the library staff when the item is returned and printing a "book available" notice for mailing to the person who requested the item
4. Printing recall notices for items on long-term loan
5. Renewal of loans
6. Notification to the library staff of overdue items and printing of overdue notices
7. Notification to the library staff of delinquent borrowers (i.e., those with unpaid fines or overdue books)

8. Circulation Systems

either at the time of an attempted loan, at the time a borrower is leaving the institution, or on request from the library

8. Calculation of fines, printing of fine notices, recording receipt of fines, and sometimes printing of fine receipts
9. Calculation and printing of statistics of various types
10. Analysis of both summary statistics and statistics for the circulation of particular items for use in acquisitions, planning of services, and for other administrative purposes
11. Provision for handling special categories of borrowers and special types of materials

A few systems also print date due slips, automatically generate orders for lost books or needed additional copies, and print mailing labels for remote borrowers.

Because of the relative ease with which they can be implemented (assuming good system design and planning, and capable systems and library personnel), circulation systems have been very popular. Hundreds have been implemented, and except for the more exotic on-line systems their existence is treated as commonplace rather than novel. Development has followed the standard progression from systems based on unit record equipment to off-line, batch processing computer systems, and finally to a sizeable number of on-line and partially on-line systems.

The typical punched-card system requires the borrower to fill out a charge record (usually in the form of a tabulating card) with his name and address, plus the author, title, and call number of the book. This information is then keypunched, and the cards arranged by date due or call number using unit record equipment. Sorters or collators are used to merge new cards in sequence, and to select records for overdue books from the files. A very considerable amount of card-handling and file manipulation is usually associated with such systems.

Off-line computer systems, as with serial record applications, are dominated by one particular system design. Usually this is called a "357-type" system, after the data collection device widely used in earlier versions, the IBM 357. This machine accepts a punched card (Fig. 8-1), endwise, in one slot, and a plastic borrower's card punched with standard rectangular holes (Fig. 8-2) in another slot. For the system to work, borrowers must therefore be issued such cards and the books must have punched cards in them. When an identification card and a book card are placed in the device, the information from each is read automatically and transmitted by by cable to a remotely located automatic card punch. Information on the loan (the loan period or date) is also transmitted at the same time. Returns are processed in a similar fashion, except that a special identification card is used to indicate that the transaction is a return, not a loan. The transaction cards thus created on the remote punch for both charges and discharges contain all required information on each transaction, and at the end of the day are carried by hand to a computer, where they are used to update a magnetic tape file of all books in circulation or not on the shelf. Overnight, this updated file is printed out and is available the next morning for consultation by library staff and patrons (see Fig. 8-3). At the same time the updating run is being made, overdues are caught, notices are printed, and statistics are compiled.

Many variations have of course been made on this basic pattern. Terminals other than the 357 have been used; return transaction cards in some cases are produced at the same time as the loan transaction cards, and the return card placed in the book; and other processing details may vary. The basic design of the system, however, remains the same.

On-line systems, which began to be implemented in the early 1970s, have one important advantage over 357-type off-line systems: the status of each item's availability is current at all times, whereas in off-line systems one day's activities are not reflected until the next day. On-line systems also eliminate the need for a bulky print-out to be produced each night, although this is not

8. Circulation Systems

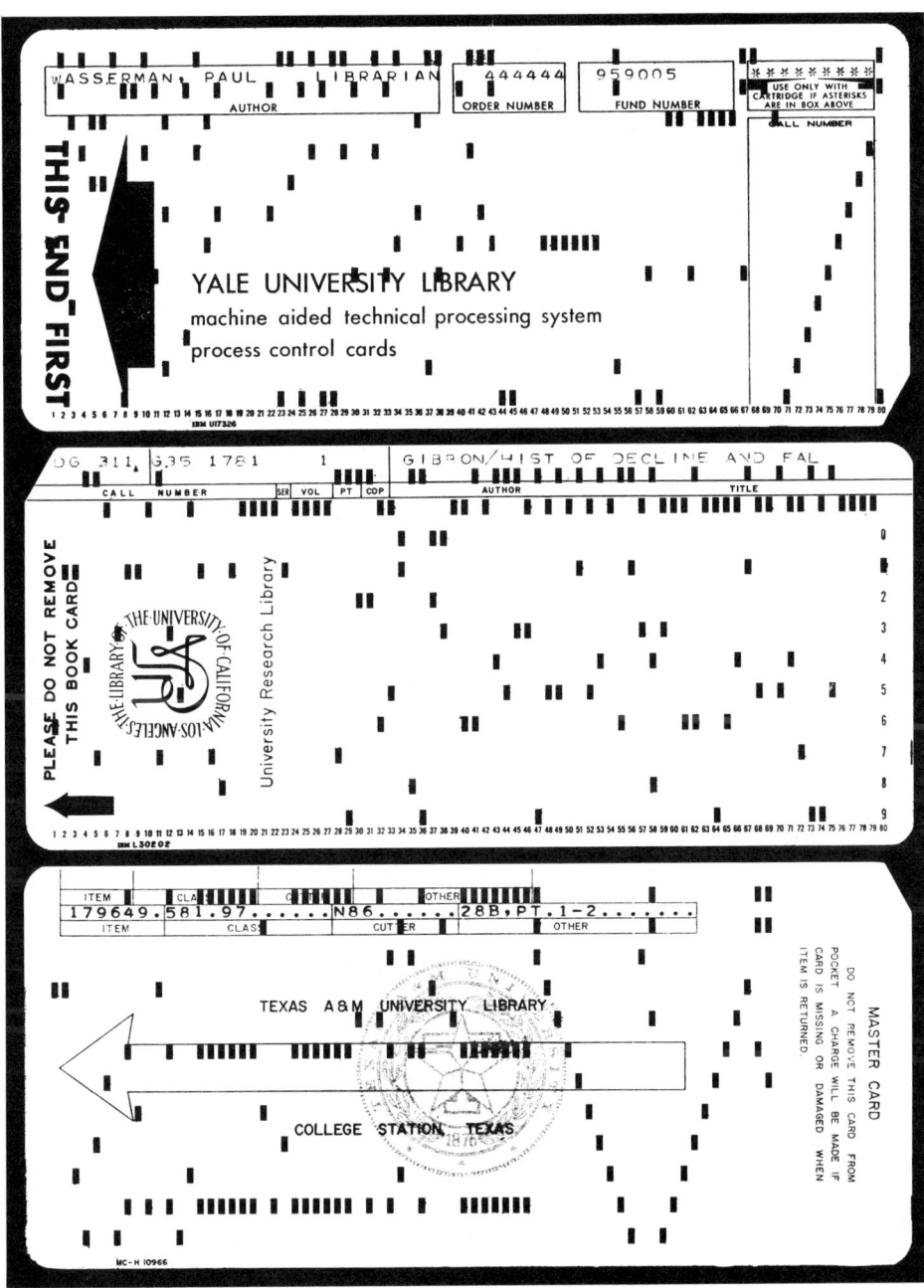

FIG. 8-1. Punched book cards.

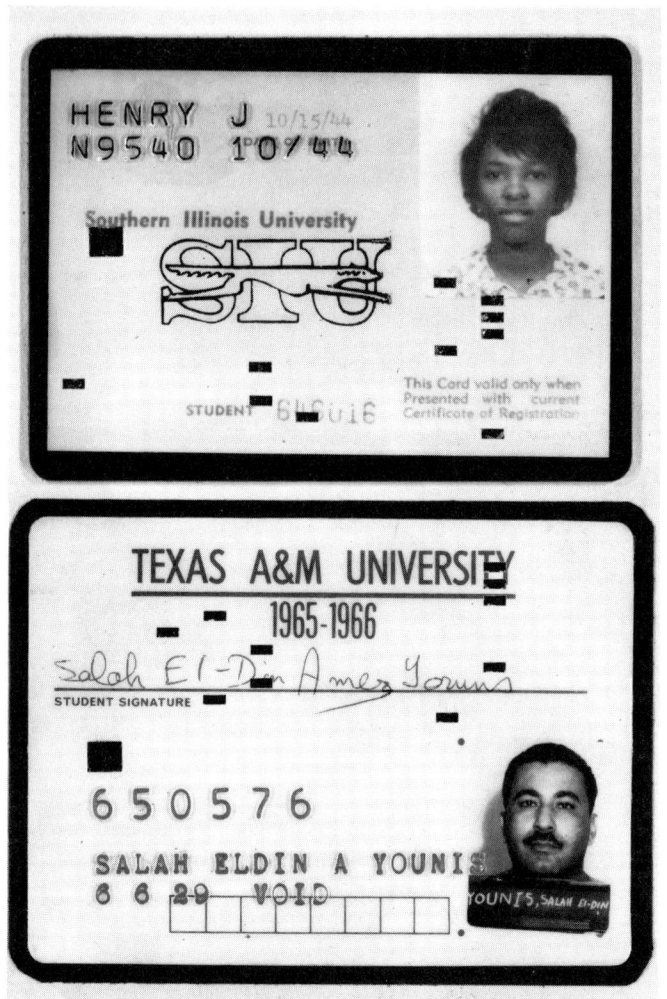

FIG. 8-2. Plastic borrower identification cards.

necessarily an advantage to library users, many of whom prefer to consult a print-out rather than wait in line to have a staff member consult a terminal. The terminals used to enter data may be the same as used in off-line systems, the IBM 1030 for example, or specially designed ones, and inquiry into the status of an item or a borrower may be on typewriter-like terminals, such as the IBM 2740,

TEXAS A+M UNIVERSITY MAIN LIBRARY — BOOKS IN CIRCULATION — AS OF 04/21/66

CALL NUMBER			ITEM	BORROWER	DATE DUE	CALL NUMBER			ITEM	BORROWER	DATE DUE
947.	H758S		362401	1613436000	05/01/66	950.	R877P		266652	3464646619	05/09/66
947.	K41E		357557	5800406033	04/26/66	951.	L359C	1964	406274	1624071000	05/15/66
947.	K96R		149161	1613168000	04/27/66	951.	L359D5		117699	1622254000	05/13/66
947.	L421H		320439	1613168000	04/27/66	951.	L364C		141567	1622254000	05/13/66
947.	M39S	1	32021.	BINDERY	03/17/66	951.	S674R		145971	3465629542	05/19/66
947.	M39S	2	32022.	BINDERY	03/17/66	951.C39	T161B		261041	3454429533	04/24/66
947.	M476R	1962	364517	1632762000	05/20/66	951.042	B427C		174546	BINDERY	02/09/66
947.	M84		5309..	5800406033	04/26/66	951.042	B732A		156210	3454769546	05/13/66
947.	O94		450231	5460801021	05/05/66	951.042	H945B	1953	233197	5449095364	05/20/66
947.	S741I		223871	5460801021	05/05/66	951.042	M819L		169238	BINDERY	02/09/66
947.	S956S		116247	5460801021	05/05/66	951.042	N866M		225859	1612877000	04/18/66
947.	W599S		351681	5800406032	04/26/66	951.0425	S637B		110779	5461121774	05/15/66
947.	W945C	1963	361298	1632762000	05/20/66	951.0425	W183C		279840	1622254000	05/13/66
947.08	J74T		344022	1632762000	05/20/66	951.05	B261COM		402615	1659573000	05/20/66
947.08	L665R		10746.	3454360202	04/20/66	951.05	G957S		284626	3465629542	05/19/66
947.08	M825R		297177	1613436000	05/19/66	951.05	L783S		333694	3565324641	05/19/66
947.08	P228F		101901	RESERVE	02/10/66	951.05	M393N		232560	3483380339	05/20/66
947.08	S495D		215887	RESERVE	02/10/66	951.05	T164C	1, 1961-	350841	5461121774	05/15/66
947.08	S741F		347451	1632762000	05/20/66	951.05	W183C		310231	BINDERY	02/07/66
947.084	AG848H		199460	5800406032	04/26/66	951.14	F469W		415780	1652093000	05/18/66
947.084	A161S		351374	1613436000	05/01/66	951.156	B666P		186951	3465629542	05/19/66
947.084	A659H		404409	5800406033	04/26/66	951.7	C479M		349953	5461121774	05/15/66
947.084	B126D		250590	5456805605	05/20/66	951.9	D282G		233097	1630598000	05/04/66
947.084	C753P		337006	5800406033	04/26/66	951.9	H636W		193392	BINDERY	02/21/66
947.084	D951U		411905	1654774000	05/21/66	951.9	H636W		198259	BINDERY	02/21/66
947.084	E13S		177552	5456805605	05/20/66	951.9	M133K		184167	BINDERY	02/21/66
947.084	F294G		118590	5800406039	05/17/66	951.9	R958L		275760	BINDERY	02/21/66
947.084	H295G		146469	5800406032	04/26/66	951.9042	F296T		365429	BINDERY	02/07/66
947.084	P287T		235116	1654774000	05/21/66	951.9042	F296T		415790	1622950000	05/19/66
947.084	P481A		133445	1654774000	05/21/66	951.9042	F996U		339303	1633660000	05/04/66
947.084	R241H		326981	5800406032	04/26/66	951.9042	H636K		327396	5461121774	05/15/66
947.084	R813H		56717.	1607008000	05/03/66	952.033	T315B		284260	1622578000	04/14/66
947.084	S392R		283383	5800406034	04/27/66	953.	G567G		401852	3478323698	05/01/66
947.084	S674S		141326	3453426044	05/16/66	953.	L423R		205861	BINDERY	02/09/66
947.084	S782L	1	36262.	3453426044	05/16/66	954.	S7411		411874	1642007000	05/13/66
947.084	T858H	1	50043.	3434386282	04/17/66	954.	W195IN		211352	1572747000	05/19/66
947.084	V947W		414897	1654774000	05/21/66	954.04	N396S		408554	1642007000	05/13/66
947.084	W721R		147131	1652355000	05/19/66	956.	AE85S		222796	1623217000	05/07/66
947.0841	B877R	1	342811	5800406039	05/17/66	956.1	C512D		== ==355189	BINDERY	02/09/66
947.0841	B877R	2	342812	5800406039	05/17/66	959.	B981S		417368	BINDERY	03/17/66
947.0841	C319S		414926	1641160000	05/19/66	959.	B989S		344051	1641160000	05/20/66
947.0841	P133L		316459	1659573000	05/20/66	959.	T869S		406343	1584136000	05/06/66
947.0842	M896J		401007	5456805605	05/20/66	959.5	T786M		416718	3466744446	TERM
947.0842	W855C	1961	403339	5800406034	04/27/66	959.7	B947V		410399	3466744446	TERM
947.085	B344H		279630	1654774000	05/21/66	959.7	F194S	1963	366942	3327243760	05/01/66
947.085	S167N		352910	1659573000	05/20/66	959.7	F194T	1963	366163	1632210000	05/12/66
947.085	W855K		276178	5456805605	05/20/66	959.7	H224S		234650	1632210000	05/12/66
948.	O89N		5304..	1460642231	05/14/66	959.7	H772C		365215	5461121774	05/15/66
949.4	B715S		217772	1622606000	05/16/66	959.7	H772C		402634	1613436000	05/11/66
949.4	H561S		163556	1622606000	05/16/66	959.7	S529L		451371	LIB 37	05/14/66
949.6	L524R		150046	1623423000	05/20/66	959.7	T164C		342563	5467806608	05/11/66
949.702	D576C		415587	3453426044	05/16/66	959.7	W281L		364432	1633660000	04/21/66
949.8	B622R		160103	1623423000	05/20/66	960.	A258A	2	370404	1622167000	05/12/66
949.8	M345R		168041	5461121774	05/15/66	960.	B787A		303408	1622167000	05/12/66

FIG. 8-3. List of books in circulation, Texas A & M University Library.

or on visual display (cathode-ray tube) terminals with a keyboard, such as the IBM 2260. As with unit record and off-line systems, the variations from one design to the next are many and warrant study.

Unit record systems

The earliest automated circulation system--indeed, as pointed out earlier, the earliest automated system of any kind to be used in a library--was installed by Ralph Parker at the University of Texas in 1936. As with most unit record systems that followed, the borrower was required to fill out a card, writing out information on both the book and himself. At the end of the day, the date due was gang-punched into the cards, which were then manually filed by call number. Each day the file of outstanding charges was run through an IBM Model 080 sorter to select overdues. Notices were then prepared, and the borrower's number was punched into each card so that all overdues for a particular borrower could be selected at any subsequent time. This step was not performed at the time the initial loan was made, since studies showed only ten percent of the outstanding loans became overdue; delaying the punching until the book became overdue therefore reduced the keypunching of borrower's numbers by 90 percent. When the overdue books were returned, fine amounts were punched into the same card used for the charge, and at the end of the semester the cards were used to tabulate the total amount of fines due from each delinquent borrower.[1]

The University of Florida had a similar system by 1941, and an article describing it mentions others at the University of Virginia and the University of Georgia, as well as at the University of Texas.[2]

In 1948, the Detroit Public Library initiated a unit record system making use of a punched transaction card. The borrower filled out a call slip with the usual information and presented it at the desk; an attendant then took a card with a transaction number prepunched in it, transcribed this number onto the call slip, and put the punched card in the book. The call slip was placed in a file arranged by transaction number. As books were returned, the punched transaction cards were removed from them and collected. Two weeks

8. Circulation Systems

after a due date, the cards were sorted mechanically into transaction number sequence and compared with a master deck on a collator, which selected the master cards with numbers not matched in the transaction card deck. These represented overdues, which were then used to withdraw manually the matching call slips from the loan file. As a final step, the name, address, and other information on the call slip was photographed to produce an overdue notice.[3]

The Brooklyn College Library began a similar transaction card system in February 1950, but (illustrative of the differing requirements of college and public libraries) found the inability to tell who had a particular book unsatisfactory. Accordingly, a new system was begun in June 1958 which many other college and university libraries soon copied. As in the Detroit Public Library system, prepunched transaction cards were used, the transaction number was manually written on a charge record when the loan was made, and the transaction card was placed in the book. Instead of a call slip, however, a blank punch card (a "call card") was used for the charge record, and some of the information written on it by the borrower was punched into the card after the loan was made: specifically, the date due was punched from a program card in the keypunch, and the transaction number as well as the numeric part of the Cutter portion of the call number were punched by the operator. A mechanical sorter was then used to sort the call cards into sequence by Cutter number, and a collator was used to merge them into a loan file arranged in the same sequence. Only three numbers or less from the Cutter portion of the call number were used, in order to reduce the amount of keypunching necessary; up to fifty cards might appear under one number, but apparently this was few enough to make manual searching from that point practicable. The file was also kept small by creating a separate file for extended loans, although this made two places to look in order to locate a book.

As in the Detroit system, the transaction cards were taken out of the returned books and accumulated. The collator was then used to match transaction cards and loan cards, selecting those representing books which had been returned.[4]

The Montclair system

Although the Brooklyn College system just described eliminated such things as the preparation of book cards, filing book cards when the books were charged, and slipping returned books (that is, unfiling the cards and replacing them in the books), it had the disadvantage of requiring the borrower to write out, laboriously, all the required information on himself and on each book he wished to borrow. Systems which automatically read book cards and badges, such as the 357-type system described earlier, ended this imposition, and at the same time eliminated the need for repetitive keypunching of the information by the library staff. One of the landmarks of library automation, therefore, was the installation in 1942 of a prototype of the 357-type system in the Montclair, New Jersey public library. Two "specially designed book charging machines" were connected by cables to a standard reproducing keypunch, and insertion of a borrower's card and a book card automatically punched the information from each into a blank card already in the keypunch. The machine was called a "transaction machine" by its builders, IBM, but was promptly christened "Punching Judy" by the library staff. Judy's products were mechanically sorted into sequence by accession number to create a loan file, and when books were returned the book cards were mechanically duplicated, then matched against the loan file to purge cards for the returned books. The borrower's cards were actually stub cards, not plastic identification cards, but in most respects the system anticipated by over twenty-two years the next important step in the development of automated circulation systems.[5]

Computerized 357-type systems

At Southern Illinois University in Carbondale, Illinois, the Systems and Procedures Office had begun studying the library's circulation problems in December 1960. A young graduate student in management took an interest in the situation, extended the study, incorporated it in a master's thesis, then stayed on the university staff to design the system and see it into operation. Discussions

8. Circulation Systems

and improvements to the design took place in 1962 and 1963, and the system was finally put into full operation in May 1964.

The studies by the Systems and Procedures Office had revealed a marked similarity between library circulation procedures and industrial inventory control, and the key element in the new system was an industrial data collection device, the IBM 357. Introduced by IBM in 1959, this unit had been used by industry for remote recording of job processing and attendance reporting, as well as for inventory control, but had not yet been used by librarians.

SIU's first design was a "two-card" system, rather than the one-card system described earlier; that is, two transaction cards were produced at the time a loan was made rather than one. The second card was withdrawn from the keypunch and placed in the book as the loan was made; on return, the card could then be withdrawn for processing and the book sent immediately to the shelf. The advantage of this method is that rapid reshelving is possible; the disadvantage is that the keypunch must be located at the circulation desk, so that the second cards can be taken from it as each loan is recorded, and a considerable amount of noise near the circulation desk results. The cost of equipment is also increased, since a keypunch must be located at each circulation point; in the SIU system, one automatic keypunch was installed for every two 357 charging units, and for the three charging points this made a total of six 357s and three keypunches. Despite such minor disadvantages, however, the new system has been successful and widely influential.

The method used by SIU to create book cards for its collection is also of interest. The Systems and Procedures Office developed a coding sheet which could be marked with pencils and scanned optically to produce the required punched cards, thus avoiding manual keypunching (see Fig. 8-4). Students transferred call numbers from the library's shelflist to the code sheets, eight volumes to a sheet. An optical scanner at a commercial firm converted the code sheets to punched book cards which were then printed out so that the print-out could be compared with the shelflist to discover any errors.[6]

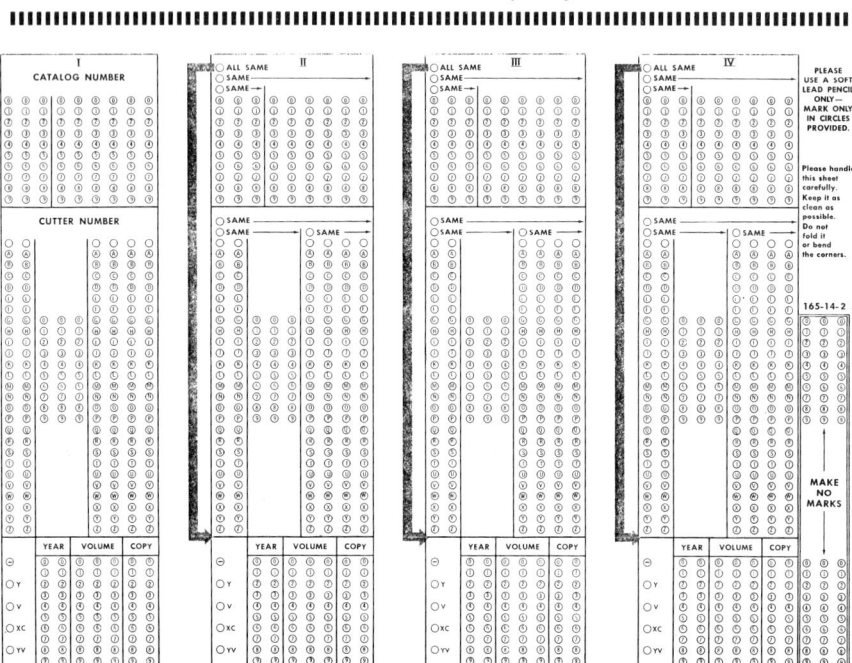

FIG. 8-4. Call number coding sheet, Southern Illinois University Library.

Other 357 systems followed SIU's in rapid succession. Florida Atlantic University implemented an almost identical one in September 1964,[7] and later that same year Rice University[8] and the University of Missouri[9] built systems using 357 devices for data collection but unit record equipment for processing. Essentially the same as SIU's up to the creation of transaction cards, these latter two systems then used sorters and collators to place the transaction cards in sequence, to match returns against the file, and to select overdues. Both of these systems were later transferred to computers.

Early in 1965 the first computerized 357 system of the one-card variety was implemented at Washington University in St. Louis. An automated cataloging system which had already been implemented produced punched book cards as a by-product, so some book cards were already available. Rather than produce book cards for the rest of

8. Circulation Systems   193

the collection in a mass effort, a procedure was worked out for creating them as each book circulated. Two identical decks of book cards, prepunched only with sequential identification numbers, were placed at the circulation desk. When a book was presented for charging and had no machine-readable book card, the old typed card was retained and one of the prepunched cards was used to make the transaction and then placed in the book. The second prepunched card was then clipped to the typed book card, and later the information from the typed card was keypunched into the new book card. This completed book card was then used to update the magnetic tape loan file. The new book card was retained in a special file, and when the book was returned the distinctive color of the dummy book card in the back of the book told the staff to retrieve the prepared book card and insert it in the book. The active portion of the collection was thus identified automatically by the borrowers, and could be converted first, and books which never circulated could be converted last or not at all. More importantly to the library at that time, the system could be put into operation months earlier than if a mass conversion had been required first. As expected, a sharp decline in the number of books presented for charging without a punched book card resulted after a few months, and the keypunch operator could then begin systematic conversion of selected portions of the collection.

The Washington University system differed from SIU's in two other significant respects. The SIU book cards contained call numbers only, in addition to control punches and a unique identification number. Washington University felt that overdue notices required further identification of the book, and that brief author and title would be desirable not only for overdues and other notices but for the daily printout of the loan file as well. Accordingly, the book cards were designed to contain truncated author and title entries as well as call number, identification number, and control punches. A special wiring of the 047 tape-to-card converter that produced the book cards from the cataloging system's punched tape enabled the author and title to be truncated and punched automatically for new books, and the brief information was already on the typed cards in the older books so the keypunch operator could transcribe it. The second variation was in the input mechanism; instead of a keyboard entry for the date due, special cartridges were used which could be set for the various loan periods at the beginning of the day, and could then be placed in a slot to input the information automatically when loan transactions were made.[10]

Texas A & M University installed a two-card system later in 1965 which made an interesting provision for processing "holds" placed by persons waiting for the return of a particular book. The identification numbers of the items for which holds were requested were punched into cards, which were then kept in accession number sequence. Before returned books were shelved, the return cards were sorted into accession number sequence, and a collator was used to match these cards against the hold cards. If a match was found, the appropriate book was removed from the book truck used for shelving, and the hold request was processed as usual.[11]

By the following year (1966), numerous other libraries had reported installation of similar systems, and one writer knew of over fifty libraries using the 357.[12] Many of these systems later switched from the 357 to the 1030, a faster, quieter, and more reliable data collection device, although the system design remained basically the same. The 1030 had other advantages over the 357 which made it increasingly popular: it needed only two wires to connect it with a remote punch instead of dozens; it utilized an automatic punch (1034) with much higher punching speed than the regular 026 punch; and it could even be connected on-line to a computer.

Because of these features, many libraries began directly with 1030 units instead of starting with 357s. Certainly the largest of the examples reported in the literature is the one at the University of British Columbia. Twenty-nine 1031 units of two types are used in this system, plus a PDP-11 minicomputer to control them and create the daily transaction tapes. The processing itself is done on a Honeywell 200 and an IBM 370 Model 155. Brief author and title information are contained on the book cards, and charging and returns

8. Circulation Systems 195

are by the one-card method. Book cards were created for those books known to have been circulated during the nine months prior to the introduction of the system, and with this as a start approximately 50 percent of the books circulated during the first year had book cards when presented for charging. Cards for the rest were generated as they circulated; by the second year, 75 percent presented for charging already had book cards, the third year 90 percent, and the fifth year 98 percent.[13]

Statistics typically gathered by such circulation systems have been particularly well used at British Columbia. Loan policies have been modified, duplicate copies of heavily used items have been obtained, and acquisition policies have been modified, all on the basis of use statistics gathered by the system.[14]

Many libraries with 357-type systems have elected not to handle reserve books with it; ordinarily there is up to one day's delay in updating the information, since the loan file typically is printed out by the computer overnight, and thus the system would be of little use for two-hour or even one-day reserves. At the University of Michigan, however, a 1030 system has been installed specifically to handle reserve books. Four 1031 terminals and a high-speed 1034 punch are used, along with a 1032 time clock. The time is automatically punched into the transaction cards by the 1032 attachment, and the time due is stamped in the book with a time clock device. (One unusual problem is that a full minute must be allowed to elapse before a returned book can be charged out again, since the system does not deal in seconds.) Transaction cards are processed by the computer at night, and a listing of fines due, the overdue notices and a statistical report are provided to the Reserve Room the next day. Approximately 1,200 fine notices and 2,300 overdue notices are produced each month. The statistics are used for scheduling staff, to determine the need for additional copies of reserve books, and in some instances to suggest to professors that their reserve lists should be revised.[15]

Several interesting variations on the 357-1030 theme should be noted. In most cases, these systems operate in basically the same

196   Library Automation Systems

fashion once the transaction records have been produced: a computer uses the records to update a master file, either on tape or disk, simultaneously adding new charges, deleting returns, noting overdues, recalls and holds, and finally producing a large print-out of the file in call number order. The variations occur in the method used to capture the basic transaction information and in the equipment which is employed.

One of the earliest and certainly the most unusual example is the system at Johns Hopkins University library. Books to be charged are placed in a wooden holder, spines to the front, along with the student identification card, and the resulting arrangement is photographed with a microfilm camera located beneath the desk (see Fig. 8-5). The film is then developed, placed on a microfilm reader, and a keypunch operator reads the call numbers and identification numbers

FIG. 8-5. Microfilm camera for circulation system, Johns Hopkins University Library.

8. Circulation Systems   197

from the screen and keypunches them to make the transaction cards
(see Fig. 8-6). When the books are returned the same process is
repeated. The entire system was devised by the university's Operations Research group and was widely publicized, but there are
obvious disadvantages: information from the books and from identification cards must be keypunched repetitively (twice for the book
each time a loan is made), microfilm development imposes at least
an overnight delay, and reading call numbers from a microfilm reader
screen is unlikely to make for fast and error-free keypunching. Despite these seeming handicaps, the system was still in operation in
1974, nine years after it had been installed.[16]

Michigan State University used a Friden Collectadata System 30
instead of a 357 or 1030. Since the university had no student identification cards when the system was designed, the Friden unit was
chosen partly on the basis of its ability to accept two punched cards

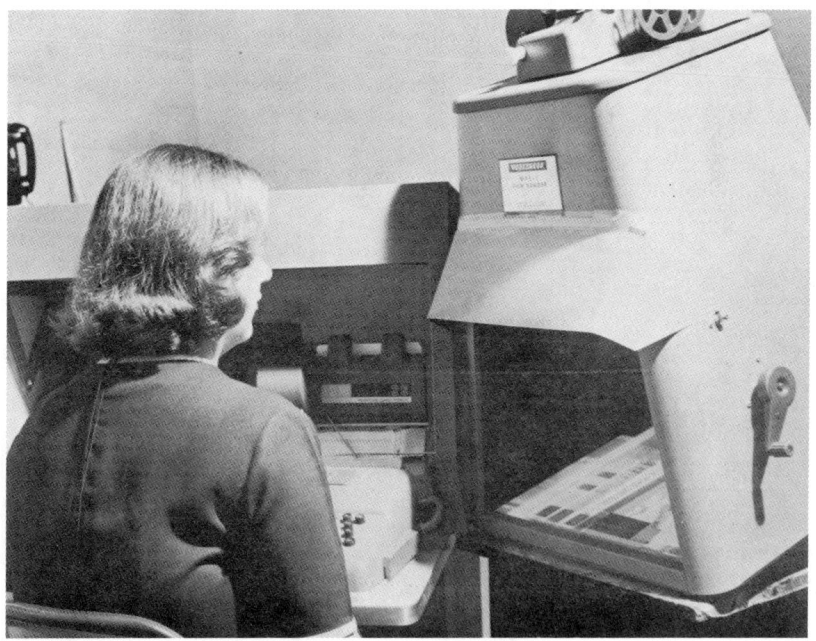

FIG. 8-6. Keypunching transaction cards from microfilm.

instead of one card and one "badge." Paper tape records of transactions are produced instead of punched cards, and the paper tape is then passed through an IBM 047 tape-to-card converter to produce punched cards. From that point on the system is basically the same as others already described.[17] Another punched tape system, using Control Data Corporation Transacter terminals, has been installed at the Santa Clara, California public library.[18]

One of the most popular alternatives to the IBM devices has been a terminal manufactured by Colorado Instruments (see Fig. 8-7). One of the earliest to use this system was the Washington State University library, which installed it in 1967. Three terminals are used, connected to a "C-Dek" incremental tape recorder which records the transactions on magnetic tape. Processing is done on an IBM 360 Model 67 operating in batch mode as a Model 65. Operating costs are

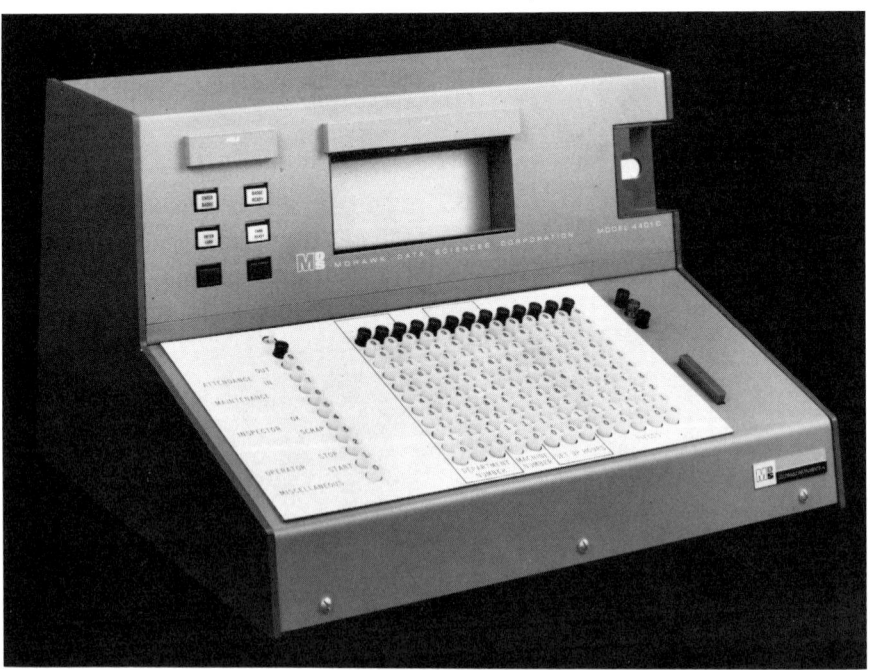

FIG. 8-7. Colorado Instruments circulation terminal.

8. Circulation Systems 199

estimated at 52 cents per transaction, and development costs at $60,000.[19] Rice University switched to Colorado Instruments terminals in 1970, and two other libraries, Syracuse University and the University of Colorado, have reported similar systems. The Syracuse installation includes a strip printer which makes self-charging possible; the student inserts his identification card and the book cards in the terminal, and in turn receives a brief print-out of the transaction which is torn off and shown to the guard at the door on leaving the library.[20] The University of Colorado system produces a 16 mm microfilm cartridge containing an updated list of books on loan instead of the conventional print-out, with estimated savings in production costs of $12,000 yearly.

The Standard Register Company manufactures a data collection device similar to the IBM and Colorado Instruments units, called a "Source Record Punch," which has also been used successfully in some libraries.[21]

Not all computer-based circulation systems have used data collection devices, machine-readable identification cards, and punched book cards, of course. Several large universities and many special libraries still use manual keypunching to capture the basic information on borrower, borrowed item and loan, then process this information by computer. The data collection technique is the same as with most unit record systems: a charge (or "call") slip is filled out by the borrower, and the information is then keypunched. Many of these systems began as unit record systems, in fact, and the processing activities were merely transferred to computers when computer time was available.

Perhaps the largest and best example of this type is the system at Harvard University's Widener Library. Almost three million volumes are housed in Widener, all without book cards. A unit record system to handle circulation of these volumes was initiated in 1963, but was redesigned to operate on a 1401 in 1968 in order to obtain a printout of books on loan. Transaction cards are still inserted in books and used to indicate returns, however, and a file of duplicate transaction cards arranged by due date is still used to trigger overdue notices. Costs are estimated at 56 cents per transaction.[22]

Columbia University has used another such system with a powerful IBM 360 Model 75 computer complex doing the processing,[23] and the University of California at Los Angeles went through several versions requiring borrowers to fill out call cards before finally converting to a 1030 system in 1966.[24] Among special library systems, two of the most notable are those at the Picatinny Arsenal in Dover, New Jersey and at IBM's Research Library in Yorktown, New York. The Picatinny system was implemented in April 1962 on a 1401, and thus was one of the earliest computerized circulation systems.[25] The IBM Thomas J. Watson Research Library uses book cards with call number and brief author and title punched in them much the same as in a 357-type system; the borrower, however, must write out his name, company employee number, department, room, telephone extension, and date on the card, and all of this information is later punched manually (rather than automatically) directly into the card. Once a week, the transaction cards thus created are used to update a magnetic tape file of the items on loan, arranged alphabetically by author. If a transaction card is missing from the deck, a return is simply assumed, and the record is erased from the tape. For the next loan, a fresh book card is punched with the book information and kept at the circulation desk awaiting the return of the item. An alphabetical author listing of items on loan is also produced, as well as a list arranged by borrower and a list of overdue items.[26]

On-line circulation systems

More on-line systems have been installed for circulation control than for any other purpose. Not all of these are full on-line systems, however, since some do not use on-line techniques for inquiry or for full interaction with the computer files. Typically, these partially on-line systems (if they may be called that) provide a means of preventing delinquent borrowers from completing loans, much as point-of-sale business systems perform credit checks on-line.

8. Circulation Systems   201

They may also provide for listing specific information on the delinquencies involved, but they do not allow on-line inquiry into the status of particular books.

The first such partially on-line system to be reported was installed at the Illinois State Library in December 1966. Four stations combining a 1031 data collection terminal and a 1033 printer were connected through an IBM 1026 transmission control unit to an IBM 1620 computer (renamed a "1710" by IBM because of the "remote processing" capabilities the addition of the 1026 made possible). When a charge is attempted in the usual way for 357 or 1030 systems, the computer checks the borrower number and if the patron is a "valid borrower" (i.e., is not delinquent) the transaction is processed. When a similar transaction is made for returns, the computer prints on the 1033 printer the call number and patron number for any holds placed on the book, and the book can then be turned over to a clerk for notification of the waiting borrower. Often transactions are not processed until night, so despite the on-line feature the records are never completely current, nor is it possible to determine through the on-line capability whether a book is charged out or not.[27] Since this is a state library, this limitation is less of a disadvantage than it would be for a university system.

A unique and technically interesting partial on-line system was implemented at Midwestern University in Wichita Falls, Texas late in 1967, using the mundane workhorse computer of the 1960s, a 1401. In 1975, it was still going strong. A 1031 and a 1033 printer are connected through a 1026 transmission control, as at Illinois. When a loan is attempted and the borrower is delinquent, his delinquencies are printed out on the 1033, and if there is no address on file for the borrower, a message is printed indicating that fact. A special inquiry capability also allows the library to list on the 1033 printer all items charged to a patron, his overdues, and any outstanding fines, a feature important for clearing students who are leaving the university. When books are returned, the printer also prints a receipt. Each book card has the loan period punched into it, so there is no need for multiple date-due cartridges or manual entry, and reserve books may be shelved with the main collection. The loan period is automatically extended or shortened if a code in the borrower's identification code so indicates--faculty, for example, have a longer loan period and citizens in the area have a shorter period.[28] Midwestern is justifiably proud of this imaginative use of a second-generation computer.

In 1972, IBM introduced a small system for circulation control with capabilities similar to the Illinois State and Midwestern systems, called the "System 7." The first installation was at the University of Pennsylvania, where it replaced a 1030 system in use since 1969. The System 7 uses IBM 2791 terminals, which accept punched book cards and plastic identification badges like the 1030, but also have provision for keying in data and an "Operator Guidance Panel" which can display up to 32 different messages to help staff members complete transactions correctly. Four terminals are installed in the main library, and one in each of three branch libraries, all on-line to the System 7's computer, a small (14,000-byte) unit with a fixed disk. Only a small amount of data is actually on-line however: the accession numbers and call numbers of books on hold for other patrons and for books on reserve, plus the borrower numbers of patrons who are delinquent or whose cards have been lost, etc. In effect, the files collectively constitute a "hold" file of books and borrowers, and serve to "trap" either books or borrowers in any of the categories mentioned. No on-line inquiry is possible; the transactions are recorded as they take place, much as in 357-type systems, and at night the information is transferred for processing to a large IBM 370 Model 168 computer at "UNI-COLL," a computer consortium serving a group of colleges and universities in the Philadelphia area. The overnight print-out feature common to 357 and 1030 systems is retained for inquiry purposes.

Other System 7 installations have been reported at American, Georgetown, and Howard Universities in Washington, D.C., the University of Ottawa and Slippery Rock State College in Pennyslvania. American University uses two 1053 printers to create receipts for

8. Circulation Systems

fines paid, and Georgetown University uses a printer for fine receipts, exit passes, and brief messages.[29]

In competition with IBM, the Singer Company is marketing the Singer 10 system with accompanying Singer Model 100 terminals. The first system was installed in the University of Maryland library early in 1973. In Maryland's case the processing is done by the library's Univac 9300 computer or the university's Univac 1108; the operation of the system itself, however, is almost identical to the System 7.[30]

On-line circulation systems with full inquiry capabilities

The first reported on-line circulation system with full capabilities for inquiry was implemented at the Bell Telephone Laboratories in Murray Hill, New Jersey in March 1968. Dubbed the BELLREL (for Bell Laboratories' Library Real-time Loan) system, it uses six IBM 1050 terminals (each consisting of a 1052 keyboard/printer and a 1056 card reader) on-line to a 370 Model 155. Two of the terminals are in Murray Hill, two at another library in Holmdel, and two more at a third library in Whippany, New Jersey, these three being the largest libraries of Bell Laboratories. Together, they make some 500,000 loans per year, and the automated system handles 75 percent of these. Ninety-two percent of all titles held (about 100,000) are recorded in the system, and inquiry as to the status of any of these items is possible; up-to-the-minute information is available on all items off the shelves and on copies still available for use. To charge an item, a book card is read by the card reader, and the borrower identification number is typed on the keyboard. If a book card is not available for the item, the book identification number is also keyed. Total elapsed time averages twenty-three seconds for a single loan, fifteen seconds per loan for multiple transactions. Returns are made by typing a return code, and then reading the book cards or typing in the book identification numbers. Holds (called "reservations" in this system) are caught at the time of return, and a loan to the waiting borrower is made automatically. An inquiry code elicits a printed response which gives the status of all copies of a work, accompanied by statistics such as the number of holds on the title. Other queries provide listings of the items charged to a particular person, circulation records of particular items, and circulation records of particular persons. In all, there are eleven different types of inquiry possible and twenty-two types of transactions. During the first year, down-time was higher than expected, due mainly to failures in equipment and the programs which came with the original computer (a 360 Model 40); no extended periods of down time have occurred, however. Costs have been appreciably higher than the former manual system, but the new system's users and developers apparently feel these are offset by the improved service made possible.[31]

Another on-line circulation system with full inquiry capabilities was implemented the same year (1968) at Eastern Illinois University. Two 1031 card-and-badge readers and one 1033 printer are located at the circulation desk, along with a 3277 visual display terminal for inquiry. Information on most circulating items can be obtained, although infrequently circulated books have been removed from the file to conserve space on the disk which stores the machine-readable records; such books must be checked out by manual means. As books are checked in, the printer provides notification of any which are overdue or on hold for another borrower, but only one hold per book can be handled by the program. A variety of inquiries can be made, in addition to inquiry on the status of particular items. One code, for example, retrieves the name, address, and telephone number of a patron, and another retrieves the first book in a classification number; if the "next" button is pressed, succeeding books in that subject classification can be displayed, providing a form of terminal browsing. A variety of statistical reports and listings is also available. The circulation history of a book can be provided, as can the borrowing history of an individual, a fact that has given rise to some anxiety regarding possible invasion of privacy. Collection use can be analyzed for subject fields, defined broadly or narrowly, and collection development policies can be modified as a result. Costs in 1970/71 were seventy-six cents per circulation,

8. Circulation Systems   205

or twenty cents per transaction, counting all transactions; it should
be noted, however, that the library is required to share in subsi-
dizing free computer time for students and faculty, as well as paying regular computer rates, and this has undoubtedly inflated the
cost of computer services.[32]

Two important on-line systems were implemented in 1970, both
at major universities. The first, at Northwestern University, is
especially noteworthy for its emphasis on self-service charging.
Four book-charging stations, each consisting of an IBM 1031 card-
and-badge reader and a 1033 printer, are available for this purpose
(see Fig. 8-8). The borrower inserts his identification card and
the book card, in response to which the printer produces a date due
slip to be torn off and placed in the book. If the identification
card or book card cannot be read by the terminal, or if the book is
charged to Reserve or to a carrel, or if the badge number is "blocked"
(because the card has been reported lost--"delinquents" are apparently not blocked) the printed slip merely says "UNPROCESSED" and the

FIG. 8-8. Northwestern University book charging station.

would-be borrower is instructed to go to the main circulation desk. Persistent problems have been experienced with paper jams in the printers, and all efforts by IBM and the university's Physics Shop have so far not solved the problem. A ticket-ejector system is scheduled for trial next, and the library hopes this will provide a solution.

Lost badges have also been a problem. Users leave them in the terminals, and others then take them; when this happens and is reported, the user's number is blocked and a new badge is issued. Blocking is done only once a day, however, so "a determined thief can charge out a considerable number of books before the number can be blocked."[33]

Inquiry is made on a single 2740 terminal at the circulation desk. Only books not on the shelves are recorded (about 50,000 to 60,000 volumes on the average) so the information available is limited. Inquiry is by call number only, and holds (called "saves" in this system) are also entered via the terminal using the inquiry feature. The computer used is a 370 Model 135 (originally a 360 Model 30), and a generalized file management system handles other university programs as well as this one. Costs are estimated at sixty-seven cents per circulation. Unlike other systems, very little management information is provided, apparently because the categories of information desired have not yet been identified. A peculiar problem is that books returned without a date-due slip are held in the circulation department and not shelved until the date due has passed, for fear someone will have intentionally withheld the slip, will find the book and insert the slip, and will then be able to carry away an uncharged book. On-line "validation of users" and "automatic regulation of loan privileges" have been considered but not implemented because of the cost and time that would be required. Despite these imperfections, some minor problems and a few peculiarities, the staff nevertheless seems pleased with the system and committed to its use.[34]

The second important on-line system implemented in 1970, the Ohio State University system, takes an approach opposite to that of

8. Circulation Systems

Northwestern so far as borrower participation is concerned. Instead of self-service charging, the Ohio State system requires the circulation staff to type the borrower's identification number and the book's call number on an IBM 2740 typewriter terminal. Returns are also processed by staff members manually keying in the call number, and only the "home" terminals (that is, the terminal or terminals in the main or branch library to which the book is assigned) can process returns, in order to prevent erroneous or mischievous return of books at other terminals.

Charging by the staff makes telephone borrowing by the patrons possible, and this feature (coupled with a campus mail and delivery service) has understandably been popular. (Circulation rose by 40 percent in the first 18 months after installation.) Over one million titles have been entered into the on-line files, and the information, although brief, is sufficient to enable the system to be used by borrowers as an on-line union catalog for the entire university. More than fifty terminals (including IBM 2260 visual display units as well as 2740 typewriter terminals) have been placed around campus, and borrowers use them to inquire as to the status of items. If no terminal is convenient, they may telephone a library staff member to perform the search for them. Inquiries are made by keying only a few characters, normally the first four letters of the author's last name and the first five letters of the first significant word of the title (foreign language articles are considered "significant," since it was felt that the majority of users would not be able to distinguish significant from nonsignificant words in foreign languages). Searches can also be made by author or by title alone, and by call number (not, however, by subject). A brief listing of items conforming to search criteria may be obtained or the full record of each item can be called up. Once the desired items are identified, the system indicates whether they are available, and if so they may be borrowed by telephone and delivered by messenger, all without physically going to the library. These features are in line with Ohio State's philosophy of encouraging decentralized library service and maximizing convenience to the user.

The use by the reference department is also of interest.

The checking of standard reference books, especially bibliographies, for those items which we hold is now being done on a large scale. The reference librarians use the terminal provided in the reference department not only for such housekeeping routines as charging to themselves the latest volume of those series labeled "latest volume in Reference," but also for answering catalog information questions. Since so much of reference work is the matching of bibliographic sources against library holdings, there is extensive use of the terminal in that department, although very little actual "charging" and "discharging" is performed.[35]

Naturally all of this is achieved at some cost, both in system development and staff time. Total costs of the system have not been reported, but the programming was contracted to IBM for $225,000, and the data conversion to another firm for approximately $95,000 (conversion of slightly more than 736,000 titles cost an average of 12.8 cents per title). The average cost per transaction has been calculated at 42 cents, counting charges, discharges, searches and clerical costs. However, if reserve transactions and their associated costs are excluded (they are still handled manually, and account for almost one-half of the transactions) the cost of other transactions rises to about a dollar.[36]

Two other on-line circulation systems which use terminals in either the 2740 series or the 2260 series in conjunction with 1030 card-and-badge readers have been reported in the literature. The University of Manitoba uses two 1031s and three 2741 typewriter terminals on-line to a 360 Model 65. A high-speed 1034 punch is used as a back-up system in case the computer is "down" for some reason, and in such a case the system functions as a regular, off-line 1030 system; transaction cards created by the 1034 are simply fed back into the computer when it is up again.

Only the books charged out are on file, and inquiry is by call number. The reply to an inquiry is the borrower's identification number, the call number of the book, the due date, any holds, and renewal information. If the computer does not find a complete record, the reply given is "book not on loan," "book loaned today,"

8. Circulation Systems

or "book returned today," the latter two messages necessitated by the fact that complete updating of loan records occurs only once a day.

Manitoba has used its system to take a step many librarians have long dreamed of, the elimination of the fine system.

> When a borrower who has overdue materials attempts to borrow again, a message is received on the 2741 informing the loan desk that "borrower # ___ has ___ books overdue," and the loan is refused. If he asks what items he has overdue another staff member shows him the overdue list.
>
> The rationale for this method of control rests in the experience of the library. The last complete year during which fines were in force, over $13,000 was collected at the main circulation desk alone. At 25 cents per day this represented 52,000 overdue days without taking into account that the maximum fine was $5.00 per item. In other words, the fine system did not achieve the objective for which it was designed. Fines were punishment for those whose means were slim, but no deterrent for those who could afford the luxury of keeping books as long as they wanted regardless of the needs of other borrowers. The change was welcomed almost unanimously by student borrowers. Faculty, who had never been subject to fines, were understandably not so enthusiastic. However, all but a few now accept this as a reasonable system of control.[37]

At Western Kentucky University in Bowling Green, a system with 6 IBM 2260 display terminals and five 1031s was implemented in 1972, on-line to a 360 Model 40. In this system, the visual display terminals are available for students and faculty to use in locating materials, a popular capability since the library is spread over ten floors in two buildings and use of the terminals saves much footwork and time if the books are already checked out. Many users record the book identification numbers from the catalog (these were added in the process of reclassification, as described in Chapter 5), check the numbers on the terminals, and only then go to the stacks to find the books which are not already checked out. Only certain information on books checked out is available at the public terminals; for obvious reasons, the programs have been written so that the terminals cannot be used to obtain the names and addresses of library users, or the identification of the borrowers of particular books.

It should be noted that searching in the Western Kentucky system is by item number only; author and title searching capabilities are planned as soon as disk storage space is available.[38]

Light-pen systems

A recent technological development which appears to be ushering in a new era of automated circulation systems is the use of "light pens" (see Fig. 8-9). A beam of light is projected from the end of the pen, bounced off self-adhesive labels which have patterns of bars printed on them, and then picked up by another part of the pen. The pattern of light and dark created by the so-called "zebra" labels is translated into a digital number, which can then be used for either off-line or on-line processing. Each book is given a label with a unique identification number, and a similar label with a unique borrower number is placed on the borrowers' identification cards.

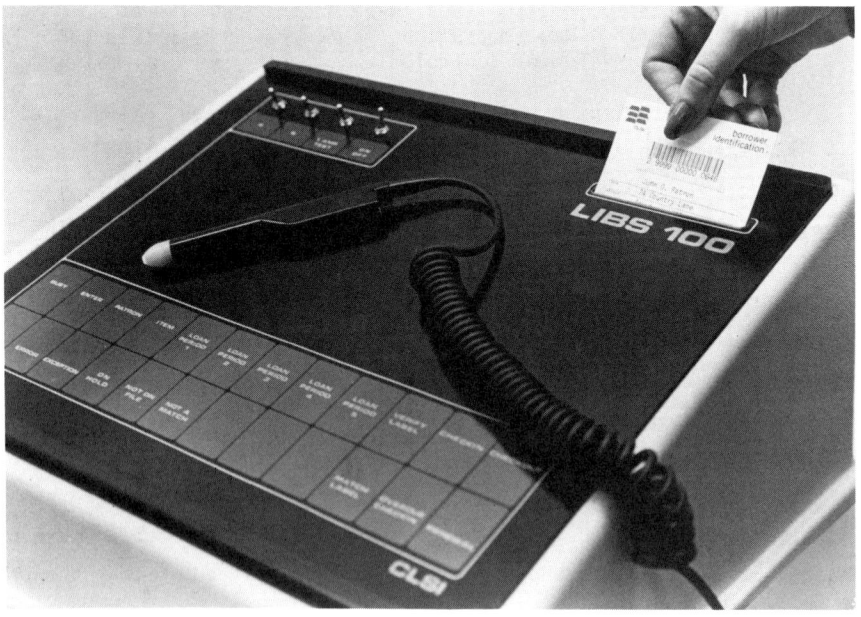

FIG. 8-9. CLSI light-pen terminal.

8. Circulation Systems 211

The advantages to the light-pen method of data capture are numerous. No preparation of punched or typed book cards is necessary, and the problem of lost or mutilated book cards is eliminated; no special borrower identification card is necessary, only a place to stick the small label; mechanical and card-jamming problems associated with card-and-badge readers are avoided; and the act of passing the light pen across the book label and the borrower label is perhaps the fastest and simplest checking-out and checking-in method possible.

Light-pen systems were first used routinely for circulation systems in Great Britain, beginning about 1972, and by the following year there were at least eight such systems in operation. All of these utilize light pens manufactured by the Plessey Company, and all are off-line. When the borrower and book numbers are read by the pen device, the information is recorded on a magnetic tape cassette housed in the unit. A converter is used to reformat the information in conventional magnetic tape form for processing off-line by computer. Plessey also makes a small electronic "trapping store" which can contain several thousand numbers in machine-readable form; with this unit added, books on hold can be trapped when they are returned, as can delinquent borrowers when they attempt to charge out more books.[39]

The first light-pen systems in the United States were implemented in 1974. The University of South Carolina library began operating an off-line system in January of that year, using Monarch light pens and labels, a PDP-11 minicomputer to collect machine-readable information, and a large IBM 360 Model 65 computer in the university's computer center to process the information each night. The list of books on loan is printed out daily, both in full-size and in computer-output-microfiche (COM). A Hazeltine 2000 visual display unit is also employed, not for inquiry but to show transactions as they occur. Much of the system was designed and built by staff members in the library, the computer center, and the university's Computer Science Department.[40]

On-line light-pen systems with full inquiry capabilities

Later in 1974, CLSI (Computer Library Services Inc.) began installation of on-line circulation systems using light pens and visual display units on-line to a small minicomputer. Each system is self-contained, and all programs are supplied by CLSI.^{41} Separate packages of programs are supplied depending on whether the library is a public library or an academic library; the first public library installation was in Marin County, California and the first academic library installation at the University of Houston.

In the latter system (called "Phred," for no particular reason), the configuration is seven visual display units, three light-pen units, and three printers, all on-line to a small PDP-11 Model 05 computer housed in the library. The total purchase price for both the circulation system and an acquisition system using the same computer was $159,100, including the programming and staff training performed by CLSI. Inquiry via terminal provides information on all books in the library, not merely on books charged out, provided of course that the bibliographic information has first been entered into the system; Houston is entering this information as books circulate the first time, except that all new books processed since implementation of the system are also entered. Searching is by author or an author-title key. Parts of some programs are still under development to solve special problems; for example, the provisions for adding an additional volume of a serial or series to the file limit the number of such volumes to one hundred, after which a second record must be constructed. Despite such isolated defects, however, the system provides remarkably smooth, efficient and economical circulation, combining the advantages discussed earlier of both on-line and light-pen technologies.

NOTES

1. Ralph H. Parker, "The Punched Card Method in Circulation Work," *Library Journal*, 61, 903-905 (December 1, 1936).

8. Circulation Systems

2. E. Carl Pratt, "International Business Machines' Use in Circulation Department, University of Florida Library," *Library Journal*, 61, 302-303 (April 1, 1942).

3. Ralph H. Parker, *Library Applications of Punched Cards: a Description of Mechanical Systems*, American Library Association, Chicago, 1952, pp. 26-27; and Arthur Yabroff, "Circulation Control at the Detroit Public Library," in *IBM Library Mechanization Symposium, Endicott, New York, May 25, 1964*, International Business Machines, White Plains, N.Y. [1965?], pp. 37-42.

4. Henry Birnbaum, *General Information Manual, IBM Circulation Control at Brooklyn College Library*, International Business Machines, White Plains, N.Y., 1960.

5. Margery Quigley, "Library Facts from International Business Machine Cards," *Library Journal*, 66, 1065-1067 (December 15, 1941); and Quigley, "Ten Years of IBM," *Library Journal*, 77, 1152-1157 (July 1952).

6. *An Automated Circulation Control System for the Delyte W. Morris Library*, Southern Illinois University, Carbondale, Illinois, 1963; L. R. DeJarnett, "Library Circulation," in *IBM Library Mechanization Symposium, Endicott, New York, May 25, 1964*, International Business Machines, White Plains, N.Y. [1965?], pp. 78-94; and Ralph E. McCoy, "Computerized Circulation Work: a Case Study of the 357 Data Collection System," *Library Resources & Technical Services*, 9, 59-65 (Winter 1965).

7. Edward Heiliger, "Florida Atlantic University Library," in *Proceedings of the 1965 Clinic on Library Applications of Data Processing*, University of Illinois Graduate School of Library Science, Urbana, 1966, pp. 92-111.

8. Frederick Ruecking, Jr., *Circulation Control at Rice University Using the IBM 357 Data Collection System*, International Business Machines, White Plains, N.Y. [1965?].

9. Ralph H. Parker, "Development of Automatic Systems at the University of Missouri Library," in *Proceedings of the 1963 Clinic on Library Applications of Data Processing*, University of Illinois Graduate School of Library Science, Urbana, 1964, pp. 48-55; and Parker, "Not a Shared System," *Library Journal*, 92, 3967-3970 (November 1, 1967).

10. Stephen R. Salmon, "Automation of Library Procedures at Washington University," *Missouri Library Association Quarterly*, 27, 11-14 (March 1966).

11. Bruce W. Stewart, "Data Processing in an Academic Library," *Wilson Library Bulletin*, 41, 388-395 (December 1966); and Stewart, "Data Processing in the Texas A & M University Library," in *Proceedings of the 1966 Clinic on Library Applications of Data Processing*, University of Illinois Graduate School of Library Science, Urbana, 1966, pp. 167-194.

12. C. D. Gull, "Automated Circulation Systems," in *Library Automation, A State of the Art Review*, American Library Association, Chicago, 1969, p. 141. See, for examples, the following: Anne Flannery and James D. Mack, *Library Systems Analysis Report Number 4, Mechanized Circulation System, Lehigh University Library*, the Library, 1966; Floyd Cammack and Donald Mann, "Institutional Implications of an Automated Circulation Study [at Oakland University]," *College & Research Libraries*, 28, 129-132 (March 1967); J. Emery Kanasy, "Circulation Control Systems [at Windsor University]" and Jack Billinton, "Circulation Control Systems [at the University of Saskatchewan]," in *Automation in Libraries*, Canadian Association of College and University Libraries, 1967, pp. 76-88 and 89-92; Patricia Ann Stockton, "An IBM 357 Circulation Procedure [at American University]," *College & Research Libraries*, 28, 35-40 (January 1967); and "Why Wait? ...", *Books and Libraries at the University of Kansas*, 4, 1-2 (February 1967).

13. Lawrence F. Buckland *et al.*, *Final Report, Phase I: Survey of Automated Library Systems*, Prepared for the California State University and Colleges, Inforonics, Inc., Maynard Mass., 1973, Appendix A, p. P 2.

14. Richard Phillips Palmer, *Case Studies in Library Computer Systems*, R. R. Bowker, New York, 1973, p. 33; and J. McRee Elrod, "Letter to the Editor," *College & Research Libraries*, 32, 145 (March 1971).

15. Palmer, *op. cit.*, pp. 13-18.

16. Benjamin Courtright, "The Johns Hopkins University Library," in *Proceedings of the 1966 Clinic on Library Applications of Data Processing*, University of Illinois Graduate School of Library Science, Urbana, 1966, pp. 18-33; news item, *Library of Congress Information Bulletin*, 23, 655-656 (November 23, 1964); *Progress Report on an Operations Research and Systems Engineering Study of a University Library* (NSF Grant GN-31), April 1963, and later reports with the same title dated June 1964 and June 1965; Robert H. Roy, "Utilization of Computer Techniques for Circulation and Inventory Control in a University Research Library," in *Minutes of the Sixty-Third Meeting, January 26, 1974, Chicago, Illinois*, Association of Research Libraries, Appendix B, pp. 20-39.

17. Frank Martin and Jack Banning, *Library Circulation Control at Michigan State University*, the University, East Lansing, Michigan, 1966.

18. *Computerized Library Operation, Santa Clara Public Library, Santa Clara, California*, Control Data Corporation, Minneapolis, Minn. [n.d.].

19. Buckland, *op. cit.*, Appendix A, p. O 1-2, and table following p. 38.

20. Buckland, *op. cit.*, Appendix A, pp. A 1-4.

8. Circulation Systems

21. See, for example, Edward Broadhead, "Automation Comes to Southern Colorado State College Library," *Colorado Academic Libraries*, 6, 5-6 (Spring 1970).
22. Palmer, *op. cit.*, pp. 19-26; Richard De Gennaro, "Automation in the Harvard College Library," *Harvard Library Bulletin*, 221-222 (July 1968); "The Use of Data Processing Equipment in Circulation Control," in *Library Technology Reports: Circulation Systems*, American Library Association, Chicago, 1965, pp. 3, 13-16.
23. Buckland, *op. cit.*, Appendix A, pp. B 1-2.
24. James R. Cox, "The Costs of Data Processing in University Libraries: In Circulation Activities," *College & Research Libraries*, 24, 492-495 (November 1963); Cox, "Circulation Control with IBM Unit Record Equipment at the University of California Library, Los Angeles; Progress and Change," in *IBM Library Mechanization Symposium, Endicott, New York, May 25, 1964*, International Business Machines, White Plains, N.Y. [1965?], pp. 95-132; "The Use of Data Processing Equipment in Circulation Control," *Library Technology Reports: Circulation Systems*, American Library Association, Chicago, 1965, pp. 3, 17-20; and Cox, "Automation Advances in the Research Library," *UCLA Librarian*, 19, 22-24 (March 1966).
25. I. Haznedari and H. Voos, "Automated Circulation at a Government R & D Installation," *Special Libraries*, 55, 77-81 (February 1964).
26. Joseph Becker, "Circulation and the Computer," *ALA Bulletin*, 58, 1008-1010 (December 1964); and "The Use of Data Processing Equipment in Circulation Control," *Library Technology Reports: Circulation Systems*, American Library Association, 1965, pp. 4, 21-24.
27. Robert E. Hamilton, "Illinois State Library Computer System," *Wilson Library Bulletin*, 43, 721-722 (March 1968); and Hamilton, "The Illinois State Library 'On-Line' Circulation Control System," in *Proceedings of the 1968 Clinic on Library Applications of Data Processing*, University of Illinois Graduate School of Library Science, Urbana, 1969, pp. 11-28.
28. Calvin J. Boyer and Jack Frost, "On-Line Circulation Control--Midwestern University Library's System Using an IBM 1401 Computer in a 'Time-Sharing' Mode," in *Proceedings of the 1969 Clinic on Library Applications of Data Processing*, University of Illinois Graduate School of Library Science, Urbana, Illinois, 1970, pp. 135-146; Charles D. Heineke and Calvin J. Boyer, "Automated Circulation System at Midwestern University," *ALA Bulletin*, 63, 1249-1254 (October 1969).
29. Lois M. Kershner, "Management Aspects of the Use of the IBM System/7 in Circulation Control," in *Proceedings of the 1974 Clinic on Library Applications of Data Processing, Applications of Minicomputers to Library and Related Problems*, University of Illinois Graduate School of Library Science, Urbana, 1975, pp. 43-54; *System/7-2790 Library Circulation Control*, University of

Pennsylvania, IBM Application Brief GK 20-0673-0; Donald D. Dennis and Patricia A. Stockton, "Automated Library Circulation System Boosts Service, Control at American University," *Special Libraries*, 65, 512-515 (December 1974).

30. "Maryland U. Using 'Point of Sale' Terminals for Book Checkout," *Advanced Technology/Libraries*, 2, 1-2 (April 1973). See also Walter G. Hamner, "The Minicomputer and Its Use in Library Operations at the University of Maryland," in *Proceedings of the 1974 Clinic on Library Applications of Data Processing: Applications of Minicomputers to Library and Related Problems*, University of Illinois Graduate School of Library Science, Urbana, 1975, pp. 32-42.

31. R. A. Kennedy, "Bell Laboratories' Library Real-Time Loan System (BELLREL)," *Journal of Library Automation*, 1, 128-146 (June 1968); *ibid.*, "Bell Laboratories On-Line Circulation Control System: One Year's Experience," in *Proceedings of the 1969 Clinic on Library Applications of Data Processing*, University of Illinois Graduate School of Library Science, Urbana, 1970, pp. 14-30.

32. Palmer, *op. cit.*, pp. 35-45; Buckland, *op. cit.*, Appendix A, pp. AA 1-3; Paladugu V. Rao and B. Joseph Szerenyi, "Booth Library On-Line Circulation System (BLOC)," *Journal of Library Automation*, 4, 86-102 (June 1971).

33. Velma Veneziano, "An Interactive Computer-Based Circulation System for Northwestern University; the Library Puts It to Work," *Journal of Library Automation*, 5, 103 (Summer 1973).

34. *Ibid.*, pp. 101-117; James S. Aagaard, "An Interactive Computer-Based Circulation System: Design and Development," *Journal of Library Automation*, 5, 3-11 (March 1972); Palmer, *op. cit.*, pp. 46-57; and Joseph T. Paulukonis, "On-Line Real-Time Self-Service Circulation at Northwestern University," in *Proceedings of the 1972 Clinic on Library Applications of Data Processing: Applications of On-Line Computers to Library Problems*, University of Illinois Graduate School of Library Science, Urbana, 1972, pp. 82-93.

35. Hugh C. Atkinson, "The Ohio State On-Line Circulation System," in *Proceedings of the 1972 Clinic on Library Applications of Data Processing: Applications of On-Line Computers to Library Problems*, University of Illinois Graduate School of Library Science, Urbana, 1972, p. 27.

36. *Ibid.*, pp. 22-28; Irene Braden Hoadley and A. Robert Thorson, eds. *An Automated On-Line Circulation System: Evaluation, Development, Use; Proceedings and Papers of an Institute Held at the Ohio State University, September 13-14, 1971*, Ohio State University Libraries, 1973; Buckland, *op. cit.*, Appendix A, pp. M 1-2; and Stephen W. Massil, "Report on a Visit to Certain Libraries in the USA, May-June 1973," *Program*, 8, 82 (April 1974).

8. Circulation Systems 217

37. Dorothy McKibbin, "On-Line Circulation Control: Three Years' Experience," *Canadian Library Journal*, 31, 214-230 (June 1974).
38. Earl E. Wassom, Patricia W. Custead and Simon P. J. Chen, "On-Line Cataloging and Circulation at Western Kentucky University: An Approach to Automated Instructional Resources Management," *LARC Reports*, 6, 29-36 (1973); and Buckland, *op. cit.*, Appendix A, pp. L 1-5.
39. C. W. J. Wilson, "Developments with Computer-based Loans Systems in the United Kingdom," *Program*, 7, 170-171 (October 1973); and Karen Senior and Deborah J. Yamanaka, "The Automated Loans System at Loughborough University of Technology," *Program*, 8, 1-21 (January 1974).
40. Kenneth E. Toombs, "Light Pen Technology in the University of South Carolina Library," *Southeastern Librarian*, 24, 27-28 (Summer 1974); and Toombs, "Light-Pen Technology at the University of South Carolina--The South Carolina Circulation System," *Journal of Library Automation*, 7, 226-227 (September 1974).
41. Dennis N. Beaumont, "The LIBS 100 System," in *Proceedings of the 1974 Clinic on Library Applications of Data Processing: Applications of Minicomputers to Library and Related Problems*, University of Illinois Graduate School of Library Science, Urbana, 1975, pp. 55-79.

Chapter 9

THE PROBLEMS OF
LIBRARY AUTOMATION SYSTEMS

The projects described in previous chapters used many techniques, some of which worked, some of which did not. The successes have normally been reported in the literature fully and in detail, and information about them is thus available to the interested reader who wants to explore further. The problems and failures, unfortunately, are not as often reported, and information about them must be gleaned from a welter of technical detail and elusive sources. The facts, when known, are not always pleasant, but if a reasonably complete picture of library automation in our time is to be drawn, they must be included, warts and all. At the risk of being gloomy, therefore, this chapter will attempt to categorize some of the known pitfalls and problems, with examples, as a guide to the wary and a warning to the earnest enthusiast.

Generally speaking, the difficulties appear to involve three groups of people--computer center and systems personnel, suppliers of hardware and software, and librarians--and three types of problems--poor planning, poor design, and poor implementation.

The computer center and systems personnel

In this category, at least seven areas of difficulty may be identified. Availability of computer processing time has been a problem for numerous library projects; the lack of priority given by the computer center to the development of library systems has been another complaint; and a third is the lack of control by the library over decisions regarding continuation of a project. The experiences of the M.I.T. library with its acquisition systems and the Florida Atlantic University library with its book catalog project serve as examples of all three of these related problems.

Comments by observers of these difficulties have been numerous and pointed. Says one:

> Too often the library has been a charity ward of the data processing center and as such has had the lowest priority. The computer center has not hesitated to dump the library in favor of higher priority jobs. ... It is very dangerous for the library to accept charity. The library must have a firm agreement as to its rights and scheduled services on the computer. If these are not nailed down, the library runs a great risk of building a perfectly good system that never becomes operational or, if operational, is suddenly terminated.
>
> This danger can hardly be exaggerated. There have been instances in which the manager of a data processing center has solicited library support, because the more jobs he had to do, the better equipment he could justify. But once the equipment was procured and installed and more high priority jobs became operational, the library soon found itself pushed right off the computer.[1]

And another:

> One of the lessons of library automation learned during the last few years is that a library cannot risk putting its critical computer-based systems onto equipment over which it has no control. This does not necessarily mean that it needs its own in-house computer. However, if it plans to rely on equipment under the administrative control of others, such as the computer center or the administrative data processing unit, it must get firm and binding commitments for the time, and must have a voice in the type and configuration of equipment to be made available. The importance of this point may be overlooked during an initial development period, when the library's need for time is minimal and flexible; it becomes extremely critical when systems such as acquisitions and circulation become totally dependent on computers.
>
> People at university computing centers are generally oriented toward scientific and research users and in a tight situation will give the library's need second priority; those in administrative data processing, because they are

9. Problems of Library Automation Systems 221

operations oriented, tend to have a somewhat better appreciation of the library's requirements. In any case, a library needs more than the expressed sympathy and good will of those who control the computing equipment--it needs firm commitments.[2]

A fourth problem involving computer centers and their personnel is what Veaner has called "system instability." In a survey of twenty-four institutions conducted in 1972, he found that "this was more the rule than the exception, especially in software, operating systems, hardware configurations, and pricing. Wherever an academic computing facility was used for library development, the same broken record always seemed to be playing: the facility was always being taken apart and put together again."[3]

The attempts by the University of Pittsburgh to implement a circulation system are illustrative:

> The circulation system was originally specified for the University computer center's 360/50's. However, the computer center informed the library that it could not handle the library processing demands. At that time, the library had an IBM 1130. A hybrid system was devised using the IBM 1130 and several IBM 1030's. There were difficulties becoming operational, and in the meantime the university computer center decided to rid themselves of the 360/50's and install two PDP-10's on a dual processing basis. The library was informed that the university computer center would begin running the library programs as soon as they were converted to the PDP-10's. After the necessary reprogramming, both systems are now on the university equipment.[4]

Rice University's experience with its circulation system affords another example. It was begun on unit record equipment, transferred to an IBM 7040, then to a Burroughs B5500, and finally to an IBM 370 Model 155. At times during the period when the system was being switched from one computer to another, the "daily" print-out of the circulation file was literally months out of date, and since the transaction records were on tape instead of punched cards there was no way of telling where the books were.

Attitudes of computer center personnel may also be a source of trouble. Ignorance of libraries and their operations has frequently led to an assumption that the problems to be solved are simple or trivial, or at best, to the glib conclusion by systems analysts and programmers that they understand both the problems and the solutions. Elitism--"the notion that the masters of the computer are inherently superior to and have better judgment than computer customers"[5]--is also common. A related problem is the fact that most of the good programmers and systems analysts are naturally interested in facing new challenges and are apt to become disinterested in library projects once they become "production" systems. And fear also may play a part; to many computer centers, it has sometimes appeared that the library, in addition to its usually well-established role on campus or in the community, could become the largest of the computer center's users, and "in some facilities this recognition may have induced a fear of being taken over or overwhelmed by the user, who would then be in a position to dominate and dictate the direction of further development and operations."[6] A host of other attitudes and emotions may affect library system projects. One system expert with long years of experience says, "I have seen computer center staff force users out of compatibility with other installations in matters that are completely standard for reasons that seem to range from downright incompetence, to an arrogant desire to exert control over other people's work, to regarding the computer as a toy for their personal amusement and a vehicle for practical jokes that verge on the malicious."[7]

A sixth problem, the high rate of turnover in systems analysts and programmers, was noted by the Washington University School of Medicine library in connection with its book catalog project.

> Not one of them was able to see it through to conclusion, or (in spite of reams of manual sheets) to provide sufficient documentation so that the person following could understand fully what had gone before. Even debugging had been sketchy. The result was a patchwork so difficult to understand that necessary changes, not anticipated when the program was first put into operation, could not now be made.[8]

Veaner's study also noted problems caused by uncertainty over who was actually in charge of the computer facility, and the unsettling effects when high administrative officials involved in its management left the institution.

9. Problems of Library Automation Systems 223

Suppliers

At least five types of problems can be identified in this category. The first is the failure of suppliers to deliver the necessary equipment. The Orange County Public Library designed and programmed a circulation system but never implemented it, simply because the company which was supposed to supply the hardware never delivered. A more common (indeed, almost universal) problem is the failure of suppliers to deliver the required software (i.e., the programs and related documentation), either on time or at all.

A third familiar problem is inadequate service response, which plagued most of the projects using paper-tape machines and still troubles most libraries using automatic typewriters. It also seems clear that some machines used in library automation projects are simply poor machines, either poorly engineered or poorly built, a case in point being the IBM 1050 which most libraries have discontinued using because of constant breakdowns.

Finally, and probably most common of all, the software supplied may be faulty, a problem which usually gets solved one way or another, but which may fatally disrupt the time schedule or the planned budget. Projects of all sizes, from MARC on down, have suffered from this difficulty.

Library staff

Perhaps the most serious problem originating with the library staff itself is the failure to distinguish legitimate research and experimentation from operational improvements, or to provide separate funds for research. Some of the developments in library automation have been funded by grants (usually given to initiate expected operational improvements, not for research) but most have been funded from the operating budgets of individual libraries. Only a few libraries have deliberately set aside a portion of their budgets for research and experimentation.

Because most experimental techniques were attempted under the guise of operational improvements, those that did not work were conidered failures by the librarians. Money that might have been used for more books or more staff had been wasted, it appeared, and mismanagement or (more charitably) misjudgement was often suggested. Yet seen properly as needed research and experimentation--the only way a profession advances--many of these "failures" were in fact successes. To the extent that they demonstrated methods which did not work, they made a valuable contribution to this part of librarianship.

The real failure of many librarians involved in these projects is the lack of reporting to the profession on the problems encountered. A few projects have been reported frankly and in full, but most have died silently, almost secretly. Perhaps because they were intended to be immediate operating improvements, their cessation was viewed with embarrassment and even shame, and those in charge refused to discuss them. In such cases, the failure goes beyond the mere missing of an opportunity to contribute to the advancement of the profession; a real harm results, because other libraries are apt to repeat the process with the same results, needlessly wasting money, manpower, and time.

Unfortunately there are far too many examples of this problem. Florida Atlantic's projects were begun with great publicity, but after implementation of the projects the profession was kept almost completely in the dark regarding how well the new systems had worked. Rumors of trouble abounded, fed by reports of staff members accepting positions elsewhere. When the Director of Library and Information Retrieval Services resigned early in 1967, "it became apparent that the experiment which had been launched with such confidence and such fanfare had failed," yet only when a later director of libraries published a summary report did many of the facts become known. "Those involved chose ... to blanket the difficulties encountered with silence, ignoring the fact that progress in a technologically oriented society is as dependent upon the analysis of projects which fail to achieve goals as it is on the resounding successes."[9]

Networks have had a particularly high mortality rate, especially those designed to do centralized processing, but reports by the librarians involved on the reasons for discontinuance tend to be elusive.

9. Problems of Library Automation Systems

ANYLTS (the Association of New York Libraries for Technical Services) began like Florida Atlantic University with a considerable amount of publicity, and some $2.5 million was reportedly spent on its development, yet when it died in 1972 there was no general report to the profession. Apparently development efforts had fallen considerably behind schedule, and the income-producing activities of the project could not sustain it after Federal funds were withdrawn. In the absence of a formal report, however, it is impossible to know for certain the reasons for its failure.

Talking too much before the fact and too little after may be failings related to a more general problem identified by Veaner in the study cited earlier: the failure of librarians to understand the entire process of development.

> Development is a new phenomenon in libraries. Most librarians were not educated to comprehend development as an iterative process, characterized by experimentation, error, feedback, and corrective measures. Accustomed to the relative stability of long-established procedures--some of which had stood for generations, even centuries--some librarians were baffled by the rapidly changing new technology, others showed impatience and a low tolerance for frustration. Many expected development projects to resemble turnkey operations, and the failure of the process to accommodate these expectations produced disappointment and an inability to cope with the computer environment.[10]

Despite the "stability of long-established procedures," another problem in many library automation projects has been that the library staff really did not understand the existing procedures, at least not with the precision and detail required for designing alternative methods of accomplishing the same tasks. As a result, systems were implemented which could not handle various exceptions to normal procedures, simply because the exceptions were not mentioned or understood, and not uncommonly the whole project failed as a result.

Library staff have also created problems by failing to agree on the desired characteristics of the final product of a system. As might be imagined, cooperative projects and networks have been particularly vulnerable to this vice. The Colorado Academic

Library Book Processing Center (CALBPC) died in part because the participants constantly disagreed on the format of the catalog cards all of them were to receive, some catalogers insisting on treating cards as works of art, others insisting on petty variations to suit "local conditions," and still others insisting on the maximum in economy. The CALBPC effort also exposed other difficulties librarians seem to have in working with each other, such as head librarians feuding or jockeying for status, institutional jealousies, and simple parochialism.[11]

Even when library staff members do agree on what they want, difficulties have frequently occurred in communicating these decisions. Veaner found that "many did not understand how to put together a specification document; particularly they did not know how to account exhaustively for all possible cases of alternatives. Librarians were unaccustomed to defining their data processing requirements quantitatively or with precision--both absolutely indispensable to the computer environment. ... Few library users understood the relationship between the system specifications and functional results, and fewer still understood the significance of performance specifications."[12]

Poor planning

Some of the problems that have troubled library automation projects are not the sole province of any one of the above groups of people, but may originate with any or all of them. The first category of such problems may be thought of generally as poor planning, and at the head of the list of planning problems may be the idea to initiate a project in the first place. There are many valid reasons to begin an automated system: to do something better, or faster, or less expensively, or to do something that can no longer be done effectively by manual systems, or to provide a new service, provided of course that the resources are available to pay for it. But many projects have been started, not for any of these reasons but because of pressure from the institution's administration to "be modern" or "automate the library," to keep up with the Joneses of the library world, to promote a personal reputation, or simply because somebody on the library staff is gadget-happy and needs a new toy. Systems

9. Problems of Library Automation Systems

thus initiated, or begun without sufficient analysis of the goals and objectives of the project, are apt to fail early, and even if they proceed past the implementation stage the lack of clearly defined objectives will make evaluation of their success difficult if not impossible.

Another problem in planning that is frequently encountered is the lack of market research--that is, the failure to establish in advance that the planned product or service is needed or wanted. The reports of the Washington University School of Medicine library on its book catalog and serials list projects provide good examples of this problem, as well as a related one: the products cost too much for the benefits derived. These twin problems--insufficient demand and inordinate costs--run through the reports of many troubled projects and seem to be the principal reasons for the failure of every example of a particular type of network not yet mentioned: the kind set up to transmit materials between libraries by facsimile transmission instead of by conventional interlibrary loan techniques.

The best-documented and most extensive such project was the Facsimile Transmission System (FACTS) in New York State, which involved fifteen libraries and ran from January 20, 1967 to March 31, 1968. An impressive amount of time and money was spent in constructing this network, but the results in terms of user response were disappointing. Apparently the principal problem was that there was little demand for the fast but expensive service the system was set up to provide. To quote from a report by its director:

> We began the experiment with the idea that the only reason to install telefacsimile is to achieve instantaneous delivery. Therefore, a turn-around time of 24 hours was established as a goal. ... In fact, the users were uninterested in receiving material in 24 hours. The Nelson Associates polled the users and asked them what period they thought appropriate for delivery of items. Out of 772 respondees, 288 voted for 5 to 10 days (this is the largest percentage), only 5 voted for the 24 hour period, and 48 people said that 20 or more days would be completely sufficient for their needs.
>
> ... As an information network, FACTS was not a success; as preventive maintenance, it was a triumph. Only 5% of the time available for transmission on the equipment was used, resulting

in a per filled request cost of around $70.

... FACTS was a failure because it cost too much. Not because it cost a lot, but because it cost too much. The product was not worth the price.[13]

Other facsimile transmission networks reporting failure for similar reasons include ones in California, Nevada, Hawaii, and Pennsylvania.[14]

Perhaps the biggest problem at the planning stage is simply wishful thinking. Unrealistic assumptions are commonly made regarding the time required to complete and implement a project, the effort involved, and most of all the cost. Assumptions regarding the benefits that will result may also be at fault, a problem experienced by the Colorado Academic Libraries Book Processing Center. It was presumed at the planning stage that larger discounts would result if book orders were pooled, but in fact this never happened. Libraries were not buying the same titles as much as had been thought, and even when they did, it was at different times so the orders could not be pooled. With the added costs of processing, bookkeeping, and paperwork at the Center, the cost was higher, in fact, than if each library had ordered its books separately.[15]

In their early enthusiasm and eagerness to get started, library system planners may also forget to do their homework--that is, to search the literature, to learn (through various means, including contact with the professional associations) of similar projects which have been attempted or implemented, and then to take the experiences of these projects into account. For a profession with the communication of information as a goal, the incidence of this failure is disturbing. The numerous information retrieval projects of the previous decade were particularly guilty in this regard, but examples exist for virtually every type of project. Even terminal-oriented circulation systems, of which hundreds now exist, continue to be developed from scratch, without building on the experience of others.

In some cases, this failure to profit from the lessons learned and the work done by other systems occurs not because of ignorance but because of what Brong and Pasternak have called the "N-I-H" or

"Not-Invented-Here" syndrome.[16] The planners know of other systems which do what they wish to do, but they refuse to adopt such systems (or even to study them) simply because they were developed by other institutions. The excuse may be that the existing systems were designed for public institutions rather than private ones (or vice versa), or that they do not accommodate "local conditions," but the real reasons are often ambition, arrogance, and indifference.

One other problem in the planning category should be mentioned. Occasionally the planning for a system is based on the existence of "soft" money--i.e., money from grants or one-time gifts or appropriations--or the assumption that such money will be available to fund the project in the future. This is both appropriate and desirable if the project is developmental or experimental, and designed either to terminate when the funds run out or to continue operating (perhaps at a reduced level) with identified, regularly budgeted funds. Incredible as it may seem, however, not a few projects have either assumed that soft money would continue to be available indefinitely, or have simply failed to consider what would happen when such funds ran out.

Poor design

The actual design of many systems also falls prey to wishful thinking and unwarranted assumptions: for example, that acquisitions data can be reused, without major changes, for catalog cards, or that serials are regular and predictable enough that irregular serials will not be a major problem. System designs may also fail to provide for editing and proofing procedures, as in the Florida Atlantic book catalog project, where it was assumed that "untrained clerical personnel could be relied on to code Library of Congress copy for keypunching without having their work revised."[17] And some systems have omitted routines for handling exceptional circumstances, which again may be due to wishful thinking.

A second problem associated with the design stage is poor choice of hardware. The machinery chosen may be satisfactory for the functions it was originally designed to perform, but unsuitable for use in another context. Equipment designed for intermittent use may fail when used in a high-volume, production environment; and conversely, equipment designed for constant use may fail when used intermittently, as was the case in the Hawaii facsimile system.[18]

Software may also be misused, as Warheit illustrates in the following example:

> Some libraries use or have used an excellent text-editing program to convert their records, such as shelflist, serials holdings, etc., into machine-readable form. But his text-editing program was designed to handle large documents and not short records like a catalog card. Therefore, it is not as efficient as it might be for shelflist conversion. Some systems people have not recognized this and continue to use the program unchanged. In one instance, at least, a systems man recognized this deficiency and made a few changes in the program. His library is now converting its catalog records at a much faster rate and at a lower cost.[19]

Occasionally the misuse of hardware or software occurs because the designer has a pet technique, or a pet piece of equipment, and attempts to apply it to every system problem, simply because it is familar and has worked for him before. A good systems designer starts by analyzing the problem, conceptualizing alternative approaches to a solution, rigorously determining the advantages and disadvantages of each approach, and selecting one. If the project is large, specifications will then be drawn up, and only then will equipment selection begin. Unfortunately poor designers sometimes reverse the process and a poor system is almost inevitable.

Occasionally, too, a particular desing or approach becomes a favorite not of a particular person but of a large number of libraries; in short, a fad. If the system design is basically a good one, such as the terminal-oriented circulation system, everyone profits; if the system design is basically bad, such as the arrival card serial control system, everyone suffers. The proof against this problem, of course, is conscientious inquiry into the actual results achieved by similar systems.

Poor implementation

Once systems reach the implementation phase, most of the problems will have already been created or encountered, but some projects

9. Problems of Library Automation Systems

still falter at this stage. A common fault is that those charged with the implementation, whether librarians, systems people, or administrative staff, fail to take the human element and human values sufficiently into account. Unless it is made clear to all staff members affected by the new system that the goal is better service or more assistance to them in their work, resistance is almost inevitable. Even when the purposes of the system are understood, fears for job security are likely to be rampant even if not expressed, and failure to provide reassurances on this score can have serious repercussions. Temporary inconveniences or additional workloads caused by the one-time necessity of converting records must be explained, and disruptions must be anticipated and counteracted. Problems only distantly related to the new system may be involved, as the experience of Northwestern University with its technical processing system indicated:

> One phenomenon demanding alertness during the implementation of the new system, particularly because it involved a computer, was the tendency to blame the system for unrelated or marginally associated problems arising during the same time period. Although automation can be held responsible for certain amounts of stress and strain and resulting conflicts, it is little understood by many librarians. Thus it often serves as a scapegoat for other kinds of difficulties (e.g., slow-downs resulting from staff turnover, problems related to absorbing processing for additional branch libraries). Faced with possibilities of this type, the only way to implement any system successfully is to have the full cooperation and dedication of the library staff who must make it work. A superbly designed system, excellently programmed, will fail if personnel lack understanding or are unwilling to contribute the extra effort needed to accomplish a major change in procedures. Although an excellent system is a necessity, Northwestern's experience indicates that attitudes are at least equally important among the many requirements for successful implementation.[20]

Presumably back-up procedures will have been incorporated in the system during the design phase, but manual back-up procedures must also be provided during implementation in the event of total system failure. The consequences of omitting this step can be disastrous, as a final example from Florida Atlantic illustrates. (Incidentally, if this chapter has seemed unduly harsh in judging this unfortunate library's early projects, it is only because they provide an astonishingly consistent illustration of how library automation projects ought not to be done.) The systems at FAU had been designed on paper at the University of Illinois at Chicago Circle, but never actually implemented; nevertheless it was apparently assumed "that the preliminary work done at Chicago made it possible to bypass manual backup systems during the period when the new computer-based systems were being tested and debugged. ... No serious discussions were ever held regarding what would happen if unforeseen difficulties arose with either the software or the hardware," the consequences of which "were serious. When the computer-based systems failed, the students and faculty were left without many of the services which even the least sophisticated library user takes for granted."[21]

Throughout design and implementation (and usually continuing some time after), documentation of the system and all procedures must also be produced, and some library systems have come to grief on this matter alone. A system may be implemented and working well, but if knowledge of the system is partly or fully in some key person's head and that person leaves or his services are otherwise lost, the solution of subsequent problems may be difficult if not impossible. All systems change, or at least should change, since any library is growing and the requirements imposed on the system consequently differ. If documentation is faulty, changing the system may be a major problem, even in some instances enough to cause its abandonment.

A final word

Any catalog of woe such as the foregoing is naturally depressing, and inevitably runs the risk of seeming overdrawn. Fortunately there have been many systems that avoid most if not all of the problems cited, and the successes probably outnumber the failures. To cite these in the interest of "balance," however, would be contrary to the purpose of this chapter, and at any rate no one expects a paper on pathology to conclude with examples of healthy patients. Library automation _is_ basically healthy, despite the problems mentioned, but it will be more so when all of those involved can discuss, openly and candidly, the difficulties and even the failures that all sooner or later experience.

NOTES

1. I. A. Warheit, "When Some Library Systems Fail," *Wilson Library Bulletin*, 46, 54 (September 1971).
2. Richard De Gennaro, "The Development and Administration of Automated Systems in Academic Libraries," *Journal of Library Automation*, 1, 85 (March 1968).
3. Allen B. Veaner, "Institutional Political and Fiscal Factors In the Development of Library Automation, 1967-71," *Journal of Library Automation*, 7, 6 (March 1974).
4. Lawrence F. Buckland et al., *Final Report, Phase I: Survey of Automated Library Systems*, Prepared for the California State University and Colleges, Inforonics, Inc., Maynard, Mass., 1973, Appendix A, pp. C 3-4.
5. Veaner, *op. cit.*, p. 7.
6. *Ibid.*, p. 7-8.
7. Michael P. Barnett, letter to the editor, *College & Research Libraries*, 32, 392 (September 1971).
8. Doris Bolef et al., "Mechanization of Library Procedures in the Medium-Sized Library: VIII. Suspension of Computer Catalog," *Bulletin of the Medical Library Association*, 57, 265.
9. H. William Axford, "Florida Atlantic University Library," in *Encyclopedia of Library and Information Science*, Marcel Dekker, New York, 1972, vol. 8, pp. 546, 555-556.
10. Veaner, *op. cit.*, p. 8.
11. In contrast with many others, the CALBPC experiences have been well and fully reported. See Richard M. Dougherty and Joan M. Maier, *Centralized Processing for Academic Libraries; the Final Report (Phase III, Jan. 1-June 30, 1969) of the Colorado Academic Libraries Book Processing Center: The First Six Months of Operation*, Scarecrow Press, Metuchen, N. J., 1971; Allen B. Veaner, *Colorado Academic Libraries Book Processing Center Report #3* [Boulder, University of Colorado?], 1971; Donald D. Hendricks, *A Report on Library Networks*, University of Illinois Graduate School of Library Science, Urbana, 1973, pp. 10-11; and numerous articles in the *Colorado Academic Library*, including Lawrence E. Leonard, "Colorado Academic Libraries Book Processing Center: a Feasibility Study Turned Feasible," 4, 1-4 (Summer 1968); Joan M. Maier, "The Colorado Academic Library Book Processing Center: A Dream Becomes a Reality," 5, 1-2 (Spring 1969);

Richard M. Dougherty, "The Colorado Academic Library Book Processing Center: Immediate Prospects and Problems," 5, 3-8 (Spring 1969); Richard M. Dougherty, "Some Reflections on the Colorado Academic Library Book Processing Center," 6, 12-16 (Autumn 1970); and Joe Hewitt, "The Colorado Academic Libraries Book Processing Center: Status Report," 7, 18-22 (Spring 1971).

12. Veaner, *op. cit.*, pp. 8-9.

13. Lynn R. Hard, *User Response to the FACTS (Facsimile Transmission System)* Network [McGill University Library, Toronto, 1971?], pp. 42, 45, 58.

14. William D. Schieber and Ralph M. Shoffner, *Telefacsimile in Libraries*, Institute of Library Research, Berkeley, California, 1968; David Heron, "Telefacsimile in Libraries: Progress and Prospects," *Unesco Bulletin for Libraries*, 23, 10 (January-February 1969); and W. Carl Jackson, "Telefacsimile at Penn State University: A Report on Operations during 1968-1969," *Library Resources & Technical Services*, 15, 223-228 (Spring 1971), and personal conversation with Roland Lloyd, Pennsylvania State University Library, January 28, 1974.

15. Donald D. Hendricks, "A Report on Library Networks," *Occasional Papers*, no. 108, University of Illinois Graduate School of Library Science, Urbana, 1973, p. 11.

16. Gerald R. Brong and Elizabeth F. Pasternak, "The N-I-H Syndrome," *Library Journal*, 95, 3877-3878 (November 15, 1970).

17. Axford, *op. cit.*, p. 553.

18. J. R. Hunt, "System in Hawaii," *ALA Bulletin*, 60, 1142-1146 (December 1966).

19. Warheit, *op. cit.*, p. 55.

20. Karen Horny, "Automation of Technical Services: Northwestern's Experience," *College & Research Libraries*, 35, 368 (September 1974).

21. Axford, *op. cit.*, p. 553.

Chapter 10

THE PROSPECTS
OF LIBRARY AUTOMATION SYSTEMS

The recent history of library automation systems is characterized by several strong trends brought about by changes both in technology and in the economic situation confronting most libraries. Unless radical changes in either technology or the economy occur, these trends seem likely to continue dominant, and to determine the course of library automation development for some time to come.

Networks

Chief among these trends and easily the most conspicuous is the heavy emphasis being placed on library networks--that is, systems involving more than one library. The entire program of the 1973 Clinic on Library Applications of Data Processing was devoted to networks,[1] and the long-awaited draft report of the National Commission on Libraries and Information Science contained as its major recommendation a proposal for a national network, evolving from the existing local and regional ones.[2] As Bierman has noted, "the folly of individual libraries proceeding on their own to develop major automated systems solely for their own use seems well recognized and accepted."[3]

Networks come in many styles and flavors. One of the most common is the cooperative center for providing catalog cards (and sometimes related cataloging products), of which the outstanding and most successful example is OCLC, the Ohio College Library Center. As mentioned earlier, many other state and regional networks are now tied into OCLC and dependent on it to a greater or lesser extent for the services they offer. These include NELINET (the New England Library Information Network of about 40 libraries);[4] FAUL (the Five Associated University Libraries of Upstate New York, which despite the name includes seven members, one of which is not a university library);[5] SUNY (the State University of New York, with seventy-two libraries); the Pittsburgh Regional Library Center; PALINET (the Pennsylvania Area Library Network); SOLINET (the Southeastern Library Network, with almost 100 members);[6] the Cooperative College Library Center in Atlanta, Georgia; and AMIGOS (which stands for nothing in particular, but includes several dozen libraries in Texas and the Southwest organized into a network by the Interuniversity Council).

A second type of network is also concerned primarily with technical processing, but attempts to provide a means of cooperative acquisitions as well as cataloging.[7] Successful ones (at least if success is measured by continued operation) include the BCL (Books for College Libraries) program in Massachusetts[8] and the College Bibliocentre program in Ontario, Canada.[9] The mortality rate for this kind of network is high, however, as the deaths of CALBPC (the Colorado Academic Library Book Processing Center) and ANYLTS (the Association of New York Libraries for Technical Services) make clear.[10]

A third type of grouping sometimes called a network is merely a loose consortium of libraries with special procedures for expediting interlibrary loans, often using teletypes. Most of these are not automated in any significant way, and so lie outside the sphere of this book, but some have been working for years to implement on-line networks for the same purposes, a prime example being NYSILL, the New York State Interlibrary Loan Network.[11]

At this writing, the largest category of networks would have to be labeled "in planning" or "in process of implementation," with some efforts dating back several years. CAPTAIN (Computer Aided Processing & Terminal Access Information Network) is intended to

10. Prospects of Library Automation Systems

handle acquisitions and processing for New Jersey's eight state colleges, but despite occasional signs of life has experienced constant difficulties in becoming fully operational.[12] MALCAP (the Maryland Academic Library Center for Automated Processing) has had a similar experience.[13] The Washington Library Network, run by the Washington State Library, is "about ready" to go on line after years of development.[14]

Others are mere gleams in various bibliothecal eyes. Indiana is planning a network through INCOLSA, the Indiana Cooperative Library Services Authority.[15] Academic librarians in the Midwestern states of Michigan, Wisconsin, Minnesota, Ohio, Illinois, Iowa, the Dakotas, Nebraska, and, curiously, Indiana have proposed one tentatively labeled MIDLNET or MILINET.[16] Stanford has offered its BALLOTS files for use by other libraries in an attempt to start CLAN (the California Library Automation Newwork).[17] The nine universities comprising the Oregon State System of Higher Education have proposed another.[18] And the Rocky Mountain states, not to be left out or outdone by anybody, have proposed SALINET, the Satellite Library Information Network, for which they have been awarded "designated user" status on the Communications Technology Satellite to be launched by the space program in late 1975.[19]

This universal interest in networks has several manifest causes. For one thing, declining library budgets and the startling increase in book and serial costs have made the need for cooperation between libraries more urgent. "Resource-sharing" has become a byword, and the resources implied are both bibliographical and financial. On-line networks enable libraries to know quickly and efficiently which books are in other libraries, and it thus becomes more feasible to share expensive sets and seldom-used works among a group of libraries, reducing the number of duplicate copies needed. Bibliographical data can be shared more effectively, too, as the OCLC system demonstrates. A final and forceful incentive is that the sources of funds for purely local automation projects have almost dried up; the Federal grants that were plentiful in the 1960s disappeared in the 1970s, foundations have been less willing to fund projects unless they were truly innovative, and most libraries' own budgets are being held static or reduced instead of being increased. Money for cooperative projects that can reasonably be expected to reduce operating costs can usually be found, but not money for local experimentation.

Several technical developments have also helped to make the network trend possible. The improvement in communication between computer systems and system users has already been noted, but it should be pointed out that this extends to communication between libraries as well. Telephones and teletype have long made some interlibrary communication possible, but on-line networks allow librarians in many different libraries literally to share the same working files and catalogs in real time, almost as if they were working in one giant library. Technology has also lowered the cost of storing units of data by several orders of magnitude and the cost of on-line terminals has declined almost as dramatically, while labor costs have continued to rise. The combined force of all these factors has made the economic argument for networks compelling.

Standards

Work in the development of standards has also facilitated networking. Without MARC as a national standard for machine-readable bibliographic data, most of the successful networks would not have been possible, and credit for this success must go not only to MARC's brilliant developers at the Library of Congress but also to the many librarians and others who worked hard to promote widespread acceptance of the standard through professional organizations such as the American Library Association (especially its Information Science and Automation Division and Resources and Technical Services Division), the American National Standards Institute and the International Standards Organization. The recent introduction of International Standard Bibliographic Descriptions for monographs and serials opens the way for standard recording of non-MARC as well as MARC records, and the International Standard Serial Number offers promise for eventual control of that sticky body of data. These and other standards activities have done much to stabilize the future of networks.

10. Prospects of Library Automation Systems

Minicomputers

The problems many libraries have experienced in using large, general-purpose institutional computers may also help account for the network trend, since a cooperative system used only for library purposes is one way of avoiding the necessity of sharing a computer with non-library users in an institutional environment. Another way around this problem, apart from networking, is the use of minicomputers, owned, controlled and used solely by a single library, and this alternative appears to be growing in popularity. Mention has already been made of the library-owned 1440 used by the University of Missouri, and 1401s have also been dedicated to library purposes, notably at Harvard. Minicomputers as currently defined are smaller than the 1400 series, however, most of them taking little more space than the average secretarial desk.[20] A favorite is Digital Equipment Corporation's PDP-11, often used as a satellite processor to feed data to and from large computers and do some processing itself, but now increasingly used on a stand-alone basis. The PDP-11s used by the University of British Columbia and the University of South Carolina for their circulation systems provide examples of the former, and the PDP-11 used by the University of Houston for its circulation system offers an example of the stand-alone type.

Commercial systems

The Houston system also illustrates another growing trend, the interest in "turn-key" systems developed and offered by commercial firms. The reasons behind this trend are similar to those for networking: they avoid the cost of local systems development, and they eliminate concerns about priority and availability. Presumably they lower the risk of failure, too, since the company supplying the system is responsible for making it work, not the library, and the system will normally have undergone a considerable amount of debugging prior to installation.

Commercial systems have had a mixed career in library automation, however. Several large companies have been active for many years in the field, but have been more successful in supplying hardware to libraries than in designing complete systems. Lack of knowledge of the market--in this case, libraries--seems to be the problem, rather than lack of technological capability; systems have been proposed which were based on the company's experience in running its own special libraries, without any apparent realization that larger libraries and libraries of different types have different problems and operate in different ways. To some extent, the failure of some commercial designs may also be due to the fact that the companies involved are large and have interest in other fields.

Smaller companies are a different story. Most of them have concentrated on the library market alone, so they tend to know the market and the business better, but they also tend to be undercapitalized and hence are prone to financial instability. Not a few have gone bankrupt, causing considerable anguish and embarassment to their customers as well as to themselves. Many of the better-run firms seem to have established themselves on a reasonably sound footing, however, and in recent years have made a significant contribution to library automation. Several have offered book catalogs successfully for so many years that the service is now routine, a few have found markets for cataloging and searching services, and "package system" companies have been successful in installing dozens of ready-made acquisitions and circulation systems.

The package (or "turn-key") systems appear to offer numerous advantages. Normally they include all necessary equipment, programs, instruction manuals and prepaid training for staff members as well as maintenance contracts and guarantees; in short, everything necessary to operate a well-defined area of library operations, such as circulation. The cost of a library systems staff is thus avoided, as is the cost of program development and testing. The months and even years of waiting for development efforts to reach fruition, so common with earlier projects, are also bypassed, and the problems of relations with a central computer center and competing for time on a large, general-purpose computer do not arise. The problem of overinflated claims, both for operation of the system and service, still makes caution necessary, however, just as caution has always

10. Prospects of Library Automation Systems 241

been necessary in the purchase of equipment alone. An additional cause for caution is that such systems are a relatively recent development, and it is just as easy for their designers to underestimate the difficulty of automating library operations as it was for library systems staffs before them. For some types of projects and in some libraries, moreover, a local, in-house effort may continue to be the only feasible alternative, and without continued experimentation little further progress in the field is likely to result. Commercial firms do have risk capital, however, and most libraries do not, so the availability of well-designed and fully supported commercial systems offers a welcome alternative for library automation to many libraries in the future.

Future developments

Assuming that the trends mentioned above continue, the development of library automation in the near future can be predicted with some degree of confidence. For catalog card production, very few new projects are likely to be initiated by individual libraries. Most libraries instead will choose to join a network tied to OCLC or a similar service, using it for catalog searching and resource sharing as well as for card production.

Attempts to use such networks for cooperative acquisitions are less likely to succeed, and seem destined to fall into disfavor. Acquisitions work is more likely to be done on commercial package systems, or on systems designed locally. The Collaborative Library Systems Development effort of Columbia, Chicago, and Stanford universities found that acquisition procedures differed so widely that a joint effort at systems development in this field was impractical.[21] This situation is unlikely to change in the near future, and local systems will therefore continue to be built, with an increased use of on-line techniques.

Book catalogs will probably remain popular with public libraries, where the ease of producing multiple copies makes them particularly attractive, but most of them will come from one of the various commercial book catalog services rather than from new projects initiated by the libraries themselves. Academic libraries will continue to use book catalogs to a lesser extent, although the increasing need to share resources and the concomitant need to make existing resources more widely known may lead to a greater use of book catalogs than heretofore.

Circulation control will be dominated by commercial, standalone systems, which appear likely to increase rapidly; a recent telephone poll revealed literally dozens of libraries planning to order or already installing such systems.[22]

Only in serials control is the picture still cloudy. The CONSER project is energetic and exciting at the moment, and the fact that OCLC, with its proven record of achievement, will host the project offers hope for its success. The experience of most other serials projects, however, offers very little encouragement, and CONSER's approach to the problems engendered by the "baffling bibliographic instability" of serials offers very little more. If CONSER and OCLC working together can solve these problems and provide an on-line serials system similar to the one at UCLA's Biomedical Library, the improvement in library operations and service may be enormous. If they fail, it may be years before another attempt is made.

Predictions based on current trends of course ignore one important factor. Technological advances are often unpredictable, and frequently the most exciting and the most significant are those which can least be foreseen. The odds are probably excellent that one or more real breakthroughs will occur within the next decade and offer a new approach, perhaps even begin a new era in library automation. The excesses, misguided enthusiasms and unfortunate mistakes that sometimes clouded early efforts, slowed progress and diminished support were merely growing pains, we may hope, and the reports of most recent projects show an expertise in planning, design and execution that augurs well. When breakthroughs come, therefore, it seems reasonable to think that the profession will be ready for them, and eager to put them to effective use.

10. Prospects of Library Automation Systems

NOTES

1. *Proceedings of the 1973 Clinic on Library Applications of Data Processing: Networking and Other Forms of Cooperation*, University of Illinois Graduate School of Library Science, Urbana, 1973.

2. *A New National Program of Library and Information Science*, National Commission on Library and Information Science, Washington, 1973. Reprinted in *Special Libraries*, 64, 583-590 (December 1973).

3. Kenneth J. Bierman, "Library Automation," in *Annual Review of Information Science and Technology*, vol. 9, American Society for Information Science, Washington, 1974, p. 136.

4. See Ann T. Curran, "Library Networks: Cataloging and Bibliographic Aspects," in *Proceedings of the 1969 Clinic on Library Applications of Data Processing*, University of Illinois Graduate School of Library Science, Urbana, 1970, pp. 31-41; and John P. McDonald, "NELINET: One Approach to Library Automation," in *Collaborative Library Systems Development*, M.I.T. Press, Cambridge, Massachusetts, 1971, pp. 102-105.

5. See David Kaser, "FAUL: A Consortium Approach to Library Automation," in *Collaborative Library Systems Development*, M.I.T. Press, Cambridge, Massachusetts, 1971, pp. 106-109.

6. See news items in *Wilson Library Bulletin*, 49, 18 (September 1974) and *Journal of Library Automation*, 7, 144 (June 1974).

7. Two rather different networks have emanated from the Washington University School of Medicine library, one providing serial holdings information on a batch basis, the other providing catalog cards, both for medical libraries. The projects are described by Estelle Brodman in "Backing Into Network Operations," *Proceedings of the 1973 Clinic on Library Applications of Data Processing: Networking and Other Forms of Cooperation*, University of Illinois Graduate School of Library Science, Urbana, 1973, pp. 9-23.

8. See "Massachusetts Central Book Processing Center Effects Savings for State-Supported Institutions," *College & Research Libraries News*, no. 4, 89-90 (April 1971); Lawrence F. Buckland et al., *Final Report, Phase I: Survey of Automated Library Systems*, Prepared for the California State University and Colleges, Inforonics, Inc., Maynard, Mass., 1973, Appendix A, p. D-E 4; "Massachusetts Central Library Processing Center Report," *JOLA Technical Communications*, 3, 5-6 (May/June 1972); and "Hammer Outlines Central Processing Difficulties," *Advanced Technology/Libraries*, 2, 1-2 (June 1973).

9. See Gordon H. Wright, "An Ontario Libraries' Network, or Cooperative Entanglement," in *Proceedings of the 1973 Clinic on Library Automation of Data Processing: Networking and Other Forms of Cooperation*, University of Illinois Graduate School of Library Science, Urbana, 1973, pp. 68-101.

10. See Chapter 9.

11. Peter J. Paulson, "Networks, Automation and Technical Services: Experience and Experiments in New York State," *Library Resources & Technical Services*, 13, 518 (Fall 1969).

12. "New Jersey Has Captain, But Captain Needs A Commander," *Advanced Technology/Libraries*, 3, 1-2 (May 1974).

13. "Maryland Academic Libraries' Automation Center," *Information Retrieval and Library Automation Letter*, 9, 12 (March 1974).

14. *Advanced Technology/Libraries*, 4, 3 (January 1975), and oral report by Ralph Franklin at the Midwinter meeting of ALA's COLA Discussion Group, Chicago, January 19, 1975.

15. "Indiana Cooperative Library Services Authority," *Journal of Library Automation*, 7, 316 (December 1974).

16. "Midwest Library Network Under Study," *Library of Congress Information Bulletin*, 33, 405-406 (December 6, 1975); and "Regional Projects and Activities," *Journal of Library Automation*, 8, 73-74 (March 1975).

17. "Stanford's BALLOTS On-Line Files Publicly Available through SPIRES September 16, 1974," *Journal of Library Automation*, 7, 316-317 (December 1974).

18. "Oregon Alters Network Plans; Competitive Bidding Likely," *Advanced Technology/Libraries*, 3, 2-3 (April 1974).

19. "SALINET--Satellite Library Information Network," *Journal of Library Automation*, 7, 228-229 (September 1974).

20. For further information on mini-computers, see three papers in the *Proceedings of the 1974 Clinic on Library Applications of Data Processing: Applications of Minicomputers to Library and Related Problems*, University of Illinois Graduate School of Library Science, Urbana, 1975: J. L. Divilbiss, "A Hardware Tutorial," pp. 3-10; James F. Corey, "Configurations and Software: A Tutorial," pp. 11-27; and Audrey N. Grosch, "Minicomputers--Characteristics, Economics and Selection for an Integrated Library Management System," pp. 158-169.

21. Paul J. Fasana, "The Collaborative Library Systems Development Project (CLSDP): A Mechanisn for Inter-University Cooperation," in *Collaborative Library Systems Development*, M.I.T. Press, Cambridge, Massachusetts, 1971, pp. 231-232.

22. By the author, September 1974.

BIBLIOGRAPHY

As in the text, reports of projects which are not yet operational have for the most part been omitted, as have news notes and papers on specialized aspects of the subject. An attempt has been made to include only those articles likely to remain significant or useful for several years, but the reader will understand that such an attempt is hazardous at best.

The bibliography is arranged, first, by broad category or type of application; second, under each category, in reverse chronological order, so that the most recent articles appear first; and finally in alphabetical sequence by author. Items starred are for first reading.

General Bibliography

Continuing bibliographic coverage is provided by:

**Annual Review of Information Science and Technology*, v. 1, 1966- (Publisher varies).

The following three bibliographies, used together as a series, provide coverage through 1971:

Billingsley, Alice, "Bibliography of Library Automation," *American Libraries*, 3, 289-312 (March 1972).

Mason, Charlene, "Bibliography of Library Automation," *ALA Bulletin*, 63, 1117-1134 (September 1969).

McCune, Lois C., and Stephen R. Salmon, "Bibliography of Library Automation," *ALA Bulletin*, 61, 674-694 (June 1967).

Bibliography

General and Miscellaneous

1975

* De Gennaro, Richard, "Library Automation: The Second Decade," *Journal of Library Automation*, 8, 3-4 (March 1975).

1974

* Veaner, Allen B., "Institutional Political and Fiscal Factors in the Development of Library Automation, 1967-71," *Journal of Library Automation*, 7, 5-26 (March 1974).

1973

* Buckland, Lawrence F. et al., *Final Report, Phase I. Survey of Automated Library Systems, Prepared for the California State University and Colleges*, Inforonics, Inc., Maynard, Massachusetts, 1973.

* Palmer, Richard Phillips, *Case Studies in Library Computer Systems*, R. R. Bowker, New York, 1973.

1972

Avram, Henriette D., "Library Automation: A Balanced View," *Library Resources & Technical Services*, 16, 11-18 (Winter 1972).

Avram, Henriette D., Lenore S. Maruyama, and John C. Rather (eds.) "Automation Activities in the Processing Department of the Library of Congress," *Library Resources & Technical Services*, 16, 195-239 (Spring 1972).

Kilgour, Frederick, "Evolving, Computerizing, Personalizing," *American Libraries*, 3, 141-147 (February 1972).

* Markuson, Barbara Evans et al., *Guidelines for Library Automation: a Handbook for Federal and Other Libraries*, System Development Corporation, Santa Monica, California, 1972.

Mason, Ellsworth, "Automation, or Russian Roulette?" *Proceedings of the 1972 Clinic on Library Applications of Data Processing*, University of Illinois Graduate School of Library Science, Urbana, 1972, pp. 138-156.

Warheit, I. A., "On-Line Interactive Systems in Libraries, Now and in the Future," *Proceedings of the 1972 Clinic on Library Applications of Data Processing*, University of Illinois Graduate School of Library Science, Urbana, 1972, pp. 3-21.

1971

Balmforth, C. K., and N. S. M. Cox (eds.) *Interface: Library Automation with Special Reference to Computing Activity*, M.I.T. Press, Cambridge, Mass., 1971.

Fasana, Paul J., and Allen Veaner (eds.) *Collaborative Library Systems Development*, M.I.T. Press, Cambridge, Mass., 1971.

LARC Association, *A Survey of Automated Activities in the Libraries of the U.S. and Canada*, 2d edition, compiled and edited by Frank S. Patrinostro, LARC Association, Tempe, Arizona, 1971.

McAllister, Caryl, "On-Line Library Housekeeping Systems: a Survey," *Special Libraries*, 62, 457-468 (November 1971).

Mason, Ellsworth, "Along the Academic Way," *Library Journal*, 96, 1671-1676 (May 15, 1971).

Mason, Ellsworth, "The Great Gas Bubble Prick't, or, Computers Revealed by a Gentleman of Quality," *College & Research Libraries*, 32, 183-196 (May 1971).

Weber, David C., "Personnel Aspects of Library Automation," *Journal of Library Automation*, 4, 27-37 (March 1971).

1970

Bierman, Kenneth John, and Betty Jean Blue, "A MARC-Based SDI Service," *Journal of Library Automation*, 3, 304-319 (December 1970).

*Hayes, Robert M., and Joseph Becker, *Handbook of Data Processing for Libraries*, Wiley-Becker-Hayes, New York, 1970.

Jacob, Mary Ellen L., "Standardized Costs for Automated Library Systems," *Journal of Library Automation*, 3, 207-217 (September 1970).

Locke, William N., "Computer Costs for Large Libraries," *Datamation*, 16, 69-74 (February 1970).

Markuson, Barbara Evans, "An Overview of Library Systems and Automation," *Datamation*, 16, 60-68 (February 1970).

Veaner, Allen B., "Major Decision Points in Library Automation," *College & Research Libraries*, 31, 299-312 (September 1970).

Veaner, Allen B., "The Application of Computers to Library Technical Processing," *College & Research Libraries*, 31, 36-42 (January 1970).

Warheit, I. A., "Design of Library Systems for Implementation with Interactive Computers," *Journal of Library Automation*, 3, 65-78 (March 1970).

1969

Dougherty, Richard M., "The Colorado Academic Libraries Book Processing Center Study," *Library Resources & Technical Services*, 13, 115, 136-141 (Winter 1969).

Kilgour, Frederick G., "The Economic Goal of Library Automation," *College & Research Libraries*, 30, 307-311 (July 1969).

Overmyer, LaVahn, *Library Automation: a Critical Review*, U.S. Office of Education Bureau of Research, Washington, D.C. (December 1969).

1968

De Gennaro, Richard, "Automation in the Harvard College Library," *Harvard Library Bulletin*, 16, 217-236 (July 1968).

* De Gennaro, Richard, "The Development and Administration of Automated Systems in Academic Libraries," *Journal of Library Automation*, 1, 75-91 (March 1968).

* Kimber, R. T., *Automation in Libraries*, Pergamon Press, New York, 1968.

1967

* Cox, N. S. M., J. D. Dews, and J. L. Dolby, *The Computer and the Library; the Role of the Computer in the Organization and Handling of Information in Libraries*, Archon Books, Hamden, Conn., 1967.

Fasana, Paul J., "Determining the Cost of Library Automation," *ALA Bulletin*, 61, 656-661 (June 1967).

Harrison, John, and Peter Laslett (eds.), *The Brasenose Conference on the Automation of Libraries, Proceedings of the Anglo-American Conference on the Mechanization of Library Services 30 June - 3 July 1966*, Mansell, London, 1967.

Shera, Jesse H., "Librarians against Machines," *Science*, 156, 746-750 (May 12, 1967).

1966

Markuson, Barbara Evans, "A System Development Study for the Library of Congress Automation Program," *The Library Quarterly*, 36, 197-273 (July 1966).

Papazian, Pierre, "The Old Order and the New Breed; or Will Automation Spoil Mel Dewey?" *ALA Bulletin*, 60, 644-646 (June 1966).

Salmon, Stephen R., "Automation of Library Procedures at Washington University," *Missouri Library Association Quarterly*, 27, 11-14 (March 1966).

Stewart, Bruce Warren, "Data Processing in Academic Library," *Wilson Library Bulletin*, 41, 388-395 (December 1966).

Stewart, Bruce Warren, "Data Processing in the Texas A & M University Library," in *Proceedings of the 1966 Clinic on Library Applications of Data Processing*, University of Illinois Graduate School of Library Science, Urbana, 1966, pp. 167-181.

Stuart-Stubbs, Basil, *Conference on Computers in Canadian Libraries, Université Laval, Quebec, March 21-22, 1966, A Report Prepared for the Canadian Association of College and University Libraries*, University of British Columbia Library, Vancouver, 1966.

Vickery, B. C., "The Future of Libraries," *The Library Association Record*, 68, 252-260 (July 1966).

Bibliography

Welsh, William J., "Compatibility of Systems," in Harvey, John (ed.) *Data Processing in Public and University Libraries*, Spartan Books, Washington, D.C., 1966, pp. 79-93.

White, Herbert S., "To the Barricades! The Computers are Coming!" *Special Libraries*, 57, 631-635 (November 1966).

1965

Hammer, Donald P., "Automated Operations in a University Library; A Summary," *College & Research Libraries*, 26, 19-29, 44 (January 1965).

Hayes, Robert M., "Implications for Librarianship of Computer Technology," in Goldhor, Herbert (ed.) *Proceedings of the 1964 Clinic on Library Applications of Data Processing*, University of Illinois Graduate School of Library Science, Urbana, 1965, pp. 1-6.

Licklider, J. C. R., *Libraries of the Future*, M.I.T. Press, Cambridge, Mass., 1965.

Howe, Mary T., "Mechanization in the Decatur Public Library," in *IBM Library Mechanization Symposium, Endicott, N.Y., May 25, 1964, Proceedings*, White Plains, N.Y., 1965, pp. 1-13.

Overhage, Carl F. J., and R. Joyce Harmon (eds.) *Intrex: Report of a Planning Conference on Information Transfer Experiments, September 3, 1965*, M.I.T. Press, Cambridge, Mass., 1965.

Parker, Ralph H., "The Machine and the Librarian," *Library Resources & Technical Services*, 9, 100-103 (Winter 1965).

Weiss, Rudi, "The State of Automation? A Survey of Machinery Used in Technical Services Departments in New York State Libraries," *Library Resources & Technical Services*, 9, 289-302 (Summer 1965).

Before 1965

Brodman, Estelle, and Chester R. Gough, *Computers in Medical and University Libraries; a Review of the Situation in the U.S. in 1964*, Washington University School of Medicine, St. Louis, 1964.

Clapp, Verner W., "Mechanization and Automation in American Libraries," *Libri*, 14, 369-375 (1964).

Clapp, Verner W., *The Future of the Research Library*, University of Illinois Press, Urbana, Illinois, 1964.

Griffin, Hillis L., "Estimating Data Processing Costs in Libraries," *College & Research Libraries*, 25, 400-403 (September 1964).

Markuson, Barbara Evans (ed.) *Libraries and Automation: Proceedings, Conference on Libraries and Automation, Airlie Foundation, 1963*, Library of Congress, Washington, D.C., 1964.

Parker, Ralph H., "Development of Automatic Systems at the University of Missouri Library," in Goldhor, Herbert (ed.) *Proceedings of the*

1963 Clinic on Library Applications of Data Processing, University of Illinois Graduate School of Library Science, Urbana, 1964, pp. 48-55.

Parker, Ralph H., "What Every Librarian Should Know About Automation," *Wilson Library Bulletin*, 38, 752-754 (May 1964).

Schultz, Claire K., "Automation of Reference Work," *Library Trends*, 12, 413-424 (January 1964).

Stein, Theodore, "Automation & Library Systems," *Library Journal*, 89, 2723-2734 (July 1964).

King, Gilbert W. et al., *Automation and the Library of Congress*, Library of Congress, Washington, D.C., 1963.

Lipetz, Ben-Ami, "Labor Costs, Conversion Costs, and Compatibility in Document Control Systems," *American Documentation*, 14, 117-122 (April 1963).

Swanson, Don R., "Library Goals and the Role of Automation," *Special Libraries*, 53, 466-471 (October 1962).

Parker, Ralph H., *Library Applications of Punched Cards; A Description of Mechanical Systems*, American Library Association, Chicago, Illinois, 1952.

Bush, Vannevar, "As We May Think," *Atlantic Monthly*, 176, 106-107 (July 1945).

Integrated Systems

1975

Brudvig, Glenn L., "The Development of a Minicomputer System for the University of Minnesota Bio-medical Library," in *Proceedings of the 1974 Clinic on Library Applications of Data Processing: Applications of Minicomputers to Library and Related Problems*, University of Illinois Graduate School of Library Science, Urbana, 1975, pp. 170-190.

Davison, Wayne, "Minicomputers and Library Automation: The Stanford Experience," in *Proceedings of the 1974 Clinic on Library Applications of Data Processing: Applications of Minicomputers to Library and Related Problems*, University of Illinois Graduate School of Library Science, Urbana, 1975, pp. 80-95.

Payne, Charles T., "The University of Chicago Library Data Management System," in *Proceedings of the 1974 Clinic on Library Applications of Data Processing: Applications of Minicomputers to Library and Related Problems*, University of Illinois Graduate School of Library Science, Urbana, 1975, pp. 105-119.

Project BALLOTS and the Stanford University Libraries, "Stanford University's BALLOTS System," *Journal of Library Automation*, 8, 31-50 (March 1975).

1974

Bentley, Jane F., and Leo J. Cooney, "Automation at the Redstone Scientific Information Center--An Integrated System," *Library Resources & Technical Services*, 18, 259-267 (Summer 1974).

Horny, Karen, "Automation of Technical Services: Northwestern's Experience," *College & Research Libraries*, 35, 364-369 (September 1974).

1973

"BALLOTS-MARC Operations at Stanford University," *Library of Congress Information Bulletin*, 32, 130-131 (April 13, 1973).

Hammer, Donald P., and James S. Sokoloski, "The Massachusetts Central Library Processing Service," in *Proceedings of the 1973 Clinic on Library Applications of Data Processing*, University of Illinois Graduate School of Library Science, Urbana, 1973, pp. 124-149.

Stone, Sandra E., *History of Automation at Yale University Library*, Yale University Library, New Haven, Connecticut, 1973.

1972

*Epstein, A. H. et al., *Bibliographic Automation of Large Library Operations Using a Time-Sharing System: Phase I, Final Report*, Stanford University Library, Stanford, California, 1972, ED 049 786.

Epstein, A. H. et al., *Bibliographic Automation of Large Library Operations Using a Time-Sharing System: Phase II, Part I (July 1970-June 1972), Final Report*, Stanford University Libraries, Stanford, California, 1972, ED 060 883.

Epstein, A. H., and Allen B. Veaner, "A User's View of BALLOTS," in *Proceedings of the 1972 Clinic on Library Applications of Data Processing*, University of Illinois Graduate School of Library Science, Urbana, 1972, pp. 109-137.

Kountz, John C., "BIBLIOS Revisited," *Journal of Library Automation*, 5, 63-86 (June 1972).

1971

Payne, Charles T., "The Chicago Experience," in *Collaborative Library Systems Development*, Cambridge, Mass., M.I.T. Press, 1971, pp. 5-10.

Payne, Charles T., and Kenney Hecht, "The University of Chicago's Book Processing System," in *Collaborative Library Systems Development*, Cambridge, Mass., M.I.T. Press, 1971, pp. 183-192.

Veaner, Allen, Hank Epstein, and John Schroeder, "The Stanford Experience," in *Collaborative Library Systems Development*, M.I.T. Press, Cambridge, Mass., 1971, pp. 42-68.

1970

Cady, Glee et al., *System Scope for Library Automation and Generalized Information Storage and Retrieval at Stanford University*, Stanford University, Stanford, California, 1970.

Kountz, John C., and Robert E. Norton, "BIBLIOS: a Modular System for Library Automation," *Datamation*, 16, 79-83 (February 1970).

1969

Black, Donald V., "Library Information System Time-Sharing on a Large, General-Purpose Computer," in *Proceedings of the 1968 Clinic on Library Applications of Data Processing*, University of Illinois Graduate School of Library Science, Urbana, 1969, pp. 139-154.

Kountz, John C., and Robert Norton, "BIBLIOS--A Modular Approach to Total Library ADP," in *American Society for Information Science: Proceedings*, v. 6, *Cooperating Information Societies*, Greenwood, Westport, Conn., 1969, pp. 39-50.

1968

Boylan, Merle N. et al., *Automated Acquisition, Cataloging, and Circulation in a Large Research Library*, Lawrence Radiation Laboratory, University of California, Livermore, California, 1968.

Fussler, Herman H., and Charles T. Payne, *Development of an Integrated, Computer-Based, Bibliographical Data System for a Large University Library; Annual Report to the National Science Foundation from the University of Chicago Library, 1967/68*, University of Chicago Library, Chicago, Illinois, 1968. ED 022 514.

Jansen, Guenter A., *Univac Electronic Data Processing in the Public Library Systems of Long Island*, Univac Division, Sperry Rand Corporation, Washington, D.C., 1968 (?).

Scott, Jack W., "An Integrated Computer Based Technical Processing System in a Small College Library," *Journal of Library Automation*, 1, 149-158 (September 1968).

University of Chicago Library, *Development of an Integrated, Computer Based, Bibliographical Data System for a Large University Library*, Chicago, 1968. PB 179 426.

Weisbrod, David L., "An Integrated Computerized Bibliographic System for Libraries," *Drexel Library Quarterly*, 4, 214-232 (July 1968).

1967

Payne, Charles T., "An Integrated, Computer-Based Bibliographic Data System for a Large University Library: Problems and Progress at the University of Chicago," in *Proceedings of the 1967 Clinic on Library Applications of Data Processing*, University of Illinois Graduate School of Library Science, Urbana, 1967, pp. 29-40.

Bibliography

1966

Alanen, Sally, David E. Sparks, and Frederick G. Kilgour, "A Computer-monitored Library Technical Processing System," in *Progress in Information Science and Technology; Proceedings of the American Documentation Institute 1966 Annual Meeting, October 3-7, 1966, Santa Monica, California*, Adrianne Press, n.p., 1966, pp. 419-426.

Batts, Nathalie C., "Data Analysis of Science Monograph Order/Cataloging Forms," *Special Libraries*, 57, 583-586 (October 1966).

Geddes, Andrew, "Data Processing in a Cooperative System--Opportunities for Service," in Harvey, John (ed.) *Data Processing in Public and University Libraries*, Spartan Books, Washington, D.C., 1966, pp. 25-35.

1965

Burns, Lorin R., "The Use of IBM Unit Record Equipment in the Lake County Public Library," in *IBM Library Mechanization Symposium, Endicott, N.Y., May 25, 1964*, pp. 15-35.

Moore, Evelyn A., Estelle Brodman, and Geraldine S. Cohen, "Mechanization of Library Procedures in the Medium-Sized Medical Library: III. Acquisitions and Cataloging," *Bulletin of the Medical Library Association*, 53, 305-328 (July 1965).

Acquisitions

1972

Auld, Larry, and Robert Baker, "LOLITA: An On-Line Book Order and Fund Accounting System," in *Proceedings of the 1972 Clinic on Library Applications of Data Processing*, University of Illinois Graduate School of Library Science, Urbana, 1972, pp. 29-53.

Carter, Ruth C., "Automation of Acquisitions at Parkland College," *Journal of Library Automation*, 5, 118-136 (June 1972).

1971

"Library Acquisitions Information System (LAIS)," *LARC Reports*, 4, 1-68 (1971).

1970

Burgess, Thomas K., "Criteria for Design of an On-Line Acquisitions System at Washington State University Library," in *Proceedings of the 1969 Clinic on Library Applications of Data Processing*, University of Illinois Graduate School of Library Science, Urbana, 1970, pp. 50-66.

* Dunlap, Connie R., "Mechanization of Acquisition Processes," in Melvin J. Voigt (ed.) *Advances in Librarianship*, v. 1, Academic Press, New York, 1970, pp. 37-55.

Kennedy, James H., and James S. Sokoloski, "Man-Machine Considerations of an Operational On-Line University Library Acquisition System," in *Proceedings of the American Society for Information Science, v. 7: The Information-Conscious Society*, n.p., 1970, pp. 65-67.

Spigai, Frances G., and Thomas Mahan, "On-Line Acquisitions by LOLITA," *Journal of Library Automation*, 3, 276-294 (December 1970).

1969

Cage, Alvin C., "Data Processing Applications for Acquisitions at the TSU Library," *Proceedings of the Second Texas Conference on Library Automation*, March 27, 1969, n.p., n.d., pp. 35-57.

* Dunlap, Connie, "The Automation of Acquisitions Systems," in *Library Automation, a State of the Art Review*, American Library Association, Chicago, 1969, pp. 37-43.

Evans, Glyn, and Estelle Brodman, *The Redesign of the Automated Acquisitions-Catalog System at Washington University School of Medicine Library*, the Library, St. Louis, 1969.

Kilgour, Frederick G., "Effect of Computerization on Acquisitions," *Program*, 3, 95-103 (November 1969).

Teare, Robert F., "Experience to Date in Automated Acquisitions at Honnold Library," in *Proceedings of the American Society for Information Science, v. 6: Cooperating Information Societies*, Greenwood Publishing Corp., Westport, Conn., 1969, pp. 29-38.

Thomson, James W., and Robert H. Muller, "The Computer-Based Book Order System at the University of Michigan Library: A Review and Evaluation," in *Proceedings of the 1968 Clinic on Library Applications of Data Processing*, University of Illinois Graduate School of Library Science, Urbana, 1969, pp. 54-78.

Widener Library Acquisitions System, Harvard University Library, Cambridge, Mass., [1969?].

1968

Burgess, Thomas K., and L. Ames, *LOLA: Library On-Line Acquisition Sub-System*, Washington State University Systems Office, Pullman, Washington, 1968.

Jansen, Guenter A., *Univac Electronic Data Processing in the Public Library Systems of Long Island*, Univac Division, Sperry Rand Corporation, Washington, D.C., [1968?].

1967

Dobb, T. C., "Simon Fraser's Automated Acquisitions System, April 1st, 1966 to April 1st, 1967," in *Automation in Libraries*, Canadian Association of College and University Libraries, n.p., 1967, pp. 25-36.

Dunlap, Connie, "Automated Acquisitions Procedures at the University of Michigan Library," *Library Resources & Technical Services*, 11 192-202 (Spring 1967).

Macpherson, John F., "Automated Acquisition at University of Western Ontario," in *Automation in Libraries*, Canadian Association of College and University Libraries, n.p., 1967, pp. 37-42.

Shaw, Ralph R., "Control of Book Funds at the University of Hawaii Library," *Library Resources & Technical Services*, 11, 380-382 (Summer 1967).

Vagianos, Louis, "Acquisitions: Policies, Procedures, and Problems," in *Automation in Libraries*, Canadian Association of College and University Libraries, n.p., 1967, pp. 1-24.

1966

Corbin, John B., "The Acquisitions Program of the Centralized Processing Center of the Texas State Library," in *Proceedings [of the] First Texas Conference on Library Automation*, March 23-24, 1966, Texas Library & Historical Commission, Austin, Texas, 1966, pp. 36-39.

Line, Maurice B., "Automation of Acquisition Records and Routine in the University Library, Newcastle upon Tyne," *Program*, no. 2, June 1966.

1965

Burns, Lorin R., "The Use of IBM Unit Record Equipment in the Lake County Public Library," in *IBM Library Mechanization Symposium, Endicott, New York, May 25, 1964*, International Business Machines, White Plains, New York [1965], pp. 15-35.

Cox, Carl R., "The Mechanization of Acquisition and Circulation Procedures at the University of Maryland Library," in *IBM Library Mechanization Symposium, Endicott, New York, May 25, 1964*, International Business Machines, White Plains, New York [1965], pp. 206-235.

Howe, Mary T., "Mechanization in the Decatur Public Library," in *IBM Library Mechanization Symposium, Endicott, New York, May 25, 1964*, International Business Machines, White Plains, N.Y. [1965], pp. 1-13.

Minder, Thomas L., "Automation--the Acquisitions Program at the Pennsylvania State University Library," in *IBM Library Mechanization Symposium, Endicott, New York, May 25, 1964*, International Business Machines, White Plains, N.Y. [1965], pp. 145-156.

Minder, Thomas L., and Gerald Lazorick, "Automation of the Penn State University Acquisitions Department," in *IBM Library Mechanization Symposium, Endicott, New York, May 25, 1964*, International Business Machines, White Plains, N.Y. [1965], pp. 157-163.

Moore, Evelyn A., Estelle Brodman, and Geraldine S. Cohen, "Mechanization of Library Procedures in the Medium-sized Medical Library: III. Acquisition and Catalog," *Bulletin of the Medical Library Association*, 53, 305-328 (July 1965).

Morrissey, Eleanor F., "A Mechanized Book Order and Accounting Routine," *Southeastern Librarian*, 15, 143-148 (Fall 1965).

Schultheiss, Louis A., "Data Processing Aids in Acquisitions Work," *Library Resources & Technical Services*, 9, 66-72 (Winter 1965).

Before 1965

Randall, G. E., and Roger P. Bristol, "PIL (Processing Information List); Or A Computer-Controlled Processing Record," *Special Libraries*, 55, 82-85 (February 1964).

Culbertson, Don S., "The Costs of Data Processing in University Libraries; In Book Acquisition and Cataloging," *College & Research Libraries*, 24, 487-489 (November 1963).

Parker, Ralph H., "Automatic Records System at the University of Missouri Library," *College & Research Libraries*, 23, 231-232, 264-265 (May 1962).

Keller, Alton H., "Book Records on Punched Cards," *Library Journal*, 71, 1785-1786 (December 1946).

Moffitt, Alexander, "Punched Card Records in Serial Acquisitions," *College & Research Libraries*, 7, 10-13 (January 1946).

Parker, Ralph H., "Development of Automatic Systems at the University of Missouri Library," in *Proceedings of the 1963 Clinic on Library Applications of Data Processing*, University of Illinois Graduate School of Library Science, Urbana, 1964, pp. 46-48.

Cataloging (General)

1974

Butler, Brett, "Automatic Format Recognition of MARC Bibliographic Elements: a Review and Projection," *Journal of Library Automation*, 7, 27-42 (March 1974).

*Overhage, Carl F. J., and J. Francis Reintjes, "Project Intrex: a General Review," *Information Storage and Retrieval*, 10, 157-188 (May/June 1974).

1973

U.S. Library of Congress, RECON Working Task Force, *National Aspects of Creating and Using MARC/RECON Records*, Washington, D.C., 1973.

1972

Chen, Simon P. J., "On-Line and Real-Time Cataloging," *American Libraries*, 3, 117-119 (February 1972).

*U.S. Library of Congress, MARC Development Office, *Books: A MARC Format; Specification for Magnetic Tapes Containing Catalog Records for Books*, 5th edition, U.S. Government Printing Office, Washington, D.C., 1972.

Van Dyke, Vern J., and Nancy L. Ayer, "Multipurpose Cataloging and Indexing System (CAIN) at the National Agricultural Library," *Journal of Library Automation*, 5, 21-29 (March 1972).

Winik, Ruth, "Reference Function in an On-Line Catalog," *Special Libraries*, 63, 217-221 (May/June 1972).

1971

American National Standards Institute Committee Z39, *American National Standard Format for Bibliographic Information Interchange on Magnetic Tape*, American National Standards Institute, New York, 1971.

Avram, Henriette D., "The Evolving MARC System: The Concept of a Data Utility," in *Proceedings of the 1970 Clinic on Library Applications of Data Processing: MARC Uses and Users*, University of Illinois Graduate School of Library Science, Urbana, 1971, pp. 1-26.

Kennedy, John P., "File Size and the Cost of Processing MARC Records," *Journal of Library Automation*, 4, 1-12 (March 1971).

Shoffner, Ralph M., "Some Implications of Automatic Recognition of Bibliographic Elements," *Journal of the American Society for Information Science*, 22, 275-282 (July/August 1971).

1970

Curran, Ann T., "Library Networks: Cataloging and Bibliographic Aspects," in *Proceedings of the 1969 Clinic on Library Applications of Data Processing*, University of Illinois Graduate School of Library Science, Urbana, 1970, pp. 31-41.

De Gennaro, Richard, "A National Bibliographic Data Base in Machine-Readable Form: Progress and Prospects," *Library Trends*, 18, 537-550 (April 1970).

*Kilgour, Frederick G., "Concept of an On-Line Computerized Library Catalog," *Journal of Library Automation*, 3, 1-11 (March 1970).

U.S. Library of Congress, MARC Development Office, *Films: A MARC Format*, Library of Congress, Washington, D.C., 1970.

U.S. Library of Congress, Information Systems Office, *Format Recognition Process for MARC Records: a Logical Design*, American Library Association, Chicago, 1970.

U.S. Library of Congress, Information Systems Office, *Maps: A MARC Format*, Library of Congress, Washington, D.C., 1970.

1969

Avram, Henriette D., "Implications of Project MARC," in *Library Automation: a State of the Art Review*, American Library Association, Chicago, 1969, pp. 79-89.

Avram, Henriette D., et al., "MARC Program Research and Development: a Progress Report," *Journal of Library Automation*, 2, 250-253 (December 1969).

Benenfeld, Alan R., "Generation and Encoding of the Project Intrex Augmented Catalog Data Base," in *Proceedings of the 1968 Clinic on Library Applications of Data Processing*, University of Illinois Graduate School of Library Science, Urbana, 1969, pp. 155-198.

Dolby, J. L., and V. J. Forsyth, "An Analysis of Cost Factors in Maintaining and Updating Card Catalogs," *Journal of Library Automation*, 2, 218-241 (December 1969).

U.S. Library of Congress, RECON Working Task Force, *Conversion of Retrospective Catalog Records to Machine-Readable Form: A Study of the Feasibility of a National Bibliographic Service*, Library of Congress, Washington, D.C., 1969.

U.S. Library of Congress, Information Systems Office, *MARC Manuals Used by the Library of Congress*, v. 1 to 4, American Library Association, Information Science and Automation Division, Chicago, 1969.

1968

Avram, Henriette D., "MARC is a Four-Letter Word," *Library Journal*, 93, 2601-2605 (July 1968).

Chapin, Richard E., and Dale H. Pretzer, "Comparative Costs for Converting Shelf List Records to Machine Readable Form," *Journal of Library Automation*, 1, 66-74 (March 1968).

U.S. Library of Congress, Information Systems Office, *The MARC Pilot Experience: An Informal Summary*, Library of Congress, Washington, D.C., 1968, pp. 9-13.

1967

Weiss, Irvin J., and Emilie V. Wiggins, "Computer-Aided Centralized Cataloging at the National Library of Medicine," *Library Resources & Technical Services*, 11, 83-96 (Winter 1967).

1966

Buckland, Lawrence F., *The Recording of Library of Congress Bibliographical Data in Machine Form: A Report Prepared for the Council on Library Resources, Inc.*, Rev., Council on Library Resources, Inc., Washington, D.C., 1966.

U.S. Library of Congress, Information Systems Office, *A Preliminary Report on the MARC (Machine Readable Catalog) Pilot Project*, Washington, D.C., 1966.

1965

Avram, H. D., R. S. Freitag, and K. D. Guiles, *Planning Memorandum No. 3: A Proposed Format for a Standardized Machine Readable Catalog Record*, Library of Congress, Washington, D.C., 1965.

Massachusetts Institute of Technology, Project Intrex, *Semiannual Activity Report, 15 September 1965-*, Massachusetts Institute of Technology, Cambridge, Mass.

Before 1965

Buckland, Lawrence F., "Problems Confronting Machine Processing of Shared Catalog Data," in Association of Research Libraries, *Minutes of the Sixty-Fourth Meeting*, June 27, 1964, pp. 13-24.

Buckland, Lawrence F., *The Recording of Library of Congress Bibliographical Data in Machine Form*, Inforonics, Inc., Maynard, Mass., 1964.

Simonton, Wesley C., "The Computerized Catalog: Possible, Feasible, Desirable?" *Library Resources & Technical Services*, 8, 399-407 (Fall 1964).

Swanson, Don R., "Dialogues with a Catalog," *The Library Quarterly*, 34, 113-125 (January 1964).

Cataloging (Catalog Card Production)

1974

Bowden, Virginia M., and Ruby B. Miller, "MARCIVE: A Cooperative Automated Library System," *Journal of Library Automation*, 7, 183-200 (September 1974).

M. M. Williamson, "MT/ST and MCRS at the University of Houston Libraries," in *RLMS Micro-File: Current State of Catalog Card Reproduction*, American Library Association, Chicago, 1974, pp. 74-88.

1973

*Hopkins, Judith, "The Ohio College Library Center," *Library Resources & Technical Services*, 17, 308-319 (Summer 1973).

Kniesner, Dan L., and Betty J. Meyer, "On-Line Computer Techniques in Shared Cataloging," *Library Resources & Technical Services*, 17, 225-230 (Spring 1973).

Long, Philip L., "OCLC: From Concept to Functioning Network," in *Proceedings of the 1973 Clinic on Library Applications of Data Processing*, University of Illinois Graduate School of Library Science, Urbana, 1973, pp. 165-170.

Miller, Ellen Wasby, and B. J. Hodges, "Shawnee Mission's On-Line Cataloging System: The First Two Years," in *Proceedings of the 1972 Clinic on Library Applications of Data Processing*, University of Illinois Graduate School of Library Science, Urbana, 1972, pp. 94-108.

Ohmes, Frances, and J. F. Jones, "The Other Half of Cataloging," *Library Resources & Technical Services*, 17, 320-329 (Summer 1973).

"On-Line Cataloging and Circulation at Western Kentucky University: An Approach to Automated Instructional Resources Management," *The LARC Reports*, 6, no. 1 (1973).

1972

Miller, Ruby B., and Robert A. Houze, "New Horizons in Computer Applications at Trinity University Library," *Texas Library Journal*, 48, 227-229, 254-255 (November 1972).

1971

Miller, Ellen Wasby, and B. J. Hodges, "Shawnee Mission's On-Line Cataloging System," *Journal of Library Automation*, 4, 13-26 (March 1971).

1970

Blair, John R., and Ruby Snyder, "An Automated Library System: Project LEEDS," *American Libraries*, 5, 172-173 (February 1970).

Kilgour, Frederick G., "A Regional Network: Ohio College Library Center," *Datamation*, 16, 87-89 (February 1970).

Kilgour, Frederick G., Philip L. Long, and Eugene B. Leiderman, "Retrieval of Bibliographic Entries From a Name-Title Catalog by Use of Truncated Search Keys," in *Proceedings of the American Society for Information Science, v. 7, The Information-Conscious Society*, the Society, Washington, D.C., 1970, pp. 79-82.

Salmon, Stephen R., "Development of the Card Automated Reproduction and Distribution System (CARDS) at the Library of Congress," in *Proceedings of the 1969 Clinic on Library Applications of Data Processing*, University of Illinois Graduate School of Library Science, Urbana, 1970, pp. 98-113.

Tom, Ellen, and Sue Reed, *SCOPE in Cataloging*, Guelph University Library, Guelph, Ontario, 1970. ED 045 108.

1969

Breiland, Mildred, "Centralized Data Processing for Libraries in the Albuquerque Public Schools," *Drexel Library Quarterly*, 5, 92-100 (April 1969).

Kennedy, John P., "A Local MARC Project: The Georgia Tech Library," in *Proceedings of the 1968 Clinic on Library Applications of Data Processing*, University of Illinois Graduate School of Library Science, Urbana, 1969, pp. 206-212.

Kilgour, Frederick G., "Initial System Design for the Ohio College Library Center: A Case History," in *Proceedings of the 1968 Clinic on Library Applications of Data Processing*, University of Illinois Graduate School of Library Science, Urbana, 1969, pp. 54-78.

Bibliography

Reynolds, Michael, "Indiana University Regional Campus Libraries: Toward a System of Academic Libraries," in *Proceedings of the 1968 Clinic on Library Applications of Data Processing*, University of Illinois Graduate School of Library Science, Urbana, 1969, pp. 89-138.

1968

Hirst, Robert I., "Adapting the IBM MT/ST for Library Applications; a Manual for Planning," *Special Libraries*, 59, 626-633 (October 1968).

Kilgour, Frederick G., "Costs of Library Catalog Cards Produced by Computer," *Journal of Library Automation*, 1, 121-127 (June 1968).

Murrill, Donald P., "Production of Library Catalog Cards and Bulletin Using an IBM 1620 Computer and an IBM 870 Document Writing System," *Journal of Library Automation*, 1, 198-212 (September 1968).

Scott, Jack W., "An Integrated Computer Based Technical Processing System in a Small College Library," *Journal of Library Automation*, 1, 149-158 (September 1968).

1967

Luckett, George R., "Partial Library Automation with the Flexowriter Automatic Writing Machine," *Library Resources & Technical Services*, 10, 207-210 (Fall 1967).

1966

Curley, Walter W., "The Data Processing Program in Operation at the Suffolk Cooperative Library System, Patchogue, N.Y.," in *Proceedings of the 1965 Clinic on Library Applications of Data Processing*, University of Illinois Graduate School of Library Science, Urbana, 1966, pp. 15-42.

Dodendorf, Mary Seely, "870 Document Writing System of International Business Machine Corporation in the Library Section, Los Angeles City Schools," in *Proceedings of the 1965 Clinic on Applications of Data Processing*, University of Illinois Graduate School of Library Science, Urbana, 1966, pp. 43-64.

Kilgour, Frederick G., "Library Catalogue Production on Small Computers," *American Documentation*, 17, 124-131 (July 1966).

Lane, David O., "Automatic Catalog Card Production," *Library Resources & Technical Services*, 10, 383-386 (Summer 1966).

Salmon, Stephen R., "Automation of Library Procedures at Washington University," *Missouri Library Association Quarterly*, 27, 11-14 (March 1966).

1965

Kilgour, Frederick G., "Development of Computerization of Catalogs in Medical and Scientific Libraries," in *Proceedings of the 1964 Clinic on Library Applications of Data Processing*, University of Illinois Graduate School of Library Science, Urbana, 1965, pp. 25-35.

Kilgour, Frederick G., "Mechanization of Cataloguing Procedure," *Bulletin of the Medical Library Association*, 53, 142-161 (April 1965).

Before 1965

Moore, Milton, "Flexowriter Versus Multilith: A Time and Cost Study," *California Librarian*, 25, 257-259 (October 1964).

Nicolaus, John J., *The Automated Approach to Technical Information Retrieval: Library Applications*, Bureau of Ships, Washington, D.C., 1964.

Parker, Ralph H., "Development of Automatic Systems at the University of Missouri Library," in *Proceedings of the 1963 Clinic on Library Applications of Data Processing*, University of Illinois Graduate School of Library Science, Urbana, 1964, pp. 43-62.

Fasana, Paul J., "Automating Cataloging Functions in Conventional Libraries," *Library Resources & Technical Services*, 7, 350-363 (Fall 1963).

International Business Machines Corp., *Library Processing for the Albuquerque Public School System*, International Business Machines Corp., White Plains, N.Y. [1962?].

Johnson, Noel W., "Automated Catalog Card Reproduction," *Library Journal*, 85, 725-726 (February 15, 1960).

Luckett, George R., "Partial Library Automation with the Flexowriter Automatic Writing Machine," *Library Resources & Technical Services*, 1, 207-210 (Fall 1957).

Cataloging (Book Catalogs)

1973

Gibson, Liz, "BIBCON--A General Purpose Software System for MARC-Based Book Catalog Production," *Journal of Library Automation*, 6, 237-256 (December 1973).

*Malinconico, S. Michael, and James A. Rizzolo, "The New York Public Library Automated Book Catalog Subsystem," *Journal of Library Automation*, 6, 3-36 (March 1973).

1972

Kountz, John C., "BIBLIOS Revisited," *Journal of Library Automation*, 5, 63-85 (June 1972).

McGrath, William E., and Donald Simon, "Regional Numerical Union Catalog on Computer Output Microfiche," *Journal of Library Automation*, 5, 217-229 (December 1972).

1971

Kieffer, Paula, "Book Catalog--To Have or Not to Have," *Library Resources & Technical Services*, 15, 290-296 (Summer 1971).

Pulsifer, Josephine S., "MARC Book Catalog Production in Washington State," in *Proceedings of the 1970 Clinic on Library Applications of Data Processing: MARC Uses and Users*, University of Illinois Graduate School of Library Science, Urbana, 1971, pp. 53-65.

* Tauber, Maurice F., and Hilda S. Feinberg, *Book Catalogs*, Scarecrow Press, Metuchen, N.J., 1971.

1970

De Gennaro, Richard, "Harvard University's Widener Library Shelflist Conversion and Publication Program," *College & Research Libraries*, 31, 318-331 (September 1970).

"Library Automation and the New York Public Library and the Association of New York Libraries for Technical Services," *The LARC Reports*, 3, 1-103 (Fall 1970).

Piternick, George, "The Machine and Cataloging," in Melvin J. Voigt (ed.) *Advances in Librarianship*, v. 1, Academic Press, New York, 1970, pp. 1-35.

1969

Bolef, Doris, Lynda Von Wagoner, and Estelle Brodman, "Mechanization of Library Procedures in the Medium-Sized Medical Library: VIII. Suspension of Computer Catalog," *Bulletin of the Medical Library Association*, 5, 264-266 (July 1969).

Cartwright, Kelley L., "Automated Production of Book Catalogs," in *Library Automation; a State of the Art Review*, American Library Association, Chicago, 1969, pp. 55-78.

Dolby, James, V. J. Forsyth, and R. L. Resnikoff, *Computerized Library Catalogs: Their Growth, Cost, and Utility*, M.I.T. Press, Cambridge, Mass., 1969.

Evans, Glyn, *The Redesign of the Automated Acquisitions-Catalog System at Washington University School of Medicine Library*, the Library, 1969.

International Business Machines Corporation, *Library Automation--Computer Produced Book Catalog*, White Plains, N.Y., 1969.

1968

Henderson, James W., and Joseph A. Rosenthal (eds.) *Library Catalogs: Their Preservation and Maintenance by Photographic and Automated Techniques*, M.I.T. Press, Cambridge, Mass., 1968.

Johnson, Richard D., "A Book Catalog at Stanford," *Journal of Library Automation*, 1, 13-50 (March 1968).

Kountz, John C., "Cost Comparison of Computer Versus Manual Catalog Maintenance," *Journal of Library Automation*, 1, 159-177 (September 1968).

Scott, Jack W., "An Integrated Computer Based Technical Processing System in a Small College Library," *Journal of Library Automation*, 1, 149-158 (September 1968).

1967

*Cartwright, Kelley L., and Ralph M. Shoffner, *Catalogs in Book Form: A Research Study of their Implications for the California State Library and the California Union Catalog, with a Design for their Implementation*, Institute of Library Research, University of California, Berkeley, Calif., 1967.

Kozumplik, W. A., and R. T. Lange, "Computer-Produced Microfilm Library Catalog," *American Documentation*, 18, 67-80 (April 1967).

Weinstein, Edward A., and Virginia George, "Computer Produced Book Catalogs: Entry Form and Content," *Library Resources & Technical Services*, 2, 185-191 (Spring 1967).

1966

Bregzis, Ritvars, "The ONULP Bibliographic Control System: An Evaluation," in *Proceedings of the 1965 Clinic on Library Applications of Data Processing*, University of Illinois Graduate School of Library Science, Urbana, 1966, pp. 112-140.

*Hayes, Robert M., Ralph M. Shoffner, and David C. Weber, "The Economics of Book Catalog Production," *Library Resources & Technical Services*, 10, 57-90 (Winter 1966).

Kieffer, Paula, "The Baltimore County Public Library Book Catalog," *Library Resources & Technical Services*, 10, 133-141 (Spring 1966).

McCaslin, O. R., "The Book Catalog Program of the Austin Public Library: The Programmer's Viewpoint," in *Proceedings of the First Texas Conference on Library Mechanization*, Texas Library & Historical Commission, Austin, Texas, 1966, pp. 17-20.

McCurdy, May Lea, "The Book Catalog Program of the Austin Public Library: The Librarian's Viewpoint," in *Proceedings of the First Texas Conference on Library Mechanization*, Texas Library & Historical Commission, Austin, Texas, 1966, pp. 13-16.

Moreland, George B., "An Unsophisticated Approach to Book Catalog and Circulation Control," in Harvey, John (ed.) *Data Processing in Public and University Libraries*, Spartan Books, Washington, D.C., 1966, pp. 53-63.

Richmond, Phyllis A., "Note on Updating and Searching Computerized Catalogs," *Library Resources & Technical Services*, 10, 155-160 (Spring 1966).

Bibliography 265

1965

Bregzis, Ritvars, "The Ontario New Universities Library Project--An Automated Bibliographic Data Control System," *College & Research Libraries*, 26, 495-508 (November 1965).

Burns, Lorin R., "The Use of IBM Unit Record Equipment in the Lake County Public Library," in *IBM Library Mechanization Symposium, Endicott, N.Y., May 25, 1964*, International Business Machines, White Plains, N.Y., 1965, pp. 15-36.

De Gennaro, Richard, "A Computer Produced Shelf List," *College & Research Libraries*, 26, 311-315, 353 (July 1965).

Jones, Robert C., "A Book Catalog for Libraries--Prepared by Camera and Computer," *Library Resources & Technical Services*, 9, 205-206 (Spring 1965).

Matta, Seoud Makram, *The Card Catalog in a Large Research Library: Present Condition and Future Possibilities in the New York Public Library*, a thesis submitted to the faculty of Columbia University, D.L.S. (1965).

Moore, Evelyn A., Estelle Brodman, and Geraldine S. Cohen, "Mechanization of Library Procedures in the Medium-Sized Medical Library: III. Acquisitions and Cataloging," *Bulletin of the Medical Library Association*, 53, 305-328 (July 1965).

Moreland, George B., "Montgomery County (Maryland) Book Catalog," in *IBM Library Mechanization Symposium, Endicott, N.Y., May 25, 1964*, International Business Machines, White Plains, N.Y., 1965, pp. 43-60.

Pizer, Irwin H., "Book Catalogs Versus Card Catalogs," *Bulletin of the Medical Library Association*, 53, 225-238 (April 1965).

Robinson, Charles W., "The Book Catalog: Diving In," *Wilson Library Bulletin*, 40, 262-268 (November 1965).

Before 1965

Becker, Joseph, "Automatic Preparation of Book Catalogs," *ALA Bulletin*, 58, 714-718 (September 1964).

Brown, Margaret C., "A Book Catalog at Work," *Library Resources & Technical Services*, 8, 349-358 (Fall 1964).

Harris, Ira, "Reader Services Aspects of Book Catalogs," *Library Resources & Technical Services*, 8, 391-398 (Fall 1964).

Hayes, Robert M., and Ralph M. Shoffner, *The Economics of Book Catalog Production*, Advanced Information Systems Division, Sherman Oaks, Calif., 1964.

Henderson, John D., "The Book Catalogs of the Los Angeles County Public Library," in *Proceedings of the 1963 Clinic on Library Applications of Data Processing*, University of Illinois Graduate School of Library Science, Urbana, 1964, pp. 18-32.

Jones, Bob, "The Compact Book Catalog By Photographic Process," *Library Resources & Technical Services*, 8, 366-369 (Fall 1964).

Kennedy, James H., and Merle N. Boylan, *IBM 1401 Computer Produced and Maintained Printed Book Catalogs at the Lawrence Radiation Laboratory*, University of California, Lawrence Radiation Laboratory, Livermore, Calif., 1964.

MacQuarrie, Catherine, "The Metamorphosis of the Book Catalogs," *Library Resources & Technical Services*, 8, 370-378 (Fall 1964).

Moreland, George B., "Montgomery County Book Catalog," *Library Resources & Technical Services*, 8, 379-389 (Fall 1964).

Parker, Ralph H., "Book Catalogs," *Library Resources & Technical Services*, 8, 344-348 (Fall 1964).

Richmond, Phyllis A., "Book Catalogs as Supplements to Card Catalogs," *Library Resources & Technical Services*, 8, 359-365 (Fall 1964).

Weinstein, Edward A., and Joan Spry, "Boeing SLIP: Computer Produced and Maintained Printed Book Catalogs," *American Docomentation*, 15, 185-190 (July 1964).

Kingery, Robert Ernest, and Maurice F. Tauber (eds.) *Book Catalogs*, Scarecrow Press, New York, 1963.

Richmond, Phyllis A., "A Short Title Catalog Made with IBM Tabulating Equipment," *Library Resources & Technical Services*, 7, 81-85 (Winter 1963).

Griffin, Marjorie, "Printed Book Catalogs," *Special Libraries*, 51, 496-499 (November 1960).

Hewitson, Theodore, "The Book Catalog of the Los Angeles County Public Library: Its Function and Use," *Library Resources & Technical Services*, 4, 228-232 (Summer 1960).

MacDonald, Ruth M., "Book Catalogs and Card Catalogs," *Library Resources & Technical Services*, 4, 228-232 (Summer 1960).

MacQuarrie, Catherine, and Beryl L. Martin, "Book Catalog of the Los Angeles County Public Library: How It Is Being Made," *Library Resources & Technical Services*, 4, 208-227 (Summer 1960).

Dewey, Harry, "Punched Card Catalogs--Theory and Technique," *American Documentation*, 10, 36-40 (January 1959).

MacQuarrie, Catherine, "IBM Book Catalog," *Library Journal*, 82, 630-634 (March 1, 1957).

Alvord, Dorothy, "King County Public Library Does It with IBM," *PNLA Quarterly*, 16, 123-131 (January 1952).

Bibliography

Cataloging (Filing Rules)

1972

*Rather, John C., "Filing Arrangement in the Library of Congress Catalogs," *Library Resources & Technical Services*, 16, 240-261 (Spring 1972).

1970

*Cartwright, Kelley L., "Mechanization and Library Filing Rules," in Melvin J. Voigt (ed.) *Advances in Librarianship*, v. 1, Academic Press, New York, 1970, pp. 59-94.

1967

Nugent, William R., "The Mechanization of the Filing Rules of the Dictionary Catalogs of the Library of Congress," *Library Resources & Technical Services*, 11, 145-166 (Spring 1967).

1966

Hines, Theodore C., and Jessica L. Harris, *Computer Filing of Index, Bibliographic, and Catalog Entries*, Bro-Dart Foundation, Newark, N.J., 1966.

1965

Perreault, Jean M., "The Computer and Catalog Filing Rules," *Library Resources & Technical Services*, 9, 325-331 (Summer 1965).

Popecki, Joseph T., "A Filing System for the Machine Age," *Library Resources & Technical Services*, 9, 333-337 (Summer 1965).

Weinstein, Edward A., and Virginia George, "Notes Toward a Code for Computer-Produced Printed Book Catalogs," *Library Resources & Technical Services*, 9, 319-324 (Summer 1965).

Before 1965

Hines, Theodore C., "Machine Arrangement of Alphanumeric Concordance, Thesaurus, and Index Entries: The Need for Compatible Standard Rules," in *Automation and Scientific Communication; Short Papers Contributed to the Theme Sessions of the 26th Annual Meeting of the American Documentation Institute*, the Institute, Washington, D.C., 1963, v. 1, pp. 7-8.

Gull, C. Dake, "How Will Electronic Information Systems Affect Cataloging Rules?" *Library Resources & Technical Services*, 5, 135-139 (Spring 1961).

Serials

1975

Anable, Richard, "CONSER: An Update," *Journal of Library Automation*, 8, 26-30 (March 1975).

Livingston, Lawrence, *The CONSER Project: Current Status and Plans*, a paper presented to the Association of Research Libraries, January 18, 1975.

1974

Harp, Vivian, and Gertrude Heard, "Automated Periodicals System at a Community College Library," *Journal of Library Automation*, 7, 83-96 (June 1974).

*Livingston, Lawrence, "A Composite Effort to Build an On-Line National Serials Data Base (A Paper for Presentation at the ARL Midwinter Meeting, Chicago, 19 January 1974)," *Journal of Library Automation*, 7, 61 (March 1974).

Saffady, William, "A Computer Output Microfilm Serials List for Patron Use," *Journal of Library Automation*, 7, 263-266 (December 1974).

Upham, Lois, "CONSER: Cooperative Conversion of Serials Project," *Library of Congress Information Bulletin*, 33, A247-A248 (November 29, 1974).

1973

*Anable, Richard, "The Ad Hoc Discussion Group on Serials Data Bases: Its History, Current Position, and Future," *Journal of Library Automation*, 6, 207-214 (December 1973).

*Fayollat, James, "On-Line Serials Control System in a Large Biomedical Library, Part III: Comparison of On-Line and Batch Operations and Cost Analysis," *Journal of the American Society for Information Science*, 24, 80-86 (March-April 1973).

Grosch, Audrey N., "A Regional Serials Program Under National Serials Data Program Auspices: Discussion Paper Prepared for Ad Hoc Serials Discussion Group," *Journal of Library Automation*, 6, 201-206 (December 1973).

1972

Fayollat, James, "On-Line Serials Control System in a Large Biomedical Library, Part II: Evaluation of Retrieval Features," *Journal of the American Society for Information Science*, 23, 353-358 (November-December 1972).

*Fayollat, James, "On-Line Serials Control System in a Large Biomedical Library, Part I: Description of the System," *Journal of the American Society for Information Science*, 23, 318-322 (September-October 1972).

Bibliography

Johnson, Donald W., *Toward a National Serials Data Program: Final Report of the National Serials Pilot Project*, Association of Research Libraries, Washington, D.C., 1972. ED 063 099, available from the Association.

1971

American National Standards Institute Committee Z39, *American National Standard for an Identification Number for Serial Publications*, American National Standards Institute, New York, 1971.

*Bosseau, Don L., "The Computer in Serials Processing and Control," in Melvin J. Voigt (ed.) *Advances in Librarianship*, v. 2, Seminar Press, New York, 1971, pp. 104-164.

Condit, Anna R., "Optical Mark Sensing of Serials Check-In Records: A New Approach to Serials Automation," in *Proceedings of the American Society for Information Science, Annual Meeting, 34th, Denver, Colorado, 7-11 November 1971, v. 8: Communications for Decision-Makers*, Greenwood Pub. Co., Westport, Conn., 1971, pp. 287-290.

Koenig, Michael E. D. et al., "SCOPE: A Cost Analysis of an Automated Serials Record System," *Journal of Library Automation*, 4, 129-140 (September 1971).

Wilkinson, W. A., and Loretta A. Stock, "Machine-Assisted Serials Control; Bindery Preparation and Claims Control," *Special Libraries*, 62, 529-534 (December 1971).

1970

Bosseau, Don L., "The University of California at San Diego Serials System--Revisited," *Program*, 4, 1-29 (January 1970).

*De Varennes, Rosario, "On-Line Serials System at Laval University Library," *Journal of Library Automation*, 3, 128-141 (June 1970).

Norris, Jean A., and Robert E. Joerger, "University of Florida Libraries Automated Union Serials List," in *Proceedings of the American Society for Information Science, v. 7: The Information Conscious Society*, n.p., 1970, pp. 73-78.

U.S. Library of Congress, Information Systems Office, *Serials: a MARC Format*, Library of Congress, Washington, D.C., 1970.

Verity, J. B., and E. L. Crocker, "A Computer-Based System for Serials Records at Lawrence Radiation Laboratory," *Journal of the American Society for Information Science*, 21, 247-253 (July-August 1970).

1969

Belch, David E., "The Computer-Controlled Periodicals Systems at the San Francisco Public Library, *Library Resources & Technical Services*, 13, 531-532 (Fall 1969).

Black, Donald V., and Donald M. Bethe, "Library Serials Control Using a General-Purpose Data Management System," in *Proceedings of the American Society for Information Science, v. 6, Cooperating Information Societies*, n.p., 1969, pp. 5-11.

Crismond, Linda F., and Sylvia B. Fatzer, "Automated Serials Check-In and Binding Procedures at the San Francisco Public Library," in *Proceedings of the American Society for Information Science, v. 6, Cooperating Information Societies*, n.p., 1969, pp. 13-20.

Crismond, Linda F., "A Computer System for Periodicals," *Library Journal*, 94, 3619-3621 (October 15, 1969).

DeChief, Helene, "Automation of Serials at the Canadian National Railways," *The LARC Reports*, 2, 35-41 (June 1969).

DeChief, Helene, "Automation of Serials at the Canadian National Railways - Part 2, Ordering," *The LARC Reports*, 2, 12-29 (September 1969).

Dolby, J. L., H. L. Resnikoff, and J. W. Tukey, "A Ruly Code for Serials," in *Proceedings of the American Society for Information Science, v. 6: Cooperating Information Societies*, Greenwood Pub. Co., Westport, Conn., 1969, pp. 113-124.

Grosch, Audrey N., "University of Minnesota Bio-Medical Library Serials System," *Special Libraries*, 60, 349-360 (July-August 1969).

Kozlow, Robert D., "Genesis of a Serials List," in *Proceedings of the 1968 Clinic on Library Applications of Data Processing*, University of Illinois Graduate School of Library Science, Urbana, 1969, pp. 219-220.

Schwartz, Shula, and Patricia A. Bottalico, "Automation of Serials," in *Proceedings of the Second Texas Conference on Library Automation*, n.p., 1969, pp. 1-23.

*Stewart, Bruce W., "Automated Serials Systems in Perspective," in *Library Automation: A State of the Art Review*, Chicago, American Library Association, 1969, pp. 131-148.

1968

Grosch, Audrey N., *University of Minnesota Bio-Medical Library Serials Control System; Comprehensive Report*, University of Minnesota Libraries, Minneapolis, 1968.

Roper, Fred W., "A Computer-Based Serials Control System for a Large Biomedical Library," *American Documentation*, 19, 151-157 (April 1968).

Strom, Karen D., "Software Design for Bio-Medical Library Serials Control System," in *Proceedings of the American Society for Information Science, v. 5: Information Transfer*, Greenwood, New York, 1968, pp. 267-275.

1967

Clyde, Eric, "Progress in the Automation of Serials at the National Science Library," in *Automation in Libraries*, Canadian Association of College and University Libraries, 1967, pp. 64-75.

De Varennes, Rosario, "Computerized Serials Record at Laval University: a Progress Report," *Canadian Library*, 24, 122-123 (September 1967).

McDonald, R. W., "Serial Systems," in *Automation in Libraries*, Canadian Association of College and University Libraries, n.p., 1967, pp. 43-48.

Wilkinson, W. A., "A System for Machine-Assisted Serials Control," *Special Libraries*, 58, 149-153 (March 1967).

1966

Curran, Ann T., "The Mechanization of the Serial Records for the Moving and Merging of the Boston Medical and Harvard Medical Serials," *Library Resources & Technical Services*, 10, 362-372 (Summer 1966).

Eyman, Eleanor G. et al., "Periodicals Automation at Miami-Dade Junior College," *Library Resources & Technical Services*, 10, 341-361 (Summer 1966).

McGrath, William E., and Helen Kolbe, "A Simple Mechanized, Non-Computerized System for Serials Control in Small Academic Libraries: A Primer," *Library Resources & Technical Services*, 10, 373-382 (Summer 1966).

Stewart, Bruce Warren, "Data Processing in an Academic Library," *Wilson Library Bulletin*, 41, 388-395 (December 1966).

Stewart, Bruce Warren, "Data Processing in the Texas A & M University Library," *Proceedings of the 1966 Clinic on Library Applications of Data Processing*, University of Illinois School of Library Science, Urbana, 1966, pp. 167-181.

Stewart, Bruce Warren, *The Serials Mechanization of the Texas A & M University Library; Proceedings of the First Texas Conference on Library Mechanization*, n.p., 1966, pp. 40-45.

1965

Culbertson, Don S., "Computerized Serial Records," *Library Resources & Technical Services*, 9, 53-58 (Winter 1965).

Hammer, Donald, "Reflections on the Development of an Automated Serials System," *Library Resources & Technical Services*, 9, 225-230 (Spring 1965).

Randall, G. E., "Unit Record System for Serial Control in a Special Library," *IBM Library Mechanization Symposium, Endicott, N.Y., May 25, 1964*, International Business Machines, Inc., White Plains, N.Y., 1965, pp. 237-245.

Schultheiss, Louis A., "Two Serial Control Card Files Developed at the University of Illinois, Chicago," *Library Resources & Technical Services*, 9, 271-287 (Summer 1965).

Stewart, Bruce Warren, *A Computerized Serials Record for the Texas A & M University Library*, The Library, Texas A & M University, College Station, Texas, 1965.

Before 1965

Becker, Joseph, "Automating the Serial Record," *ALA Bulletin*, 58, 557-560 (June 1964).

Becker, Joseph, "The MEDLARS Project," *ALA Bulletin*, 58, 227-230 (March 1964).

Lebowitz, Abraham I., and Walter A. Kee, "Mechanized Serial Record at the Atomic Energy Commission Headquarters Library," *Documentation Progress*, 7, 4-5 (November 1964).

Vdovin, George et al., *Serials Computer Project; Final Report*, University of California at San Diego, La Jolla, Calif., 1964.

Pizer, Irwin H., Donald R. Franz, and Estelle Brodman, "Mechanization of Library Procedures in the Medium-Sized Medical Library: I. The Serial Record," *Bulletin of the Medical Library Association*, 51, 313-338 (July 1963).

Vdovin, George et al., "Computer Processing of Serial Records," *Library Resources & Technical Services*, 7, 71-80 (Winter 1963).

Voigt, Melvin J., "The Costs of Data Processing in University Libraries: In Serials Handling," *College & Research Libraries*, 24, 489-491 (November 1963).

McCann, Anne, "Applications of Machines to Library Techniques: Periodicals," *American Documentation*, 12, 260-265 (October 1961).

Anthony, L. J., and J. E. Hailstone, "Use of Punched Cards in Preparation of Lists of Periodicals," *Aslib Proceedings*, 12, 348-360 (October 1960).

Young, H. H., "Use of Punched Cards in the Serials Acquisitions Department of the University of Texas," *Special Libraries Association Texas Chapter Bulletin*, 11, 1-3 (1959).

Nicholson, Natalie, and William Thurston, "Serials and Journals in the MIT Libraries," *American Documentation*, 9, 304-307 (October 1958).

Moffitt, Alexander, "Punched Card Records in Serials Acquisition," *College & Research Libraries*, 7, 10-13 (January 1946).

Bibliography

Circulation

1975

Beaumont, Dennis N., "The LIBS 100 System," in *Proceedings of the 1974 Clinic on Library Applications of Data Processing: Applications of Minicomputers to Library and Related Problems*, University of Illinois Graduate School of Library Science, Urbana, 1975, pp. 55-79.

Hamner, Walter G., "The Minicomputer and its Use in Library Operations at the University of Maryland," in *Proceedings of the 1974 Clinic on Library Applications of Data Processing: Applications of Minicomputers to Library and Related Problems*, University of Illinois Graduate School of Library Science, Urbana, 1975, pp. 32-42.

Kershner, Lois M., "Management Aspects of the Use of the IBM System/7 in Circulation Control," in *Proceedings of the 1974 Clinic on Library Applications of Data Processing: Applications of Minicomputers to Library and Related Problems*, University of Illinois Graduate School of Library Science, Urbana, 1975, pp. 43-54.

McGee, Rob, "The University of Chicago Library's JRL 1000 Circulation Terminal and Bar-Coded Labels," *Journal of Library Automation*, 8, 5-25 (March 1975).

1974

*Atkinson, Hugh C., "Circulation Automation," in Melvin J. Voigt (ed.) *Advances in Librarianship*, v. 4, Academic Press, New York, 1974, pp. 63-75.

Dennis, Donald D., and Patricia A. Stockton, "Automated Library Circulation System Boosts Service, Control at American University," *Special Libraries*, 65, 512-515 (December 1974).

McKibbin, Dorothy, "On-Line Circulation Control: Three Years' Experience," *Canadian Library Journal*, 31, 214-230 (June 1974).

Roy, Robert H., "Utilization of Computer Techniques for Circulation and Inventory Control in a University Research Library," in *Minutes of the Sixty-third Meeting, January 26, 1974, Chicago, Illinois*, Association of Research Libraries, Appendix B, pp. 20-39.

Senior, Karen, and Deborah J. Yamanka, "The Automated Loans System at Loughborough University of Technology," *Program*, 8, 1-21 (January 1974).

Toombs, Kenneth E., "Light-Pen Technology at the University of South Carolina--The South Carolina Circulation System," *Journal of Library Automation*, 7, 226-227 (September 1974).

Toombs, Kenneth E., "Light Pen Technology in the University of South Carolina Library," *Southeastern Librarian*, 24, 27-28 (Summer 1974).

1973

Burgess, Thomas K., "Cost Effectiveness Model for Comparing Various Circulation Systems," *Journal of Library Automation*, 6, 75-86 (June 1973).

Hoadley, Irene Braden, and A. Robert Thorson (eds.) *An Automated On-Line Circulation System: Evaluation, Development, Use; Proceedings and Papers of an Institute Held at the Ohio State University, September 13-14, 1971*, Ohio State University Libraries, Columbus, Ohio, 1973.

Veneziano, Velma, "An Interactive Computer-Based Circulation System for Northwestern University; the Library Puts It to Work," *Journal of Library Automation*, 5, 101-117 (Summer 1973).

Wassom, Earl E., Patricia W. Custead, and Simon P. J. Chen, "On-Line Cataloging and Circulation at Western Kentucky University: An Approach to Automated Instructional Resources Management," *LARC Reports*, 6, 29-36 (1973).

Wilson, C. W. J., "Developments with Computer-based Loans Systems in the United Kingdom," *Program*, 7, 170-171 (October 1973).

1972

Aagaard, James S., "An Interactive Computer-Based Circulation System: Design and Development," *Journal of Library Automation*, 5, 3-11 (March 1972).

Atkinson, Hugh C., "The Ohio State On-Line Circulation System," in *Proceedings of the 1972 Clinic on Library Applications of Data Processing: Applications of On-Line Computers to Library Problems*, University of Illinois Graduate School of Library Science, Urbana, 1972, pp. 22-28.

McGee, Rob, "Key Factors of Circulation System Analysis and Design," *College & Research Libraries*, 33, 127-139 (March 1972).

*McGee, Robert S., "Two Types of Designs for On-Line Circulation Systems," *Journal of Library Automation*, 5, 184-202 (September 1972).

Paulukonis, Joseph T., "On-Line Real-Time Self-Service Circulation at Northwestern University," in *Proceedings of the 1972 Clinic on Library Applications of Data Processing: Applications of On-Line Computers to Library Problems*, University of Illinois Graduate School of Library Science, Urbana, 1972, pp. 82-93.

Bibliography

1971

"On-Line, Real Time Circulation; a Report on the Northwestern University Library System," *The LARC Reports*, 3, 1-54 (Winter 1970-71).

Rao, Paladugu V., and B. Joseph Szereni, "Booth Library On-Line Circulation System (BLOC)," *Journal of Library Automation*, 4, 86-102 (June 1971).

Shumilak, Edward E., *An Online Interactive Book-Library-Management System*, NASA Technical Note NASA Tn D-7052, National Aeronautics and Space Administration, Washington, D.C., 1971.

1970

Boyer, Calvin J., and Jack Frost, "On-Line Circulation Control--Midwestern University Library's System Using an IBM 1401 Computer in a 'Time-Sharing' Mode," in *Proceedings of the 1969 Clinic on Library Applications of Data Processing*, University of Illinois Graduate School of Library Science, Urbana, 1970, pp. 135-146.

Kennedy, Robert A., "Bell Laboratories On-Line Circulation Control System: One Year's Experience," in *Proceedings of the 1969 Clinic on Library Applications of Data Processing*, University of Illinois Graduate School of Library Science, Urbana, 1970, pp. 14-30.

1969

Blau, Edmond J., "An Automated Circulation System for a Medium-Sized Scientific Library," in *Proceedings of the American Society for Information Science, v. 6, Cooperating Information Societies*, Greenwood Pub. Co., Westport, Conn., 1969, pp. 21-28.

Boyd, Anne H., and Philip E. J. Walden, "A Simplified On-Line Circulation System," *Program*, 3, 47-65 (July 1969).

Boyer, Calvin, "On-Line Circulation Control System at Midwestern University," *The LARC Reports*, 2, 44-58 (March 1969).

Campbell, G. R., "The Circulation System of the McPherson Library, University of Victoria," *The LARC Reports*, 2, 26-43 (March 1969).

*Gull, C. D., "Automated Circulation Systems," in *Library Automation: A State of the Art Review*, American Library Association, Chicago, 1969, pp. 138-148.

Hamilton, Robert E., "The Illinois State Library 'On-Line' Circulation Control System," in *Proceedings of the 1968 Clinic on Library Applications of Data Processing*, University of Illinois Graduate School of Library Science, Urbana, 1969, pp. 11-28.

Heineke, Charles D., and Calvin J. Boyer, "Automated Circulation System at Midwestern University," *ALA Bulletin*, 63, 1249-1254 (October 1969).

1968

Auld, Lawrence, "Automated Book Order and Circulation Control Procedures at the Oakland University Library," *Journal of Library Automation*, 1, 93-109 (June 1968).

Chappell, D. L., "Automation Circulation Procedures at Utah State University," *The LARC Reports*, 1, 10/1-10/18 (July 1968).

De Gennaro, Richard, "Automation in the Harvard College Library," *Harvard Library Bulletin*, 16, 221-222 (July 1968).

Hamilton, Robert E., "Illinois State Library Computer System," *Wilson Library Bulletin*, 43, 721-722 (March 1968).

Henry, Otha, and Matt Roberts, "The Evolution of Automated Circulation Procedures in the Washington University Libraries," *The LARC Reports*, 1, 11/1-11/27 (July 1968).

Kennedy, R. A., "Bell Laboratories' Library Real-Time Loan System (BELLREL)," *Journal of Library Automation*, 1, 128-146 (June 1968).

Kimber, Richard T., "The Cost of an On-Line Circulation System," *Program*, 2, 81-94 (October 1968).

Kimber, Richard T., "An Operational Computerized Circulation System with On-Line Interrogation Capability," *Program*, 2, 75-80 (October 1968).

1967

*American Library Association, Library Technology Program, *Three Systems of Circulation Control*, American Library Association, Chicago, 1967.

Billinton, Jack, "Circulation Control Systems [at the University of Saskatchewan]," in *Automation in Libraries*, Canadian Association of College and University Libraries, n.p., 1967, pp. 89-92.

Cammack, Floyd, and Donald Mann, "Institutional Implications of Automated Circulation Study [at Oakland University]," *College & Research Libraries*, 28, 129-132 (March 1967).

Kanasy, J. Emery, "Circulation Control Systems [at Windsor University]," in *Automation in Libraries*, Canadian Association of College and University Libraries, n.p., 1967, pp. 76-88.

Kimber, Richard T., "Conversational Circulation," *Libri*, 17, 131-141 (1967).

Parker, Ralph H., "Not a Shared System," *Library Journal*, 92, 3967-3970 (November 1, 1967).

Stockton, Patricia Ann, "An IBM Circulation Procedure," *College & Research Libraries*, 28, 35-40 (January 1967).

1966

Courtright, Benjamin, "The Johns Hopkins University Library," in *Proceedings of the 1969 Clinic on Library Applications of Data*

Processing, University of Illinois Graduate School of Library Science, Urbana, 1966, pp. 18-33.

Cox, James R., "Automation Advances in the Research Library," *UCLA Librarian*, 19, 22-24 (March 1966).

Flannery, Anne, and James D. Mack, *Library Systems Analysis Report Number 4, Mechanized Circulation System, Lehigh University Library*, the Library, 1966.

Kimber, Richard T., "Studies at the Queen's University of Belfast on Real-Time Computer Control of Book Circulation," *Journal of Documentation*, 22, 116-122 (June 1966).

Martin, Frank, and Jack Banning, *Library Ciruclation Control at Michigan State University*, the University, East Lansing, Michigan, 1966.

Ruecking, Frederick, "The Circulation System of the Fondren Library, Rice University," in Corbin, John B. (ed.) *Proceedings of the Texas Conference on Library Mechanization, Austin, 1966*, Texas Library & Historical Commission, Austin, 1966, pp. 21-30.

Verhoeff, J., "The Delft Circulation System," *Libri*, 16, 1-9 (1966).

Salmon, Stephen R., "Automation of Library Procedures at Washington University," *Missouri Library Association Quarterly*, 27, 11-14 (March 1966).

Stewart, Bruce W., "Data Processing in Academic Library," *Wilson Library Bulletin*, 41, 388-395 (December 1966).

Stewart, Bruce W., "Data Processing in the Texas A & M University Library," in *Proceedings of the 1966 Clinic on Library Applications of Data Processing*, University of Illinois Graduate School of Library Science, Urbana, 1966, pp. 167-194.

1965

* American Library Association, Library Technology Project, *The Use of Data Processing Equipment in Circulation Control*, American Library Association, Chicago, 1965.

Cox, Carl R., "The Mechanization of Acquisition and Circulation Procedures at the University of Maryland Library," in *IBM Library Mechanization Symposium, Endicott, N.Y., May 25, 1964*, International Business Machines Corp., White Plains, N.Y., 1965, pp. 205-236.

Cox, James R., "Circulation Control with IBM Unit Record Equipment at UCLA," in *IBM Library Mechanization Symposium, Endicott, N.Y., May 25, 1964*, International Business Machines Corp., White Plains, N.Y., 1965, pp. 95-132.

Harris, Michael H., "The 357 Data Collection System for Circulation Control," *College & Research Libraries*, 26, 119-120, 158 (March 1965).

De Jarnett, L. R., "Library Circulation Control Using IBM 357's at Southern Illinois University," in *IBM Library Mechanization Symposium, Endicott, N.Y., May 25, 1964*, International Business Machines Corp., White Plains, N.Y., 1965, pp. 77-94.

McCoy, Ralph E., "Computerized Circulation Work: A Case Study of the 357 Data Collection System," *Library Resources & Technical Services*, 9, 59-65 (Winter 1965).

Ruecking, Frederick, Jr., *Circulation Control at Rice University Using the IBM 357 Data Collection System*, International Business Machines, White Plains, N.Y., 1965.

Yabroff, Arthur, "Circulation Control at the Detroit Public Library," in *IBM Library Mechanization Symposium, Endicott, N.Y., May 25, 1964*, International Business Machines Corp., White Plains, N.Y., 1965, pp. 37-42.

Before 1965

An Automated Circulation Control System for the Delyte W. Morris Library, Southern Illinois University, Carbondale, Illinois, 1963.

Becker, Joseph, "Circulation and the Computer," *ALA Bulletin*, 58, 1007-1010 (December 1964).

Courtright, Benjamin F., *Progress Report on an Operations Research and Systems Study of a University Library*, The Johns Hopkins University, Baltimore, 1964.

Cox, James R., *IBM Circulation Control at the University of California Library, Los Angeles: Progress and Change*, UCLA Library, Los Angeles, 1964.

Griffin, Marjorie, "IBM Advanced Systems Development Library in Transition," in Goldhor, Herbert (ed.) *Proceedings of the 1963 Clinic on Library Applications of Data Processing*, University of Illinois Graduate School of Library Science, Urbana, 1964, pp. 79-95.

Haznedari, I., and H. Voos, "Automated Circulation at a Government R & D Installation," *Special Libraries*, 55, 77-81 (February 1964).

Kennedy, James H., *IBM 1401 Computer Produced and Maintained Library Circulation Records*, University of California, Lawrence Radiation Laboratory, Livermore, California, 1964.

Kraft, Donald, *IBM Library Circulation Systems*, IBM Corporation, Chicago, Illinois, 1964.

Pizer, Irwin H., Isabelle T. Anderson, and Estelle Brodman, "Mechanization of Library Procedures in the Medium-Sized Medical Library: II. Circulation Records," *Bulletin of the Medical Library Association*, 52, 370-385 (April 1964).

Bibliography

Ruecking, Frederick, "Selecting a Circulation-Control System: A Mathematical Approach," *College & Research Libraries*, 25, 385-390 (September 1964).

Trueswell, Richard W., "Two Characteristics of Circulation and Their Effect on the Implementation of Mechanized Circulation Control Systems," *College & Research Libraries*, 25, 284-291 (July 1964).

Weyhrauch, Ernest E., "Automation in the Reserved Books Room," *Library Journal*, 89, 2294-2296 (June 1, 1964).

Cox, James R., "The Costs of Data Processing In University Libraries: In Circulation Activities," *College & Research Libraries*, 24, 492-495 (November 1963).

Howe, Mary T., and Mary K. Weidner, "Data Processing in the Decatur Public Library," *Illinois Libraries*, 44, 593-597 (November 1962).

Fry, George, and Associates, *Study of Circulation Control Systems: Public Libraries, College and University Libraries, Special Libraries*, American Library Association, Chicago, Illinois, 1961.

Birnbaum, Henry, *General Information Manual: IBM Circulation Control at Brooklyn College Library*, International Business Machines, White Plains, N.Y., 1960.

Quigley, Margery C., "Ten Years of IBM," *Library Journal*, 78, 1152-1157 (July 1952).

Pratt, Carl, "International Business Machines' Use in Circulation Department, University of Florida Library," *Library Journal*, 61, 302-303 (April 1, 1942).

Quigley, Margery, "Library Facts from International Business Machines Cards," *Library Journal*, 66, 1065-1067 (December 15, 1941).

Parker, Ralph H., "The Punched Card Method in Circulation Work," *Library Journal*, 61, 903-905 (December 1, 1936).

INDEX

including identification of all acronyms

A

Abbott Laboratories, 151
Abel, Richard, & Co., 90
Abridged Index Medicus Teletypewriter Exchange (*see* AIM-TWX)
Acquisitions, 7, 9, 13-34, 63, 89-90, 113, 116, 236, 240-241 (*see also* Serials acquisitions)
Ad Hoc Discussion Group on Serials Data Bases, 170-171
AFR (*see* Automatic Field Recognition)
Air Force Cambridge Research Library, 49, 82
AIM-TWX (Abridged Index Medicus Teletypewriter Exchange), 167, 168
Albuquerque (New Mexico) Public Schools, 44-45, 55
American Library Association, 80, 171-172, 238
American National Standards Institute, 80, 238
American Society for Information Science (ASIS), 172
American University, 202
AMIGOS Bibliographic Network, 109, 236
Anaheim (California) Public Library, 48
ANYLTS (Association of New York Libraries for Technical Services), 225, 236
Argonne National Laboratory, 74
Arizona State University, 27

ARL (*see* Association of Research Libraries)
Arrival card systems, 149-151, 154-159
ASIS (*see* American Society for Information Science)
Association of New York Libraries for Technical Services (*see* ANYLTS)
Association of Research Libraries, 169-171
Atomic Energy Commission Headquarters, 157
"Augmented catalog," 121
Authority control, 40, 97, 119, 134, 138, 144
Automata Optical Mark Reader, 159
Automatic Field Recognition (AFR), 93
Automatic typewriters, 41, 44-49, 223 (*see also* IBM MTST, 1050; Friden Flexowriters; Dura Mach 10; CPT)

B

BACKFILE, 168
BALLOTS (Bibliographic Automation of Large Library Operations Using a Time-Sharing System), 7, 32-33, 113-116, 142, 237
Baltimore County (Maryland) Public Library, 63-64, 131, 134, 139
Bar-coded labels (*see* Zebra labels)

BCL (Books for College Libraries) Project, 89, 236
Beehive Medical Electronics OCLC 100 terminal, 107
BELLREL (Bell Laboratories Real-time Loan) System, 203
Bell Telephone Laboratories, 7, 203
Bibliographic Automation of Large Library Operations Using a Time-Shared System (*see* BALLOTS)
Bibliographic Network (*see* BIBNET)
Bibliographies, 39, 98, 165-166
BIBLIOS (Book Inventory Building Library Information Oriented System), 28, 94-96
BIBNET (Bibliographic Network), 116
Billings, John Shaw, 1-2
Boeing Company, 58, 129, 132, 134
Book cards, 39, 89, 111, 120
   elimination of, 211
   punched, 47, 91, 182, 184, 191-193, 195, 200, 203
Book catalogs, 4, 39, 129-132, 240-242
   arrangement of, 134-135, 137-139, 144
   by-products of acquisition system, 15, 25, 90
   off-line computer systems for, 55-68, 78, 92-99
   on-line computer systems for, 118-121
   sequential camera systems for, 49-51
   unit record systems for, 42-44
Book Inventory Building Library Information Oriented System (*see* BIBLIOS)
Book Order and Selection System (*see* BOSS)
Book plates, 39
Book pockets, 39, 89, 91-92, 111, 120-121
Books for College Libraries (*see* BCL)
BOSS (Book Order and Selection System), 30-31, 91

Boston Medical Library (*see* Countway Library of Medicine)
Boston University, 47
British Columbia, University of, 27, 47, 194-195, 239
Bro-Dart Industries, 64
Brooklyn College Library, 189-190
Buckland, Lawrence F., 73, 91
Bureau of Ships Technical Library, 52
Burroughs B5500, 89, 221
Bush, Vannevar, 5

C

CAIN (Cataloging and Indexing) System, 98-99
CALBPC (Colorado Academic Library Book Processing Center), 225-226, 228, 236
California State Library, 46, 93, 114
California Library Automation Network (*see* CLAN)
California, University of, 93, 97, 171, 173
   Institute of Library Research, 75, 93, 97
   at Irvine, 49
   Lawrence Radiation Laboratory, 157
   at Los Angeles, 47, 200
     Biomedical Library, 120, 162-165, 242
   at San Diego, 4, 154-157
Canadian Union Catalogue Task-group, 171
CANCERLINE, 169
CAPTAIN (Computer Aided Processing and Terminal Access Information Network), 236-237
CARDS (Card Automated Reproduction and Distribution Service), 85-89
Catalog cards, 44-49, 52-55, 90-92, 104-107, 111, 113, 119, 226, 235, 241
   and book catalogs, 98-99
   Library of Congress, 73, 85-90

Index

Cataloging, 39-41, 73-84, 240
(*see also* MARC)
  automatic typewriter systems, 44-49
  centralized cataloging, 40
  choice of entry, 132-134
  effect of automation on, 127-144
  form of entry, 134
  main entry concept, 132-134
  off-line computerized systems, 51-68, 85-99
  on-line computerized systems, 103-123
  sequential camera systems, 49-51
  unit card concept, 132-134
  unit-record systems, 41-44
  use of acquisitions records, 9, 28, 32-33
Cataloging and Indexing System (*see* CAIN)
Cataloging-In-Publication, 84
Cathode-ray tube terminals (*see* Terminals)
CATLINE, 168
CDC (*see* Control Data Corporation)
Character recognition, automatic, 86
CHASM (Chicago Access Support Module), 112
CHEMLINE, 169
Chicago Access Support Module (*see* CHASM)
Chicago, University of, 48, 75, 110-112, 114, 241
Circulation, 2, 4, 7, 15, 181-183, 228
  delinquent borrowers, 182-183, 200-202
  fines, 183, 188, 195, 209
  off-line computerized systems, 190-200, 221, 239
  on-line computerized systems, 116, 184-188, 200-212, 239-240, 242
  reserve books, 195, 202, 208
  telephone borrowing, 207
  357-type systems, 184, 190-199
  unit-record systems, 188-190

CLAN (California Library Automation Network), 237
Claremont Colleges (*see* Honnold Library)
Cleveland (Ohio) Public Library, 34
Cleveland State University, 47
CLSI (Computer Library Services, Inc.), 34, 212
COBOL (Common Business Oriented Language), 56, 91
Collaborative Library Systems Development, 241
College Bibliocentre, 236
Colorado Academic Library Book Processing Center (*see* CALBPC)
Colorado Instruments Terminals, 198-199
Colorado, University of, 47, 199
Columbia University, 26, 200, 241
COM (Computer-Output Microfiche or Microfilm), 23, 56, 96-98, 157, 211
Commercial systems, 116-117, 239-240, 242
Communication, 3, 6-7, 21, 25, 103, 105, 112, 160-161, 238
COMPFILE, 168
Compos-O-Line, 50-51
Computer Aided Processing and Terminal Access Information Network (*see* CAPTAIN)
Computer centers, 112, 219-222, 240
Computer Library Services, Inc. (*see* CLSI)
Computers, 2-7, 19-21, 51-52, 127-128, 139
Computer Sciences Corporation (CSC), 166-167
CONSER (Conversion of Serials), 172-175, 242
Cooperative College Library Center, 109, 236
Cornell University, 26, 49, 173
Control Data Corporation:
  equipment:
    160-A, 155
    210, 31

(Control Data Corporation)
  211, 31
  1604, 155
  3300, 31
  Transacter terminals, 198
Council on Library Resources:
  grants, 32, 74, 80, 84, 114, 170
  as operating foundation, 171, 173-174
  studies sponsored, 73-74, 80, 140
Countway Library of Medicine, 78, 154
CPT, 49
Cross-references, 40, 78, 113, 119
CRT terminals (see Terminals)
CSC (see Computer Sciences Corporation)

D

Dartmouth College, 33-34
Data bases, 106
Datapoint 2200 terminals, 116
Decatur (Illinois) Public Library, 15
Default indicators, 83
Delta Data Systems terminals, 120, 162
Derived keys, 143
Detroit Public Library, 188
Diamond Ordnance Fuze Laboratories, 151
Digidata System 30, 26
Digital Equipment Corporation:
  equipment:
    PDP-10, 221
    PDP-11, 27, 33-34, 113, 194, 211-212, 239
Divided catalogs, 55, 120, 134-135
Documentation Inc., 63
Dunlap, Connie, 29
Dura Mach 10, 47, 75

E

EAM equipment (see Unit record equipment)
Eastern Illinois University, 7, 204

Econolist, 51
Edge-punched cards, 158-159
El Centro College, 98
ELMS (Experimental Library Management System), 120-121
Equipment suppliers, 223
Experimental Library Management System (see ELMS)

F

Facsimile transmission, 227-228, 230
FACTS (Facsimile Transmission System), 227
Fasana, Paul, 172
FAUL (Five Associated University Libraries), 109, 236
Federal Library Experiment in Cooperative Cataloging (see FLECC)
Filing, 41-42, 51-52, 58, 60, 83, 105, 120, 135-142, 153-154
  non-filing symbols, 137-138
  sort keys, 138
Five Associated University Libraries (see FAUL)
FLECC (Federal Library Experiment in Cooperative Cataloging), 109
Flexowriters (see Friden Flexowriters)
Florida Atlantic University, 27, 60, 129-130, 137, 192, 220, 224-225, 229, 231-232
Florida, University of, 75, 188
Format recognition, 49, 82-83
  (see also Automatic Field Recognition)
Foto-List, 50-51
Free Library of Philadelphia, 51
Friden:
  Collectada System, 30, 197
  Flexowriters, 27, 46-47, 49, 58, 63, 89, 98

G

General Motors Research Laboratories, 151

Index

Georgetown University, 202
Georgia Institute of Technology, 47, 74, 78, 89, 97-98, 105
Georgia, University of, 188
GE Terminet terminals, 116
GRACE (Graphic Arts Composing Equipment), 68
Guelph University, 91

H

Handprinting reader, 86-87
Harris, Jessica, 139
Harvard Medical Library (see Countway Library of Medicine)
Harvard University, 26, 65-68, 74, 78, 130, 157, 199-200, 239
Hawaii State Library, 96
Hazeltine 2000 terminals, 126, 211
HECC (Higher Education Coordinating Council), 109
Hennepin County (Minnesota) Public Library, 97
Higher Education Coordinating Council (see HECC)
Hines, Theodore, 139
Hollerith, Herman, 1-2
Honeywell-GE (General Electric) equipment:
  200, 27, 194
  635, 33, 159
Honnold Library, 25
Houston, University of, 49, 212, 239
Howard University, 202

I

IBM (International Business Machines Corporation), 52, 128
  Advanced System Development Division Library, 121
  equipment, named:
    Cardatype, 15
    MTST (Magnetic Tape Selectric Typewriter), 26, 48-49

(IBM)
  Multi-Function Card Machine, 158
  Selectric typewriter, 48
  Series 50, 15
  System 7, 202-203
  equipment, numbered:
    026, 194
    047, 47, 193, 198
    080, 188
    129, 27
    357, 24, 29, 184, 191-192, 194, 200-201
    360, 23-24, 26-29, 33-34, 52, 91-92, 104, 112-113, 116, 119-120, 153-154, 160-162, 167, 198, 200, 204, 206, 208-209, 211, 221
    370, 25, 30, 32, 92, 104, 112, 118, 160, 168-169, 194, 202-203, 206, 221
    402, 14, 17, 42
    403, 2, 15, 21, 50
    407, 14, 18, 23, 44, 50, 154
    513, 42
    526, 17
    709, 52
    826, 25
    870, 27, 47-48, 52
    1026, 201
    1030, 186, 194-195, 200-202, 208, 221
    1031, 194-195, 201, 204-205, 208-209
    1032, 195
    1033, 201, 204-205
    1034, 24, 194-195, 208
    1050, 29, 48, 111, 203, 223
    1052, 203
    1053, 202
    1056, 203
    1130, 221
    1401, 17, 19, 21-23, 25, 34, 52, 56, 58, 63, 65, 153-154, 157, 160, 200-201, 239
    1404, 158
    1410, 63, 162
    1440, 25, 98, 239
    1460, 23, 28, 60, 153
    1620, 159, 201
    1710, 201

(IBM)
  2260, 30, 121, 161-162, 188, 207-209
  2740, 32, 104, 118, 186, 206-208
  2741, 30, 104, 113, 119, 121, 208
  2791, 202
  3277, 204
  7010, 153
  7040, 25, 221
  7072, 17, 157
  7074, 23
  7090, 65
  7094, 25, 52, 56, 58
  Formation, 2
  Research Laboratory, San Jose, California, 151
  Thomas J. Watson Research Center Library, Yorktown Heights, New York, 17-19, 152, 200
IDC (*see* Information Dynamics Corporation)
Illinois Research and Reference Network (*see* IRRN)
Illinois State Library, 201
Illinois, University of, 153-154
  at Chicago Circle, 21-23, 152, 232
INCOLSA (Indiana Cooperative Library Services Authority), 237
Indiana Cooperative Library Services Authority (*see* INCOLSA)
Indiana University, 74
  Regional Campus Libraries, 55
Information Dynamics Corporation, 116-117
Information Transfer Experiment (*see* INTREX)
Inovar Corp., 96
Integrated Systems, 8-9, 32, 63, 110-112
Interlibrary loans, 120, 227, 236
International Business Machines Corp. (*see* IBM)
International Serials Data System (ISDS), 170, 172, 174
International Standard Bibliographic Description for Monographs (ISBD(M)), 238
International Standard Bibliographic Description for Serials (ISBD(S)), 172, 238
International Standard Book Number (*see* ISBN)
International Standard Serial Number (ISSN), 170, 172, 174
International Standards Organisation, 238
INTREX (Information Transfer Experiment), 4-5, 7, 121-123
IRRN (Illinois Research and Reference Network), 109
ISBD(M) (*see* International Standard Bibliographic Description for Monographs)
ISBD(S) (*see* International Standard Bibliographic Description for Serials)
ISBN (International Standard Book Number), 111, 116-117
ISDS (*see* International Serials Data System)
ISSN (*see* International Standard Serial Number)

J

Johns Hopkins University, 196-197
Joint Committee on the Union List of Serials, 171
Joint University Libraries, 15, 17, 25

K

Kansas, University of, 153, 159
Kilgour, Frederick, 107, 143-144
King County (Washington) Public Library, 2, 42, 92
King Report, 4

L

Labels, 39, 47, 89, 91-92, 111, 113, 119, 121

Index

Lake County (Indiana) Public Library, 15, 42-43
Laval University (*see* Université Laval)
Lear Sigler Terminals, 162
LENDS (Library Extended Catalog Access and New Delivery Service), 97
Library automation:
 back-up procedures, 231-232
 costs, 227-228
 defined, 1
 documentation, 232
 fads, 230
 funds for, 229, 237-238, 241
 implementation, 230-232
 planning, 226-229
 problems, 219-233
 prospects, 235-242
 specifications, 226
 system design, 229-230
Library Extended Catalog Access and New Delivery Service (*see* LENDS)
Library Information System Time-Sharing (*see* LISTS)
Library of Congress, 5, 80, 91, 120, 144, 238 (*see also* MARC)
 and CONSER, 173-174
 and the National Serials Data Program, 169-171
 book catalogs, 2, 42
 Card Division Mechanization Project, 83, 85-89
 catalog cards, 73-75
 filing rules, 141-142
 Official Catalog, 84
 order division system, 9, 25
Library On-Line Information and Text Access (*see* LOLITA)
Light pens (*see* Terminals)
Lincoln Laboratory, 152-153
Linde Company, 151
Linotron, 68, 99
List-O-Matic, 50
LISTS (Library Information System Time-Sharing), 116
Lithoid (*see* Compos-O-Line)
LOLITA (Library On-Line Information and Text Access), 31-32

Loraine County (Ohio) Community College, 98
Los Angeles City Public Schools, 48
Los Angeles County Public Library, 43-44, 51, 130, 134
Louisiana Numerical Register, 98

M

Machine-Readable Cataloging (*see* MARC)
MALCAP (Maryland Academic Library Center for Automated Processing), 237
Manitoba, University of, 208-209
MARC (Machine-Readable Cataloging), 5, 7, 73-85, 131-132, 175
 default indicators, 83
 expansion of, 83-84
 filing and filing indicators, 83, 141-142
 format recognition, use of by, 82-83
 MARC II format, 80, 111
 Pilot Project, 73-80, 92
 serials format, 170, 174
 as standard, 73, 84, 238
 use of, 32-33, 78, 90-94, 96, 105-107, 113-114, 117, 120, 144
MARCIVE (MARC IV, facetiously), 91-92
Marin County (California) Public Library, 212
Maryland Academic Library Center for Automated Processing (*see* MALCAP)
Maryland, University of, 25, 203
Massachusetts Institute of Technology, 7, 30, 121, 220
Massachusetts, University of, 30-31, 89-91
MEDFILE, 168
MEDLARS (Medical Literature Analysis and Retrieval System), 4, 68, 165-169
MEDLINE (MEDlars-on-LINE), 165, 168-169
Miami-Dade Junior College, 158-159

Michigan State University, 197-198
Michigan, University of, 23-24, 153, 195
Microcatalogs, 143-144
Microforms, 122, 129
MIDLNET (Midwestern Library Network), 237
Midwestern University, 201
MILINET (see MIDLNET)
Minicomputers, 112, 116, 239
Minnesota Union List of Serials, 173-174
Minnesota, University of, Biomedical Library, 159
Missouri, University of, 15-17, 25, 46, 75, 192, 239
Monarch Company, 211
Monsanto Company, 159-160
Montclair (New Jersey) Public Library, 2, 190
Montgomery County (Maryland) Public Library, 44, 74
Moraine Valley Community College, 160

N

Nassau County (New York) Library System, 21, 55, 74
National Agricultural Library, 74, 98-99, 169-170, 173
National Commission on Libraries and Information Science (see NCLIS)
National Library of Canada, 171, 173-174
National Library of Medicine, 4, 68, 120, 130, 165-170, 173
National Serials Data Program (NSDP), 169-171, 173
NCLIS (National Commission on Libraries and Information Science), 235
NELINET (New England Library Information Network), 109, 236
Networks, 224-228, 235-239, 241
New Bedford (Massachusetts) Public Library, 64
New England Library Information Network (see NELINET)

New Mexico State Library, 117
New York Public Library, 97, 118-119, 134, 172
New York State Interlibrary Loan Network (see NYSILL)
New York State Library, 42, 159, 173
Northwestern University, 32, 104-105, 171, 205-206, 231
NSDP (see National Serials Data Program)
Nugent, William R., 140
NYSILL (New York State Interlibrary Loan) Network, 236

O

OCLC (Ohio College Library Center), 7, 33
 and CONSER, 171, 173-174, 242
 history of, 106-110
 networks using, 109-110, 236-237, 241
 problems of, 110, 114, 119
 searching techniques, 143
Ohio State University, 158, 206-207
On-line systems, 5-7, 238
 for acquisitions, 29-34, 241
 for cataloging, 103-123, 142-143, 241
 for circulation control, 184-188, 200-212
 for serials control, 160-169
ONULP (Ontario New Universities Library Project), 4, 56, 130, 132
Orange County (California) Public Library, 28, 94-96
ORBIT, 117
Oregon State System of Higher Education, 237
Oregon State University, 31-32
OTIS (Oregon Total Information System), 104
Ottawa, University of, 202

P

PALINET (Pennsylvania Area Library Network), 109, 236

Index

Paper tape machines, 27, 29, 45-48, 75, 89, 158-159, 193, 198, 223
Parker, Ralph, 2, 188
Parkland College, 27
PDP computers (*see* Digital Equipment Corporation)
Pennsylvania Area Library Network (*see* PALINET)
Pennsylvania State University, 23
Pennsylvania, University of, 202
Permuted titles, 58, 132
Pfizer, Inc., 157
Phillip Morris Research Library, 55
Photocomposition, 56, 65, 68, 87, 93-94, 97, 99, 129
Phred, 212
Picatinny Arsenal, 200
PIL (Processing Information List), 19, 22
Pittsburgh Regional Library Center, 109, 236
Pittsburgh, University of, 221
PLAN (Public Library Automation Network), 114-116
Plessey Company, 211
Processing Information List (*see* PIL)
Programmers, 222
Public Library Automation Network (*see* PLAN)
Purdue University, 158

R

Raisin Valley (Michigan) Library Consortium, 96
Random access, 166
Rather, John C., 141, 143-144
RCA equipment:
  Spectra 70, 28, 155
  Videocomp, 87, 97, 118, 129
Recognition Equipment Inc., 86
RECON (Retrospective Conversion) Project, 80-82
Redstone Scientific Information Center, 75
Reference work, 121, 163, 208
Registers, 92-93, 130
Research and development, 223-225

Resource sharing, 237, 241-242
Retrospective Conversion Project (*see* RECON)
Rice University, 75, 78, 192, 199, 221
Rochester, University of, 42, 129-130
Ruecking algorithm, 116-117

S

St. Louis Junior College District, 64
St. Louis University, 15, 17
SALINET (Satellite Library Information Network), 237
Sanders 804 terminals, 33, 113
San Francisco Public Library, 158
Santa Clara (California) Public Library, 198
Satellite Library Information Network (*see* SALINET)
SCOPE (Systematic Computerized Processing), 91
SDC (*see* System Development Corporation)
SDI (Selective Dissemination of Information), 78
SDILINE, 168
Searching:
  in circulation systems, 207, 212
  for interlibrary loan purposes, 117
  in on-line cataloging systems, 107-108, 113, 143, 240-241
  for reference purposes, 163, 166, 168-169
Selective Dissemination of Information (*see* SDI)
Sequential card cameras, 49-51
Serials, 4, 7, 33, 147-175, 242
  acquisitions, 151
  binding, 150, 157, 160, 163-165
  check-in cards, 160
  check-in lists, 155, 159
  claiming, 150-151, 157, 160, 163
  frequency code, 157
  key title, 170
  lists, 148-150, 152-154, 157, 159-160, 170

(Serials)
  renewals, 150-152, 160
  routing, 150-151, 160
SERLINE, 168
SHARP (Ships Analysis and Retrieval Project), 52
Shawnee Mission (Kansas) Public Schools, 104
Shelflists, 65-68, 130
Shera, Jesse, 4
Ships Analysis and Retrieval Project (see SHARP)
Singer 10 system, 203
Slippery Rock (Pennsylvania) State College, 202
Software suppliers, 223
SOLINET (Southeastern Library Network), 109, 236
South Carolina, University of, 211, 239
South Dakota School of Mines and Technology, 152
Southeastern Library Network (see SOLINET)
Southern Illinois University, 4, 190-193
Spiras LTE Terminals, 107
SPIRES (Stanford Physics Information Retrieval System), 113
Standard Register Source Record Punch, 199
Standards, 5, 73, 80, 84, 238
Stanford Physics Information Retrieval System (see SPIRES)
Stanford University, 7, 32-33, 64, 113-114, 130, 138, 142, 237, 241
State University of New York (see SUNY)
Suffolk County (New York) Library System, 21, 55
SUNY (State University of New York), 109, 171, 173, 236
Swarthmore College, 160
Syracuse University, 32, 199
Systematic Computerized Processing (see SCOPE)
System Development Corporation (SDC), 116-117, 167

T

Tabulating equipment (see Unit record equipment)
Technical Information Project (see TIP)
Teletype equipment:
  33, 33
  33ASR, 105, 116
  35KSR, 31
  37KSR, 105
Terminals, 6-7, 41, 103, 129, 238
  (see also Beehive Medical Electronics OCLC 100 terminals; Colorado Instruments terminals; Control Data Corp. Transacter terminals; Datapoint 2200 terminals; Delta Data Systems terminals; GE Terminet terminals; Hazeltine 2000 terminals; IBM 357, 1030, 1031, 1050, 2260, 2740, 2741, 2791, 3277; Lear Sigler terminals; Sanders 804 terminals; Spiras LTE terminals; Teletype equipment)
  with cassettes, 116, 120
  CRT (Cathode-ray tube), 6, 31, 107, 112, 114, 116-117, 120-122, 143-144, 188, 204, 207-209
  data collection, 24, 29, 186, 202-205, 208-209
  keyboard, 29, 31, 33, 104, 111, 116, 118-119, 121, 186, 203, 206-208
  light pen, 210-212
Texas A & M University, 158, 194
Texas Medical Center, 169
Texas, University of, 2, 188
  of the Permian Basin, 98
Text, on-line access to, 122
TIP (Technical Information Project), 7
Toronto, University of, 56, 57, 78, 105-106, 129
Total systems (see Integrated systems)
TOXLINE, 168
Trinity University, 91-92

Index

Turn-key systems, 239-240
TymShare, 116, 168-169
Typography, 181

U

UCUCS (University of California Union Catalog Supplement), 93, 97
UKASE (University of Kansas Automated Serials) System, 159
U.S. Government Printing Office, 68, 99
U.S. Naval Postgraduate School, 46
Unit record equipment:
  for acquisitions, 14-15, 17-19
  for book catalogs, 2, 41-44, 128
  for catalog card production, 51-52, 128
  for circulation control, 2, 183, 188-190
  limitations of, 128, 130
  for serials control, 2
UNIVAC equipment:
  1004, 21
  1005, 21
  1008, 89, 105, 203
  9300, 25, 203
Université Laval, 7, 161, 171
University of California Union Catalog Supplement (see UCUCS)
University of Kansas Automated Serials System (see UKASE)
Upham, Lois, 173

V

Varian 73, 113

Varityper, 50
Videocomp (see RCA Videocomp)
Virginia, University of, 188
Visual display terminals (see Terminals)

W

Washington Library Network, 237
Washington State Library, 75, 78, 92, 237
Washington State University, 7, 29-30, 198-199
Washington University, St. Louis, 24, 46-47, 192-194
  School of Medicine Library, 27-28, 48, 60-63, 98, 157, 227
Watson, Thomas B., 128
Western Kentucky University, 119, 209-210
Western Union Datacom, 168-169

X

Xerox Equipment:
  Graphic printer, 105
  Sigma 5, 107, 110
  Sigma 7, 105
  Sigma 9, 110

Y

Yale University, 24-25, 52, 75, 129, 173
  Medical School, 48, 52, 107

Z

Zebra labels, 210-211

DISCARDED

JUN 2 2025